# Love Beyond Measure
## Memoirs of a Korean War Bride

*Ock Soon Crumbchrin*

### Katie Schell

*Katie Schell*

ISBN-13: 978-1491295908
ISBN-10: 1491295902

DEDICATED TO

My Mother and My Father

Ock Soon Lee and Frank Crimbchin

Cover: Impatiens are used in a Korean process
known as bongseonhwa (fingernail staining).

# TABLE OF CONTENTS

# Acknowledgments

First and foremost I must express my deepest gratitude and love to my mother, Ock Soon Lee - Pega Crimbchin, whose life journey is one filled with both unimaginable sorrow but also great joy. Her incredible story, even as I wrote it, made me look at her in awe. It has been my privilege and honor to write her memoirs in hopes that many will find encouragement and hope through her difficult journey.

I must also thank my wonderful husband, Bill Schell, whose unending patience and direction over the past eighteen months has allowed me to complete this project. As weeks turned into months, he always supported me and worked painstakingly on many technical aspects of the endeavor. One thing for sure - without his help and guidance I would still be formatting the book.

I must give special thanks to my children, Thomas Jay Dunn and Bethany Joy Friel, for being the hardworking and amazing people they are.

In addition, the many friends along the way who encouraged me and kept me on track including Brenda Galino, Tina Melisko, Susanna DeJeet, Westlyn Davis, Valerie Council-Thompson, Marty Anderson, Robin Ramsey and the Women's Group of Cornerstone Church in Export PA, whose encouragement and support will always be remembered. Thank you.

The names of some of the people in this book
have been changed to protect the innocent.

# Preface

It had been a difficult year. I had encountered grief of many kinds throughout my life but this past year was full of a grief and sorrow unknown by most. Over the past year my father was dying; and as he entered this final stage of his life, he made it clear to me that he never wanted to see me again. Yes, I loved my father although he could be very difficult and certainly had rarely shown me any kind affection.

Like all children, I loved my father. It did not matter if he was "good" or "bad", I loved my father. I did not understand him; I only knew him as the strict disciplinarian in my life. I did not know him when he was a child. I did not know him when he met his first true love. I did not know him when he was a young man full of youthful energy and had his own hopes and dreams. I only knew him as my father; and now as my dying father.

I knew my father as a very stern and unaffectionate man not given to encouraging words of support or spontaneous acts of kindness towards his children. Now at the end of his life, I learned of a deep seeded bitterness that had grown in his heart for over 35 years. The bitterness was towards me, his oldest daughter, over a misunderstanding that had occurred many years ago.

I tried to see my father once after he told me he never wanted to see me again. It did not go well. I never saw him again until over a year later on the day he died. He was breathing his last breaths and was unaware of my presence.

After my father's death, I sat down to write. I began writing about my mother and her incredible journey to America. Thirty years ago, she had put her story on cassette tapes and gave them to me. I searched my cluttered office and finally found the long lost tapes and began writing her story. I wrote and wrote and finally came to the part in the story where my father was trying to bring her out of war torn Korea to America. I called my mother on several occasions in an attempt to capture the details of the long and arduous process. My mother had very few details and was unable to provide much information. It was only about one week later that my mother called me.  She said to me, "You will not believe what I found."

When my mother first arrived in the United States, my father had shown her a wooden box.  The box was 15 inches long x 12 inches wide x 5 inches deep.  It had been lovingly handmade from hardwood, sanded and stained with a dark walnut stain and topped off with a perfectly fitted lid to match the box.  My father had pointed to the box and said to my mother, "These are important papers."  That was in January of 1954.

Since my mother was illiterate and unable to read, it never occurred to her to open the box.  The box sat in her dresser drawer for over 58 years.  After my father died, my mother in her deep grief was wandering through the house, weeping for my father when she came upon the old wooden box.  That night in the middle of her deep sorrow, she opened the box.  There inside the wood stained box were the letters; dozens and dozens of letters written during the Korean War and stored for almost sixty years, untouched.

The letters were written by my father to his parents during the Korean War; letters written from war buddies to my father after he left Korea; letters written in the Korean alphabet and translated into English.  The letters were detailing the painstaking process of bringing a Korean War bride to the United States between 1952 and 1954.

The letters would tell the remarkable story of a *Love Beyond Measure.*

# Introduction
## The Burial

Monday, February 20, 2012

My name is Ock Soon Lee. I will be eighty years old this year. I am an old woman now. Today I have come to bury my husband of almost sixty years. Yes, all of my children are here, all except one, my oldest child, my son. The one I first loved. He had other plans and simply could not make it. Of course, that is the way of my family today. Half will not speak to the other half. There is so much turmoil and anger. I do not understand what has happened to us. I do not understand my own children.

Yes, we sit in this room, with bare walls of stone. The people in this room have become hard just like these walls of stone. Yes, I have seven children, twenty grandchildren and even five great grandchildren. Will my grandchildren and great grandchildren have hearts of stone too?

My husband and I worked our entire lives to raise this family. Now we gather here to bury his ashes. My heart is broken. In this room sit my twenty-six adult children and grandchildren. I have not even counted the spouses and boyfriends who are gathered here today. Yet not one person can get up to say one kind thing about the man I loved so deeply. Not one kind thing.

Oh, if only they knew. If only they knew the man I once knew; the man who loved me unconditionally when no one else could. If only they knew the man who rescued me from a life of utter poverty, near starvation and even death. If only they knew *that* man.

Maybe then, one person could say one kind thing.

# PART ONE

Lee Pock Soon

# 1
# My Mother, My Father
## Eomeoni, Abeoji

### A small village in South Korea 1938

My memory of my parents is one of happiness and joy. Both my *Eomeoni* (Mother) and my *Abeoji* (Father) loved me so very much. I was an only child whom they named Lee Pock Soon. I remember Eomeoni was ill much of the time and spent a lot of time in bed. Abeoji was a kind and gentle man who took care of both Eomeoni and me. I remember Abeoji always carried me on his back. He did not want my precious feet to touch the ground. No matter where we were going, my transportation was on my Abeoji's back. I was his love and his joy.

Abeoji was a land owner and had rice paddies which he allowed other people to work. Although the Japanese were buying up a lot of the farm land in Korea, Abeoji was able to secure his own loan and maintain his family's land.[1] Abeoji was not wealthy but he did not work in the fields like the other men. He was able to stay home and take care of both my ill Eomeoni and myself. Our life was better because Abeoji was always there for us.

I remember one spring day it was so beautiful outside. I was probably four or five years old. The sunshine even made Eomeoni feel a little better. We went for a long walk that beautiful day deep into the woods. The wildflowers and fern were sprouting and we could hear the birds singing in the distance. We came upon a nest in the ground full of small speckled eggs. Eomeoni picked up the eggs and very carefully

---

[1] Japanese Rule 1910-1945 was a period of oppression with a primary agricultural goal to increase rice production in Korea to meet Japan's growing need. Farmland was overtaken by the Japanese and great quantities of rice exported to Japan. 1932-1936 per capita consumption of rice among Koreans declined to half of the level between 1912 and 1916.
http://countrystudies.us/south-korea/7.htm

placed them in her apron. We took them home and cooked them. Together we sat down and ate those eggs for supper. I remember that was such a happy day together with both of my parents.

I remember in the village there was a *satang namja* (candy man). Satang namja would come to the village with his oxen pulling an old wooden wagon. In the back of his wagon was a large slab of caramel. Satang namja had very large metal scissors. When he came to the village he would clang-clang-clang his scissors. All the children would come running to see if they could get a piece of that candy. Satang namja would trade his candy for anything, an old worn out pair of shoes, pieces of metal or tin, rags or swatches of cloth, even Eomeoni's hair. Eomeoni would save her hair and even my hair. Then whenever we heard the clang-clang-clang of satang namja's scissors, she would get that hair and give it to me. I would run out to satang namja to trade him for just a snip of that delicious caramel. He would then snip off a piece of candy for me. It was such a special treat. When I was a child, I often wondered what that old man did with my Eomeoni's hair. He would trade a piece of his candy for any junk you had. I remember satang namja and his wonderful caramel.

I remember one day I took a nap. When I woke up all ten of my fingers were wrapped in something like gauze. My fingers looked pink in that gauze. I woke up and I was shocked. I thought I was bleeding and I started to cry. I did not know at the time, but Abeoji had gone out into the field and picked some flowers. Korean people call it *bongseonhwa* (fingernail staining). Abeoji had picked the bongseonhwa, and mashed the petals. He then placed them on each of my fingernails and wrapped them while I was sleeping. When I woke up, Abeoji opened the wrappings one by one to show me how pretty my painted fingernails were. I remember that.

I remember when I was about five years old, I lost my first tooth. Abeoji took me outside and told me to throw my tooth up onto the roof. He told me a *ggachee* (magpie) would come and get my tooth. The ggachee will bring me a new tooth. I remember that.

Then one day Abeoji told me he was going to go to see his relatives. His relatives were getting together for *Gije* (death anniversary).[2] I do not know whose death anniversary they were honoring but I know the Korean people get together to honor the person and then have a very big feast. They cook all kinds of food, eat and drink and have a good time. Abeoji went on this journey to see his family. He had no transportation so he walked a very long distance. He was gone for several days. Then late one night, he returned home.

He was so proud of himself since he had brought all kinds of food and treats home for my mother and me. He brought *tteok* (rice cakes), *jeok* (grilled pork) and *jeon* (Korean pancakes). But the one thing he was most excited about was the satang! The satang was special because it was shaped like a little round ball. He had never seen round satang like that before. He woke me up in the middle of the night to have me eat that satang. He was so excited to share it with me because he knew how much I loved satang. Father told me it was called *nun-al satang* (eyeball candy). I woke up and ate the special nun-al satang. Then I quickly fell back to sleep.

I woke up the next morning, but Abeoji did not wake up. Abeoji was still lying in his bed. This was most unusual since he always woke up first and then he would come to wake me up. This was the first time Abeoji laid in his bed and did not get up. Eomeoni told me he was very sick and I should not bother him. So I stayed away from him that day and I left him alone to sleep.

One day went by and he still did not get out of the bed. Two days went by and he still lay in his bed, sick. I kept shaking my father and telling him to get up and come to play with me. But he did not answer me, he was too sick. This went on for about ten days and then he passed away. When my father passed away, I did not realize I was never going to see him again. I was only about five years old and I did not know what death was. I

---

[2] Gije is the custom where the family of the deceased gathers together and prepares special dishes. They present the dishes on a death anniversary table. The spirit of the deceased is invited to join in the meal. *http://traditionscustoms.com*

went to the funeral with my mother. All the women were crying. I cried too only because everyone was crying. But I did not understand death.

Someday I would learn what death was all about.

# 2
# My Grandmother
## Halmeoni

### 1939 (Age 6)

After Abeoji's funeral, Eomeoni became very ill. I was too young to comprehend exactly what type of illness Eomeoni had but I knew without Abeoji's help, she was unable to care for me. She sent me to stay with my *Halmeoni* (Grandmother).

Winter was coming and it was getting colder and colder outside. The ground was already frozen. I went to stay with Halmeoni who would care for me, but I was able to help her also. Together we would be company for each other. I was there for several months when one day I overheard my *Sahmchon* (Uncle) say to Halmeoni, "Pock Soon's Eomeoni died last night."

I heard those words and I could not believe it. I knew what death was. I was screaming and screaming. Neither Halmeoni nor Sahmchon could comfort me. I wept uncontrollably. How could this be happening? I was without Abeoji and now I would not have Eomeoni either! I was inconsolable. Halmeoni did not take me to Eomeoni's funeral. I was only six years old but I would never see my mother again.

Winter was very long that year. I stayed with Halmeoni and grew to love her more and more. I missed my parents very much but Halmeoni was good to me and together we were like a little family. We had a small house with two rooms. One room we slept in and the other room was for cooking and eating. There was a fire pit off of the room which kept us warm through the winter. Sahmchon would come to make certain we had enough wood to burn and food to eat. Sometimes Sahmchon would build the fire but mostly it was just Halmeoni and I. Halmeoni kept her spinning supplies right next to the fire and she would work on her silk while we both stayed warm.

Spring finally came. In the spring, Halmeoni raised silkworms in a separate room attached to the house. The silkworms would eat the leaves from the mulberry trees.

Halmeoni and I would pick the leaves from the mulberry trees and put them in a bushel basket. Every day we would carry the bushels of leaves to the silkworm room. Halmeoni would always remind me to be very quiet as we entered the room. She did not want me to disturb the silkworms. The little worms (larvae) would eat constantly. When I am quiet and I recall entering that room, I can still hear the silkworms' gnawing on those mulberry leaves.

The larvae would eat and eat and after several weeks, maybe a month or so, they would spin themselves into a cocoon. The cocoon was made of very fine but strong fibers which Halmeoni would use to make the silk. The cocoons had the shape of little eggs. Once in the cocoon, they would change from the caterpillars and would become known as pupae. Over time, the pupae would become moths. After the moths left their cocoon, Halmeoni and I would gather all the empty cocoons and bring them to our cooking area.

Halmeoni would then boil them gently in a big pot of water in order to prepare them for the silk threads. After Halmeoni removed them from the pot, we would rinse them with the cool water. Then we would drain them and leave them out to dry. Halmeoni taught me how to prepare the dried cocoons pulling and stretching them into little soft bundles so she could spin the thread. We would sit on the floor and while I worked on the cocoons, Halmeoni would use her little wooden spindle and spin the silk thread. We had such a nice time together, just my Halmeoni and me.

Sometimes Halmeoni would take the silkworm pupae before they became moths and boil them in a pot. She would then season them with wonderful spices. Korean people call them *beondegi* (pupa). Halmeoni and I would eat the beondegi just like a snack. I remember they were quite tasty and always a treat.

I believe Halmeoni and I really enjoyed each other. We did everything together. I helped her get the water from the well so that we could cook our rice and adzuki beans. We gathered the wood and built our fires together. We picked the mulberry leaves and fed the silkworms. I went with her everywhere she went. I slept with her every night. Although I missed my parents very much, Halmeoni's kindness helped me to forget my sadness and I did not cry for my parents anymore. Halmeoni kept me very busy and the summer days passed quickly.

Once again, the weather started to get cooler and cooler. Summer was ending and autumn was coming. That autumn, Halmeoni made an outfit for me out of her silk. The outfit was all beige. It was very beautiful. I was so happy to try it on. The *hanbok* (Korean dress) fit me perfectly. I felt so pretty in that new silk hanbok. Halmeoni also made me a new pair of shoes out of straw. The people in the village would weave shoes from straw because they did not always have leather shoes. Leather shoes were very expensive and people would have to travel far into town to purchase them. Many children wore shoes woven from the straw. Halmeoni took care to make everything new for me. I was very proud of my new outfit and so happy that Halmeoni made them special for me. I put my new clothes on and danced around the room singing;

"San-toki, toki-ya.
Uh-dee-reul gah-neu-nyah?
Kang-choong, Kang-choong tee myun-suh.
Uh-dee-reul gah-neu-nyah?"

"San-go-gae go-gae-reul.
Nah-hon-jah nuhm-uh-suh.
to-shil to-shil alh-bahm-eul.
Joo-wuh-suh ol-tae-yah."[3]

---

[3]Santoki means Mountain Bunny in Korean. All Korean children know this little song which is similar in popularity like *The Itsy Bitsy Spider* is in America. http://thekoreanway.wordpress.com/2010

"Mountain bunny, bunny.
Where are you going?
Bouncing, bouncing as you're running.
Where are you going?"

"Over the mountain peaks, peaks.
I will climb them on my own.
Plump, plump chestnuts
I will find and bring."

I was singing my song to Halmeoni because of my happiness; but Halmeoni was not happy. I saw her wiping tears from her face. I did not understand why she was crying but I did know enough to stop my singing.

The next morning Halmeoni sat me on her lap, she had something important to tell me. Halmeoni explained to me that I was going to live with another foster mother. I did not understand what she was saying. I did not have any other foster mothers. I was very confused. I never heard of a foster mother and I could not understand what she was saying. All I knew was that I did not want to go away. I liked helping Halmeoni with the silkworms and I liked being with her.

Halmeoni said the foster mother was going to be very nice to me and she would have lots of candy for me. I did not care about any candy. I did not want to leave my Halmeoni. I told her I did not want to go. I told her I wanted to stay with her. Halmeoni told me I could not stay with her and I had to go. I was terrified. I began crying and begging Halmeoni to please let me stay with her. I would be good. I would help her with everything. I just wanted to stay home with her.

Halmeoni would not talk about it anymore. She dressed me up in my new silk dress and shoes and we started that day on a journey to my new foster mother's home.

There were no roads on our journey. We walked along on little rice paddy hills and walkways. We walked and walked for miles through those rice paddies. Much of the path was just mud.

I tried not to slip into the water but every once in a while, my foot slipped and my feet were covered with mud.

We started out early in the morning and walked all day. I was crying and crying and begging Halmeoni, "Don't give me away, please Halmeoni. Please don't give me away. I will be a good girl. I promise you. Please let me live with you." I was so scared. I did not know what was happening.

The journey was hard for Halmeoni also. She was crying too but she would not answer me. Eventually, we crossed over a small river and we both stopped. She talked to me again. She told me my foster mother would be very good to me and she would give me lots of candy. She took water from the river and washed my face and then dried my face with her skirt. She took off my shoes and rinsed my feet and shoes in the river. She washed away her tears with the river water. We both stood by the river and wept. To this day, I do not know the reason my grandmother gave me away. I did not cause her any problems. I simply do not know why I had to go.

It was very late in the afternoon and we finally arrived at the foster mother's house. Sure enough, there stood an old woman and in her hand was a bag of candy. The first thing she did was give me some candy. I did not want her candy but I took it and I ate it.

My foster mother had invited some of the neighbor's children to come over so I would have someone to play with. But I would not leave my grandmother's side. I hung onto her dress and would not let her go. I hung on her dress and was begging her, "Please let me go back with you. I want to go home with you." I just kept crying and sobbing.

Halemeoni told me that she had to go to the byeonso (outhouse). So I had to let go of her dress so she could go into the old outhouse. I stood outside that wooden door and was waiting for her to come out. I would not leave that door. The neighbors' children kept calling out to me, "Pock Soon, come here to play." They kept calling my name trying to take my attention away from my grandmother. Somehow, I do not know how, but my grandmother escaped from me. When I turned around and opened the wooden door, she was gone.

That was the last time I would ever see my Halemeoni. She was going into that old wooden outhouse and I was standing at that door, waiting for her to come out. I would never see her again.

# 3
## Foster Grandmother
### Halmeoni Leul Yugseong

#### Village in Korea 1940

I was only about seven years old when Halmeoni took me to that far away village and left me with a new foster mother. Actually, my foster mother was more like a *halmeoni leul yugseong* (foster grandmother). She was very old, had all white hair and a very wrinkly face. Now I had no choice. After I could not find Halmeoni, I had to stay with this ugly old woman. I had nowhere else to go. I could never find my way home. The journey had been too long and my home was now far away. This would have to be my new home.

When Halmeoni left me that day, I remember running around and around the outhouse looking for her. I was calling out to her and crying for her. I was frantic. Where could she be? I ran around and around that old outhouse, looking inside and outside but she was gone. I threw myself on the ground and wept.

When I finally stopped crying, the first thing my foster grandmother gave me was a doily and a gallon jug to put on my head to carry the water. The well was about one mile from the house. I would make three trips every day for a jug of water to carry on my head. I was only seven years old and I was not used to carrying water on my head. I tried very hard to balance it and not spill it. If I spilled too much, I might have to make four trips for water that day.

I missed Halmeoni so much. We used to get our water together every day. Our well had been very close to our house and we would help each other get the water and carry the jugs. Now I have to make the long trips alone. I had no one. I was so lonely and so scared. I missed Halmeoni and the silkworms we took care of. I missed sleeping with her and helping her with the little soft silk bundles. I missed our quiet time together and her warm hugs. Why, Halmeoni? Why? I thought about you and thought that maybe you were missing me too and you would come back to get me. Every day I looked out into that field for you. I watched for you to come back for me. One day, I saw a woman walking in that field and I thought it was you! I called out to you, "HALMEONI! HALMEONI!" I started to run to you, but it was not you. Someday, I know you will come back for me. I know you will.

My foster grandmother was very old and she always complained of all of her aches and pains. Every day I had to massage her legs over and over again. Her shoulders ached and I had to rub her shoulders and her arms. Her hair was filled with lice. It is my job to pick the lice from her hair. I did this for her every day. She was a very lonely old woman and she needed a companion. I was seven years old and I would become her constant companion.

One day she gave me a large basket and told me to go a few streets away where the carpenter was working on a house. She told me to go there and the carpenter was going to give me some wood scraps to take home to burn. We would use the wood in our fire to cook the rice and make the tea. So I put the large basket on my head and went to find the carpenter. I saw him working on a house. I did not know how old he was but he looked like an old man to me.

The first thing the carpenter did was to pick me up and put me on his back. Well, Abeoji had carried me on his back all the time. I missed my father so much and I remembered how he carried me and played with me. I remembered how he sang songs to me and took me on long walks. I remembered his love for me and the fun we had together. I found comfort when the carpenter picked me up just like my father used to do. My heart was happy and I remembered my kind father and his deep love for me.

But I did not know what was coming to me. At first I was very happy. But then that old man hurt me, he raped me. I was only seven years old. I did not know the word for what he had done to me. I walked home - painfully walked home. I lay down on the mat and cried to myself.

Halmeoni Leul Yugseong came over to me, and asked me. "Pock Soon, What is wrong with you? Why are you crying?" I told her I had a belly ache. That is what it felt like to me, a pain in my lower belly. My foster grandmother left the house and returned with the village doctor. The doctor came and asked me what hurt. I told him my belly ached. He took my right hand. He then jabbed a large needle into my right thumb. I screamed out. He reached for my other thumb, I could not pull away. He was too strong. He jabbed a big needle into my left thumb. He grabbed each of my feet and pierced each of my big toes. I screamed but it did not stop him. He told me he was healing my belly ache. That is what Korean people do to relieve pain or illness. It is called bloodletting. Now, I not only had a "belly ache" from the rape, but I had sore thumbs and sore toes too. After that day, there was always something running down my leg. I must have been infected or something.

I could not tell my foster grandmother what had happened to me. But my life changed that day. I knew I was truly alone in this world. I knew the Halmeoni I loved so much was not going to come back for me. I knew there was no one to help me anymore. I had missed my mother and my father so very much. But I learned that day not to miss them anymore. There would never be another Abeoji. He was gone forever now. I would not look for him anymore. There would never be another Eomeoni. I would never look for her anymore either. There would never be another Halmeoni. They were gone forever.

I would not look for any of them ever again.

# 4
# Servant Girl
## Hanyeo

### 1941 – 1946

Halmeoni Leul Yugseong was getting older and the winters were very hard on her. One winter she became very ill. She was coughing up blood and became very weak. Even the village doctor could not help her. I made her some *kimchi soup* (spicy Korean stew made with kimchi) and brought her herbal tea that was supposed to heal her.[4] Nothing seemed to help. After her illness, she could not take care of herself anymore. It was difficult for her to walk around and cook for herself. Many days she could barely get out of the bed and get to the outhouse. I was only nine years old and I could not take care of her by myself. I tried to cook and care for her but she needed more help than I could provide.

When Halmeoni Leul Yugseong was a young woman she was unable to bear children. Her husband wanted a son very much. She heard of a family who had a young boy whose mother had died and needed a home. She adopted the young boy and named him Park Yong. Park Yong lived several miles away. After Halmeoni Leul Yugseong became ill and was not able to live alone with me, we moved in with her son. Park Yong was married to Yi Bong Cha and together they had nine children. Mr. Park was not a kind man and he did not particularly want his adoptive mother to live with his family. They already had eleven people in the house and now he was taking in his adoptive mother and of all things, another child - me. The man, or *seogsa* (master), made my position clear as soon as I arrived. I would be a *hanyeo* (servant), and I would earn my keep.

---

[4]Kimchi (also kimchee) is a Korean dish made of vegetables, such as cabbage or radishes that are salted, seasoned, and stored in sealed containers to undergo lactic acid fermentation.

Living in this house proved to be very difficult for me. I lived in the house with them but I was not accepted as one of them. I was treated as a servant, actually a slave to all of them including the nine children. I had to obey orders from the parents as well as their children. The children were permitted to hit me, slap me and pull my hair. No one corrected them. I suffered much physical abuse by the children in this house. They were especially mean to me.

The older children went to school while I stayed home to help care for the younger children. I wanted to go to school so very badly. I would have done anything to learn to read and write like the other children. I was so jealous of them. Sometimes, I would make excuses to go to the school. Anytime it rained, I would take the umbrella and walk to the school house. This was my way to get a chance to look inside that building. The school house was always so clean, it actually sparkled. Several times a week, the younger children would take the wax and shine the school house floors. That school house and the shiny floors looked so beautiful to me. But I was not permitted to step one foot into that school house. I could only stand outside and hand the umbrella over to the teacher. Then I would walk home alone in the rain.

Rice was harder and harder to get. I had heard the Japanese were sending our rice to Japan. They wanted the Korean people to learn to grow potatoes. The Park family had a potato farm. In the spring we would plant the potatoes. In the fall, we would harvest the potatoes. The family did not have a wagon or anything like that to bring the potatoes home. Some men would carry the potatoes home on their back. My job was to carry the potatoes home on my head. Every day during harvest they would place a little cushion doily on my head and then set the basket on top of the doily. By the time I walked home, I felt like my head was stuck down into my neck.

I did the same thing over and over again, day after day, I would work in the potato fields and I would carry the potatoes home. The family took the larger potatoes to sell at the market.

They would save the little ones for the family to eat. Every night it was my job to peel the potatoes. I would peel about one half bushel of potatoes a day in order to feed the entire family. I would also cook the rice and adzuki beans. We would eat the same meal for breakfast, lunch and supper every day.

After supper the mother of the house would give me some more little potatoes to peel in preparation for breakfast. The little potatoes were the size of robin's eggs. Some were even smaller. I would have to scrape the peels off with a spoon in order not to waste too much. Every night I was so tired after working all day, but I had to peel the potatoes. Every night as I peeled the potatoes, I would find myself falling asleep. I would startle awake, peel a few more potatoes but the exhaustion would cause me to fall asleep again. I would do this every night as I tried to stay awake to finish peeling the potatoes.

One evening, I was peeling the potatoes and I fell into a sound asleep. I did not wake up until dawn. Every morning it was my job to start the fire and cook the potatoes before anyone else would awaken. When I realized that it was dawn and the potatoes were not ready, I was terrified. I hurried to think of a solution and decided to use the big potatoes. I hurried and peeled the big potatoes, built the fire and cooked them quickly in the pot. I took the little potatoes and threw them over the wall into the neighbor's yard. I actually felt very proud of myself since I came up with such a good idea and the meal was ready before anyone woke up.

Later that afternoon, I was busy gathering the clothes to take to the river to do the family washing. While I was in the back room, bundling up the clothes, I heard the neighbor speaking to the mother. The neighbor had found the potatoes and brought them to the mother. The mother was furious with me. She was so angry that I wasted her potatoes and even worse, I used some of the big potatoes which were to be sold.

She went outside and found a stick that had thorns all over it. I knew she was going to beat me with that stick so I ran as fast as I could trying to get away from her, but she chased after me. I saw a kimchi crock buried in the ground and I jumped into the crock to hide from her.[5] It did not take her long to find me. But now I was trapped in that crock. I could not get out of it or run to hide from her. She beat me with the stick full of thorns from above. She hit me over and over again in anger. She was screaming at me and calling me all sorts of evil words.

When she finally stopped beating me, I was bloody all over. After she left, I crawled out of the crock, went to the well and washed the blood from my face, my head and arms. I had open wounds all over me. I washed the blood off, but some of my wounds did not stop bleeding. I still had blood running down my face as I walked back to the house. When I got back to the house, she was still so angry she would not even look at me.

I carried a scar from that beating behind my ear for many years. I could feel that scar for a very long time. As I grew, the scar moved. I think it is now somewhere on my head.

Every day I would cook the potatoes, the beans and the rice. The mother would put the potatoes on the bottom of the pot, then the beans and finally the rice on top. Everyone would pass the pot around the table; three adults, nine children, and then me. Thirteen people. I hardly ever got any rice. I would get whatever was left on the bottom of the pot – always potatoes or beans. I was so hungry for some rice. Every night when I washed the dishes and drained the water off, I would capture any rice left over from the dirty dishes. I would eat the rice that was left over. I did not know it could hurt me because of the dirt. I would just eat it.

The family house was a traditional Korean house called a *hanok*. The hanok had three rooms. There was a large room in the center where the family gathered and had their meals. Off of this room, there was a small area for cooking and building the fires. On one side of the center room was a large room where the entire family slept. The parents and nine children slept together in this room. On the other side of the center room was a smaller

---

[5]Kimchi crocks were clay pots used to preserve the kimchi. Many times the crocks were buried in the ground to prevent freezing in winter months.

room. Many families used it as a mother-in-law room. Parents or in-laws would sleep here. My foster grandmother and I slept in the little room.

One night my foster grandmother became very ill. She was gagging and throwing up. She could not control her bowels. There were loose stools everywhere. She kept calling for me to help her. She was very, very sick. I tried to clean her and take care of her. I was crying very loudly, hoping someone would come to help us. I was probably only eleven or twelve years old.

I was certain the people across the room could hear us but no one would come to assist. They did not care enough about her or me to come and help. Finally my foster grandmother was quiet and I too fell fast asleep. When I woke up, I realized that the mother and father had come into the room to wash her and move her body into the center room for viewing. That night my foster grandmother died in that room lying next to me.

While my foster grandmother was alive, she had provided some protection for me. After she died, I had no protection. I was nothing to these people. I was their servant, their slave. I was not even a person in their eyes. I was despised and mistreated.

Every day, all I ever did was work for them. I gathered all the wood for the fire. I cooked their meals and I cleaned up after the meals. I worked in the fields. I washed all the family's clothes. I would boil the water with the crystals and soak the dirty clothes in the pot of hot water. Then I would take the clothes down to the river. In the winter months, I broke through the ice with a pick and I rinsed the clothes in ice water. My hands would get so cold I thought my fingers would freeze off. I soaked my hands in the dirty clothes water just to warm them up. Then I rinsed the clothes again in the ice water. My hands were so sore. They were always chapped and bleeding. One day a neighbor woman saw my badly chapped and bleeding hands. She told me to pee in a pan and wash my hands in the pee before I go to bed. That was supposed to heal them. So every night I did just that and it really did help to heal my hands.

Every day, all year long, that is all I did was work, work, work. I never thought about going to school anymore. I knew I would never be permitted to attend that school. I never thought about my mother or my father anymore. There was no use wishing I had them back. That would never be. I even stopped thinking about my grandmother who gave me away. All of this was far too painful for me. I just survived each day and bore the burden of hatred and abuse. I could hardly remember ever being loved by anyone. I was truly alone in the world.

After my foster grandmother died, I slept alone in the little room. Every night, I was physically exhausted because of the hard work I did all day. I would go to my room and I would fall fast asleep. The room was always dark, there was never any light. One night someone came in from the other room. I did not know who it was. Perhaps it was one of the older boys or even the father. I did not know who was in the room with me. It was so dark. I knew what he was there for. I tried to fight him off of me but he hit me and told me to be quiet or he would kill me. He raped me. After that it seemed like every night, someone would come into that little room and rape me. I could not fight them off of me. I could not tell anyone. Who would believe me or even care? Rape is just another torment I must endure.

Every day as I went about my work, I was always looking for somewhere safe that I could go to hide at night. Many nights I would hide in the cow shed and I would sleep there with that old cow and the manure. I preferred to sleep in there rather than be raped at night. Sometimes when it was too cold to sleep outside with the cow, I would find a place to hide in the cooking area. But even on those cold nights they always seemed to look for me and find me.

One night when I had to sleep in the room, I decided to tie my dress up in knots and then he would not be able to get between my legs. So I tied my skirt into knots, as many knots as would fit. I felt safe and that night I fell into a very deep sleep. I did not even know that someone had come into the room and taken my clothes off. When I woke up, I found I was naked.

I started to think that I wanted to kill myself. I did not want to live this way anymore. There was no one that cared for me. I had no one to talk to. I was nothing but a slave to those people and they abused me in every way. I just wanted to kill myself. I did not know how to do it. I just knew that I wanted to die.

One day I heard the adults talking about a woman in the village who had actually killed herself. I did not know who they were talking about or why she would do that. I listened very closely and I overheard the mother say she had swallowed the soap crystals (lye) that we mix in water to soak our clothes. I heard them say that the crystals are like poison and if you swallow them, you will die. I thought about what she had done and realized it seemed like an easy solution. I used the soap crystals all the time. I certainly had had my fill of this ugly world and I would be happy to join my parents in death.

So that night I went and got the kimchi leaf. I wrapped up some soap crystals in the leaf and I ate them. I gagged because the crystals tasted so terrible. It was a small price to pay for the peace that lay ahead. I lay down on the mat and I felt so comfortable. I was so peaceful and ready to die. I quietly fell into a very deep sleep. The next morning, I actually woke up! How could this be? What went wrong? I was so disappointed. I was not dead. I was still alive. I felt like nothing good ever happened to me.

The next day I found a rope. I put the rope in my room thinking, "Tonight I *will* kill myself." Later that night, before they came in to rape me, I put the rope around my neck and I squeezed it as hard as I could. I squeezed and squeezed and I kept telling myself, "Do not open your mouth. Keep your mouth shut and do not use that air."

I did not want to breathe. I tried so hard not to open my mouth and take a breath. But I could not keep my mouth closed. I took a breath.

It was so hard to kill myself.

# 5
# Arranged Marriage
## Jungmae Gyeolhon

### Winter of 1947 (Age 14)

The winters were always very difficult in Korea. Many times the temperature would drop well below zero. One winter evening, during a very bad blizzard, I had to go outside to gather more wood. I thought we had enough wood for the night, but the house was cold and they were burning it up very fast. I was told to go out and find more wood. So I went out into the blizzard. I was climbing over the stones and fallen trees in the woods, looking everywhere for wood for the family to burn. The snow was very deep and continued pouring down fiercely. I was alone in the blizzard; no one else would be out in such bitter cold weather.

I found a big branch and was trying to drag it back to the house. I thought that if I could get this big branch back to that house, I would not have to make many more trips in this snow. My hands and feet were freezing and the snow was falling so hard that I could barely see in front of me. I kept trying to drag that big branch through the woods. There was not one other person out in that storm getting wood. I did not own anything like a warm pair of boots or gloves. The old jacket I had on was light in weight and my old shoes were worn thin. I had a thin piece of fabric on my head. I felt like I was freezing to death.

A neighbor saw me struggling to drag that branch in the blizzard. Over the years, she had witnessed how terrible the family mistreated me. Actually everyone in the village knew just how abusive and mean they were to me.

I remembered several years ago, when I first came to the village, the good neighbor called me over to her house one day. She was sitting on the front porch. She had watched the family mistreat me earlier in the day and she must have felt sorry for me. When I got to her house, she hugged me. I had not been hugged in such a long, long time that it felt so good. Over the years, every time I saw her, I remembered that wonderful embrace. In all my lifetime, I have never forgotten that hug.

On the day of the blizzard, the good neighbor saw me trying to drag the large branch home. As I was passing her home, she called out to me and asked me to come into her house. I had no fear of her since she had been kind to me in the past. As soon as I stepped inside, she gave me a cup of warm tea to drink. Then she washed my feet and my hands with warm water. Oh, it felt so wonderful to get warmed up. I had been so very cold in the woods, I thought my fingers and toes were frozen. I was so grateful for her kindness to me.

The good neighbor had a cousin visiting her from another village. Apparently the two women had been talking about me and my terrible home life. They had devised a plan that would not only rescue me but it would also help them. The cousin asked me if I wanted to go to her village and live with her. She would be leaving on the train the next morning. The cousin told me that if I agreed, I could live with her and her family. Her home was comfortable and she would treat me much better than the family I was living with. The cousin told me that someday I could even be married to her son. I would be her future daughter-in-law. This would be a *jungmae gyeolhon* (arranged marriage).

Well, it did not take me too long to think about this offer. It sounded wonderful. Of course I would go. I would be very happy to go. I wanted to get away from that family but I did not know where to go or how to get there. I had no money and was uneducated. I told her I would certainly go with her.

The next morning we went to the train station together. The cousin bought tickets for both of us and we got on the train. I had never been on a train before and found the adventure wonderful. I was so happy to get away from that hateful family. "Huh!" I thought. "They are all probably still sitting around waiting for the fire wood. Maybe they are all freezing to death! Huh!"

I was going to have a brand new family and I was going to be their daughter-in-law. I had no fear about leaving or going somewhere new. I just wanted to get out of that house. I was so happy to finally be getting away from them.  I fell asleep on the train and rested much of the journey.

We arrived at the new village and walked to her home.  I met the son who was supposed to marry me someday.  Well he took one look at me and he hated me.  He was probably just too young to know how to treat a future wife.  He treated me very badly.  Anytime his parents were away from the house, he would invite his friends to come over to look at me.  They would come over to make jokes about me.  They would laugh at me and pull my hair.  Sometimes they even spit on me.  The arrangement was not working out.

I stayed there about a week or two and then I decided to walk away.  I did not know where I was going or what I was going to do.  I just knew I would no longer stay and be abused like that anymore.  I did not know how I was going to do it, but I knew I could survive.  I had to.  I walked all day, both morning and into the night.  Eventually I came to another town.  I did not know it at the time, but I was now in Seoul.  I had walked to the Seoul Train Station.

I found a corner in the train station and slept there.  There were no hotels at that time so there were many people sleeping everywhere in the station.  The next day, most people boarded the train and they were gone.  Since I had no money and nowhere to go, I just stayed there.  At least it was warm and I had a roof over my head.  I noticed the people who worked at the station were now watching me.  Finally one of the men come over to me and asked, "Why are you still here?  Why don't you catch a train?  You can't just stay here.  You must leave."  I explained to him, "I have no place to go.  I have no family, my parents are dead.  I don't know where I am and I have no money.  I am hungry and tired and I just need someplace to sleep."

There was a traveler at the station whose name was Kim Min Kyung.  Mr. Kim overheard the conversation and offered to take me to his mother's house.  His mother lived nearby and was raising her two grandsons.  He asked me if I would be willing to live with his mother and help her with the grandsons. Of course I would go.

As we walked to his mother's home, Mr. Kim told me all about his family. His sister was married to a soldier and she traveled with her husband on his assignments. She had left her two children with her mother while she was away. Shin was the older son and he was a teenager. Min Ho was the younger son and he was about 5 years old. His mother was getting older and could use some help with the boys.

I listened to Mr. Kim tell his stories. I was very happy to go *anywhere*. I walked with him to his mother's home but said nothing. I was just hoping to get some rice and tea.

# 6
# A New Grandmother
## Sae Halmeoni

### 1947

Kim Min Kyung and I continued on our walk to his mother's home. He asked me, "What is your name?" I told him my name was Lee Ock Soon. I don't know why but I liked the name and decided that I would never again allow anyone to call me Pock Soon. That life was over and I wanted a new start. From now on, I would be Lee Ock Soon.

The home was several miles away from the train station and we arrived there before dark. Mr. Kim's mother was very nice to me. She must have felt sorry for me and gave me warm water for my feet and hands. She also prepared some warm tea and rice. I was starving, and quickly gulped the bowl of rice. She gave me another bowl and told me to eat slowly. I had been dreaming about this rice and tea and it tasted so wonderful. I tried to eat more slowly on the second bowl. The woman was very good to me. It had been a very long time since I had someone in my life that treated me so kindly.

I soon learned that Mr. Kim's mother had three children. She had two sons, Min Kyung and Myn Hee and one daughter, Hana. Her husband had passed away several years ago. Although her sons did not live with their mother, they did come to visit her often.

Hana was married to a soldier by the name of Park Bong Cho. He was an officer in the Republic of Korea Army, (ROK). Hana and Bong Cho had two sons Shin and Min Ho. Hana traveled with Bong Cho on his assignments south of Seoul. When she traveled, Hana would leave Shin and Min Ho in the care of her mother. I was asked to stay and help care for Min Ho.

Mr. Kim's mother was a good hearted and generous woman. She treated me just like a member of her own family. I was no different. We ate together and we slept together. Every day I helped her with chores and I cared for Min Ho. I was very happy to be a part of this family. I soon called her Halmeoni just like my own grandmother. She was just like a *sae* (new) Halmeoni. Min Ho and Shin liked me and soon called me *Ajumma* (Aunt).

My life with Halmeoni was a good life. No one was abusing me or hurting me in anyway. The family was always kind and treated me with kindness. I did everything I could to help Halmeoni. Halmeoni owned her own home and I helped her clean it. We traveled to the market together and would bring back the rice and vegetables. I worked alongside her to build the fires, cook and then clean up the dishes.

Halmeoni had a well for water right in the middle of her yard. We did not have to go far to pump the water. The market was close by. We always had enough wood to burn for heating and cooking and always enough food to eat. My life was very comfortable with Halmeoni. I soon cared very deeply for Min Ho. I called him my *Dongsaeng* (little brother). He was a very gentle and sweet little boy. I spent a lot of time with Dongsaeng. We played together and took long walks. He liked me and followed me around as I did the chores. His brother, Shin, was older and had other things of interest. Hana was very happy that I had come here and was helping her mother. She told me she no longer worried about her mother and her sons the way she used to. Now that I was there, she knew her children were cared for and her mother was less burdened. Finally after many years of suffering, I had finally found a place of peace.

Then the war came.

It was a warm summer day, Sunday, June 25, 1950. Everyone was relaxing in their homes. Families had gathered together for meals. Even the soldiers were enjoying the day, relaxing in the city. We had not heard the news reports and we were unaware that the North Korean People's Army (NKPA) had invaded South Korea. We did not know that our leader, President Syngman Rhee, and his cabinet had planned to leave Seoul as soon as possible and head south for Taejon. We did not know that

President Rhee had ordered his Army not to warn the people in order to avoid panic and chaos. We were unaware that the NKPA had over 135,000 soldiers and the ROK had about 98,000 soldiers. We did not know that the NKPA was heavily armed with automatic rifles and WW II tanks while the ROK was a very weak army with little training and very poor equipment.

I was a peasant with no knowledge of politics or wars or governments and treaties. But I would soon be caught in the middle of this horrific war and an eye witness to the Communist atrocities and the death of hundreds of soldiers and civilians in the city of Seoul.

I would soon learn of death like never before.

# 7
# First Battle of Seoul
## Surprise Attack

### June 25, 1950

It was Sunday, June 25, 1950, 4:00 AM. North Korea had launched a full-scale invasion across the 38th Parallel into South Korea. Over 90,000 Russian armed North Korean People's Army (NKPA) troops launched a coordinated land, sea and air attack against South Korea. The Republic of Korea (ROK) had only eight divisions. Four divisions were deployed along the 38th parallel. The ROK had no air force, no recoilless rifles, no heavy mortars, no medium artillery and no armor. The NKPA were armed with howitzers and self-propelled 76mm guns. In addition, the NKPA had the best tanks developed in WWII, the T34/85. The ROK tried desperately to stop the tanks with hand grenades, but the tanks simply crushed the soldiers under the treads. Scores of ROK soldiers died. The city of Seoul was captured within two days. The NKPA continued to move southward. In the first week of battle, throughout South Korea, more than 34,000 ROKs (one third of their army) were killed or captured. (Retrieved from: http://www.koreanwaronline.com)

U.S. President Harry S. Truman was notified of the invasion and by early afternoon he had returned from his home in Missouri to Washington, D.C. The United Nations Security Council passed a resolution calling for immediate cessation of hostilities and withdrawal of NKPA to the north of the 38th Parallel.

On Monday, June 26, 1950, President Truman met with the Defense Department officials and authorized General Douglas MacArthur to send ammunition and equipment to prevent the loss of Seoul. The president ordered MacArthur to utilize the Air Force and Navy against all NKPA military targets south of the 38th Parallel. He was to provide ships and aircraft to evacuate American citizens.

On Wednesday, June 28, 1950, the ROK engineers blew up the Han River Bridge trapping ROK divisions still in Seoul. Between 500-800 people, both civilians and military were killed in the explosion. NKPA entered Seoul by early afternoon. The ROK would fight to save the city but by midnight, Seoul had fallen into the hands of the North Koreans. (Retrieved from: http://www.korean-war.com)

## Lee Ock Soon

I was just a peasant with no knowledge of politics or wars. But I was caught in the middle of this horrific war. The Communists crossed over the border and marched into Seoul. The tanks were huge and rolled down the streets of our city. They rolled over any soldiers who tried to shoot at them and stop them. The Communists found the government workers and brought them out to the streets and shot them. We were trapped in the city. Unfortunately, we were not the privileged ones who were advised in advance to go to Taejon. The elite government officials were advised. It was too late for us now. We had been left behind and we were unable to escape anywhere. We were stuck in Seoul amidst the Communist takeover.

Once inside the city, the Communist soldiers went door to door throughout Seoul and gathered up the educated people and government workers. They were taken into the street to punish them in public. The Communist soldiers beat them. They dragged people out of their homes and executed many in the streets. They tied government workers to poles in the middle of the street and cut off parts of their body. We saw what was happening and we obeyed. Everyone was terrified.

The ROK army was in total disarray. One young soldier ran into our home and begged us to help him. We found a hiding place in a wall between the outhouse and the neighbor's house. We were terrified that the Communists would find him and kill all of us. We knew if we asked him to go, he would be shot dead in the streets. So we could not tell him to go. He hid in the wall for several days. Eventually he would leave. We were still afraid the Communists knew he had been there and would punish us.

After Seoul was taken over by the NKPA, the Communist soldiers went house to house and rounded up all of the young men and women. Teenagers and young adults were taken from their homes. The older men were shot. Anyone who looked the least bit suspicious was shot. I was taken by the NKPA with the other young people.

We were gathered up and told that we were going to join their army.  Every day they would tell us just how evil President Syngman Rhee and the South Korean government had become.  Our president left us behind but he escaped like a coward.  They told us how lucky we were to be chosen to be a part of the NKPA.  They told us that Kim Il-Sung was a great leader and we would be a part of his great country.  They told us we would become a part of the great country of Korea.  There would be no North Korea and South Korea.  There would be just one Korea, united under Kim Il-Sung.  Once Korea was united again, everyone would have peace and wealth.

We were held in their camp and trained to be a part of the NKPA army.  Every day we learned to march.  We would perform drills up and down the streets of Seoul.  Every day they reminded us over and over again how fortunate we were to be a part of the great NKPA army and that we would win this war.  We obediently learned to march to the tune of "Raise the Red Flag."

I was in the NKPA for several weeks.  I do not remember if it was three weeks or six weeks.  But one day, all of the other young people went on a march outside of Seoul.[6]  I was left behind.  I did not understand at that time why I had not been taken with the other young people.  Later I was told that they did not want to take me because I could not read or write.  I could not pass the written test that had been given to everyone.  I was told that they did not want an illiterate person like me in their army.  I simply returned to Halmeoni's home.

When I arrived home, Halmeoni looked so old.  She had aged so much in a very short time.  She had lost weight and looked haggard and worn down.  She told me that the Communists had been using the people to work on the roads.  It did not matter if you were young or old. You had to work to build the roads.  I now joined her building roads for the NKPA.

As soon as darkness came, the Communists forced everyone out of their homes to work on the roads.  All the women

---

[6]Later I would learn that the NKPA used these young civilians to march ahead of their army in battle to explode land mines planted by US soldiers.

and children including the grandmothers were forced to work all night, every night. They told us that we were building the roads that would win the war. They intended to bring their tanks onto those roads and travel south. Some people were given picks, some had shovels but most of us worked with our bare hands. We carried the stone and moved the dirt all night long. It was very hard labor and I was so afraid that Halmeoni could not keep up. I tried to stay close to her and I carried the big rocks and left the little rocks for her. She had never worked like this before.

If you made one wrong move, you would be shot. The Communists were ruthless and they did not hesitate to shoot and kill the civilians. They seemed to know everything we did. We worked all night. Many people were shot and killed if they were not working hard enough or if it looked like they were trying to escape. I hoped they would not shoot Halmeoni. It was very dangerous to be on this work crew. Everyone was exhausted but continued to work every night. The older people were suffering greatly but the Communists had no mercy for them.

Every night for months, we were forced to work under the lights on this road headed south towards the NKPA victory.

# 8

# Second Battle of Seoul
## Operation Chromite

### September 1950

The Second Battle of Seoul was the battle to recapture the city from the North Koreans. Douglas MacArthur had promised the South Korean government that he would fight to regain control of Seoul as soon as possible.

"On September 15, 1950 Joint Task Force Seven, with more than 320 warships including 4 aircraft carriers, carried the nearly 70,000 man strong force of X Corps into the dangerous tides of Inchon harbor. Proceeded by heavy naval bombardment and under the blanket of fighting aircraft, led by the veteran 5th Marines, elements of the 1st Marine Division were landed 100 miles behind the North Korean lines and fought their way on to take Seoul, by 9/25."
(Retrieved from: http://www.koreanwaronline.com

"The battle for Seoul lay ahead. Mounting indications were that it would be far more severe than had been the action at Inchon and the advance to the Han. Every day enemy resistance had increased on the road to Yongdongpo. Aerial observers and fighter pilots reported large bodies of troops moving toward Seoul from the north. On the 17th, enemy engineer units began mining the approaches to the Han River near Seoul. About the same time, the N.K. 70th Regiment moved from Suwon to join in the battle. As they prepared to cross the Han, the marines estimated that there might be as many as 20,000 enemy troops in Seoul to defend the city."
(Retrieved from: http://www.history.army.mil/books/korea

"The Marines advanced on Seoul. The 1st Marines were on the left, the 5th Marines on the right. The 5th Marines seized Kimpo airfield on the 17th of September. Three days later, they crossed the Han River northwest of Seoul. They had three days of hard fighting to take the high ground that lies to the northwest of the city. On 25 September both the 1st and 5th Marines moved into the city." (Retrieved from: http://www.mca-marines.org)

"The U.S. Army's 7th Infantry Division had landed on the Inchon Harbor September 19. Major General Edward M. Almond ordered his troops to take position south of Seoul. The division's 2nd Battalion of the 32nd Infantry Regiment landed at Inchon and went ashore. The 7th Division's 31st Infantry Regiment came ashore and engaged in heavy fighting with the NKPA on the outskirts of Seoul. General MacArthur personally oversaw the 1st Marine Regiment as it fought its way through the NKPA on the way to Seoul.

Operation Chromite was then handed over to Major General Almond who was intent on capturing Seoul by September 25. This would mark exactly three months from the North Korean invasion. On September 22, Marines entered the city to find it heavily occupied. The fighting was fierce. Casualties on both sides were high. Almond declared Victory on September 25, despite the fact that Marines continued to fight in door to door combat for days afterwards." (Retrieved from: http://www.xtimeline.com)

## Lee Ock Soon

I remember the American Marines came to chase the Communists back. There was a very big battle. We were trapped in the middle again. Halmeoni, Shin, Min Ho and I hid under the porch. Bullets were flying everywhere. There were Army tanks and gunfights everywhere. The Marines were going from house to house looking for and shooting the Communists.

The fighting was constant. It went on for days. We were deathly afraid to come out from under the porch. We had no idea what was happening or who was winning the war. We could not get anything to eat or drink. The four of us hid in the hole, terrified that we would be shot. We heard the constant boom-boom- boom- boom. After several days, it finally stopped and then there was quiet. We waited under the porch but every once in while we would hear more shooting. We waited. We did not move. We hid.

There was a water pump in the middle of the yard. We were dying of thirst. We could tolerate the hunger but the thirst was unbearable. They asked me to go to the well to get some water. So, I snuck out of the hole and went to the pump. It had not been pumped for a while so it needed to be primed. I was hurrying as fast as I could. I was so afraid to be out in the open like that. I was pumping and pumping trying fast and hard to get the water. Then I heard a loud "**PING.**" A bullet went right through the pump disabling it. If I was bent down just a little further, my head would have been blown away. I fell to the ground on my stomach and scurried as fast as I could back to the hole under the house. I was shaking like a leaf. I was so terrified that I did not even know if I had been shot or not. I looked all over my body to see if there was any blood. I saw no blood on my body and realized that I was not wounded. I lay under the porch, my ears still ringing from the sound of the bullet hitting the metal next to my head. There would be no water today.

After several days, the fighting stopped we were able to return to the house. I decided to walk out into the streets of Seoul. I wanted to see what had happened. I walked alone down to the crossroads. There were dead bodies everywhere. Bodies were literally blown in half. The dead bodies were all swollen up. American soldiers lie dead in the streets. Communist soldiers lie dead in the streets. I saw civilians lying dead in the streets. I just walked in between the dead bodies. I did not know why, but I had no fear. All fear was gone. I was just numb. I watched the soldiers as they gathered up the body parts and placed them in a pile to burn.

I looked down the hill and saw the Marines capturing the Communists. They were making them strip down to their underwear and march in a line. Although it was very cold outside, they obeyed.

Everyone in the city was afraid, terrified. Many children were wandering around the streets with blank looks of shock etched on their faces, wandering around alone. Their parents had been killed. I came across a young mother, laying dead along the road, her baby hungrily suckling at her breast.

The Marines were in Seoul now and the fighting had stopped. We had peace once again. We cleaned up as much as we could. Much of the city had been destroyed. We searched for wood or anything to burn. It was fall and winter was coming soon. It was already getting cold. Every day I looked for wood to burn. Our pump was no longer working. We had to walk a distance to the well for water. Food was scarce. Many orphans were in the streets wandering around looking for something to eat. I would watch as the Marines drove by in their jeeps. Sometimes they would stop and give the children candy bars. I stayed away. I was afraid of the Americans. I had never seen an American before. I did not understand why they were here with guns and weapons. I heard they were here to help the Korean people, but I did not understand.

At least the fighting had stopped. Many buildings had been blown up by the bombs. All that was left were large piles of bricks and ashes. The streets were blown apart and the street car rails now pointed to the sky like jagged spears shooting up from the earth. The city of Seoul lay in ruins.

# 9

## The Journey
### Seoul to Taegu

#### The First 100 Miles

It was now fall. We were living in some kind of peace with the American Marines in Seoul to protect us. We had to work to find food to eat and wood to burn. Life was much harder now. There were so many orphans in the streets. Every day the children were searching for food. I felt so sorry for them but we were barely surviving ourselves and could not help anyone. The buildings had been blown up and many people did not have a home to live in anymore. When I traveled to the well, I saw many women carry their buckets going through the rubble in the streets. They were looking for any scraps to salvage and sell. If they could get just a little money, they could buy some food for their children. Life was very difficult but I stayed with Halmeoni and Hana. Hana had returned to live with us but Bong Cho was very busy with the war. We had the boys and we were surviving. Bong Cho was alive somewhere south of Seoul. Several months passed and we had not seen Bong Cho. Winter was coming quickly.

We had not heard any news of the battles in North Korea but we knew the fighting continued. We were hoping and waiting for Bong Cho to return to us. It was winter and he was not back.

"They came out of the hills near Unsun, North Korea, blowing bugles in the dying light of day on 1 November 1950, throwing grenades and firing their "burp" guns at the surprised American soldiers of the 8th Cavalry Regiment, 1st Cavalry Division. Those who survived the initial assaults reported how shaken the spectacle of massed Chinese infantry had left them. Thousands of Chinese had attacked from the north, northwest, and west against scattered U.S. and South Korean (Republic of Korea or ROK) units moving deep into North Korea. The Chinese seemed to come out of nowhere as they swarmed around the flanks and over the defensive positions of the surprised United Nations (UN) troops.

Within hours the ROK 15th Regiment on the 8th Cavalry's right flank collapsed, while the 1st and 2d Battalions of the 8th Cavalry fell back in disarray into the city of Unsan. By morning, with their positions being overrun and their guns falling silent, the men of the 8th Cavalry tried to withdraw, but a Chinese roadblock to their rear forced them to abandon their artillery, and the men took to the hills in small groups. Only a few scattered survivors made it back to tell their story." Stewart, R. (10-01-00). *The Korean War: The Chinese Intervention* http://www.history.army.mil

It was now winter. A messenger sent by Bong Cho came to us from outside of Seoul. Bong Cho had sent the messenger to tell us to leave Seoul immediately. We had to move as fast as we could. The Communists were coming. The messenger told us that Bong Cho would be sending someone in a jeep to pick us up. He would meet us under the bridge to Yongdongpo (Yeongdeungpo). We had to hurry. We were told do not take time to pack anything. There was no time, we had to leave immediately. The jeep would be waiting for us under the bridge today. Bong Cho would then take us to safety.

We did not take anything with us. We did not take food or clothes or blankets, nothing. Outside, everyone was leaving Seoul now and heading south towards Taeju (Daegu). The streets were filled with people walking in the snow. Others had their clothes and food bundled in blankets, carrying them on their backs. The people were terrified. Everyone was carrying something. Many had bundles on their heads. Some were pushing their wagons. Thousands and thousands of people were marching out of Seoul. The Communists were coming back again and this time they would kill everyone.

Min Ho was very sick. He had the measles. He was very weak and could not walk. I carried him on my back. We tried to hurry as fast as we could but we could not run. Halmeoni was getting older and she had difficulty keeping up with the pace. Hana and Shin were trying to help Halmeoni. We finally reached the Yongdongpo Bridge. We were shocked to find that the bridge had been blown up. We did not know what to do. We waited for some time looking for any sign of the man in the jeep who was to

42

meet us here. Hana did not want to leave. Her husband had told us to wait. We waited and waited but the jeep never came. Eventually, we knew we had to go.

The main bridge for vehicles and jeeps had been blown up. Under the bridge was an old foot bridge. We joined the others walking across the river on the old foot bridge. Some people rode across the river on small river boats.[7] Unlike the others, we had no blankets, no food and no extra clothes. We had nothing but the clothes we were wearing. How could this happen? Where was the man who was to take us to safety? Everything went wrong. Nothing had worked out as planned. We were freezing in the snow. I had to carry Min Ho on my back. He felt so heavy, but I had to keep walking. We were not prepared for the journey that lay ahead.

The snow was very deep. Once the path was made, it was easier for everyone to walk, one behind the other, in one straight line. There were so many people. As far as I could see there were people. It was so sad. Some women had one baby tied on their front and another one tied on their back. Old men and old women walked, trying to carry all of their belongings on their back. Some carried the bundles on their heads. There was no road. The ice and snow made the journey so difficult. We were heading for Taegu. We have been told that the soldiers were there and it would be safe. The soldiers could protect us. I did not know how far away Taegu was. I was just following the people. I looked back towards the city. Seoul was lit up with fire. Many had burned their homes so the Communists would not have their food or shelter. Seoul was now ablaze. Everyone was desperately trying to flee the oncoming Communist soldiers.

We walked towards the train station; we thought that maybe we could get a ride. People were all over the train. They were desperately hanging on the sides and the tops of the train. People were hanging between the cars. It was total chaos. The

---

[7] An old Korean friend would tell of her ride in the boat with a young mother whose infant child could not be quieted. She wept bitterly as she threw her baby overboard into the Han River.

conductor kept shouting at the people to get off the train. They could not move the train until all the people got off the sides. No one would get off. Everyone continued to hold on desperately. We tried to get on but we could not. Halmeoni was just too old and Min Ho was too sick to hang on. There was so much confusion. We watched as the train pulled away. The people in between the cars were crushed to death. They fell to the ground and to their deaths. The screaming continued.[8]

We walked. We followed the train tracks. We walked past the dead and the dying that fell from the train. We walked for miles and miles. I was exhausted but I had to carry Min Ho and I could not stop to rest. Min Ho was burning up with fever. I had to go on. We came to a place where the train track was crossing a river. It was absolutely terrifying. I had never experienced such fear in all my life. The rails were set very far apart high above the river. I had to leap from one rail to the other with Min Ho on my back. If I missed the rail, I would have fallen to my death in the river. I really do not know how I crossed that river on those rails. I don't know how I reached the other side. When I touched the ground, I collapsed. I fainted. I fell on the tracks and scraped my face. Halmeoni and Hana shook me awake. They told me to get up, we had to keep moving.

We continued to follow the long line of people before us. Sometimes we walked on the tracks. Sometimes we walked on the path. Many times we walked up the hills and slid down on the ice. Everything was ice and snow. The people were exhausted. All along the way, people had died. Some mothers could no longer carry their starving babies. They simply wrapped them in a blanket and left them along the path in the snow. It was so sad to see so many babies wrapped in their blankets, some crying, some silenced by death, left lying along the path. Everyone passed by and I could hear them say, "Ohhh, Ohhh", but no one could stop

---

[8] Veterans record memories of how some of the people riding on the train arrived at their destination frozen to the top of the boxcar. Flesh had frozen to metal in temperatures that would drop to twenty below zero. Source: *I Remember Korea* by Linda Granfield, story by Jim Ramsay.

and pick them up. Sometimes I would pass what I thought was a mound of snow, but a closer look revealed a dead mother and her children, gentle snow covering their dead frozen bodies. I would pass many children and babies who died along that awful journey.

At times we would come upon a little village. Many of the homes in the villages had been burned by their owners in order to keep the Communists from benefiting from the shelter. But some people had hope that they would be returning and they did not burn their homes. These were the homes that we raided for survival. Sometimes we entered the homes and found some food. We would bring whatever we found back together and share it with each other. We found some blankets and warmer clothing. We would take the items with us. These precious garments would help us to survive. Sometimes we would sleep in the homes, many people packed together like sardines in an effort to stay warm. Early the next day our journey would begin again. There was little time for sleep. We had to keep moving.

One night we found a little house in a deserted village. We ate some rice and beans together. Again that night people found anywhere to lie down and sleep together. I stayed in the little house and fell into a very deep sleep that night. When I woke up, there were dead people lying all around me. I had blood on my coat and my body. I asked the others what had happened. Everyone was crying and scared. They said to me, "What do you mean, what happened? How could you sleep through all that shooting and screaming? Surely you heard the commotion!"

I could not believe it. The Communists had entered that very house that night. They shot the people in the room with me. I do not know how I could have slept through the shooting and the killing. Maybe I was dead. Maybe I came back to life. I do not know. All I do know is that I woke up and the others were dead.

We began walking again; there were more dead bodies along the path. We just kept walking. We were starving. Occasionally we would find a house with some food but mostly, all the houses had been raided by the people before us. We walked for a total of fifteen days. We finally arrived in a town where the people had not moved south.  It was not Taegu; we had walked to Taejon, (Daejeon). Although we had been told to go to Taegu, we could go no further.  The people told us not to go to Taegu.  There are so many refugees in Taegu; they had closed the town to any new arrivals.[9]

Many people were going to stay in Taejon and we decided to stay also.  We had walked almost one hundred miles in the deep snow and bitter cold.  We had survived the starvation, the freezing temperatures and even the Communists.  Taegu was another one hundred miles away.  We knew that we could not walk any further. We stayed in Taejon.

---

[9] Seoul citizens left the city at a daily rate of 80,000 and by December 28th half of the city's one million residents had headed south (by boat, by plane, by train or by foot).
*http://www.korean-war.com/TimeLine*.
Compiled by Ed Evanhoe, November 2002.

Photo of Korean refugees, heading south from Kangning in January of 1951. The refugees were trudging through ice and snow in an attempt to escape the Communists.

Calmus, Walter, Photographer.    01/08/1951.    Signal Corps Photo. Courtesy National Archives: (Identifier 111-SC-356475).

Lee Ock Soon traveled under similar conditions in her escape from Seoul.

# 10
## Taejon
### Surviving Alone

#### December 1950

Although we had been advised to go to Taegu, we came as far as Taejon and we could not walk any further. We decided to stay here. We were hungry, tired and cold. We did not have money to rent a room or to buy any food. While we were walking on the journey we were able to find an empty house to raid and food to share. But now that we were in a town, we could not feed ourselves that way any longer.

I do not know how but somehow Hana was able to get a room for us. The room was completely empty, no pots or pans, nothing. We went out and found some old empty cans lying in the street. We brought them back and washed them out. Shin and I went from door to door at supper time begging for any leftovers. Some people would give us one spoonful of rice. Other people would give us some of their leftovers and dump them into the can. Some people would say they had already given. Some people were very mean about it, and shouted at us not to come back there again. Some people felt really guilty and sad because they did not have much to give. I met all kinds of people. We did this for three days. We would bring our cans back to the room and mix it all together. Whatever Shin and I were able to bring back, we shared with everyone.

Hana was busy going all over the town looking for a job. She offered to do anything, wash clothes, cook or clean. There simply were no jobs available. Everyone was barely surviving. Hana started to prostitute herself with the American soldiers. She sold her body to feed us and pay the rent. One day she was crying and she told me that it really hurt her to sell her body but we had to survive. She asked me to go and look for a job. She did not tell me what to do but she told me to go out and look for job. She could not support all of us any longer. So I went out door to door asking for a job. I would do any work that anyone needed to have done. But there were no jobs. No one had money to pay anyone to work for them.

I kept walking and walking and walking. Finally it was dark. I was standing on a street corner when a man came around the corner. He had two wooden blocks in his hands and he was banging them together making noise to remind people of the curfew. There were many Communists who had been sneaking into the city at night to set off bombs. Because of this everyone in the village had to know the town password. If you were out on the streets after curfew and you did not know the town's password, you were suspected to be a Communist.

The man stopped and asked me, "What is the password?" I told the man that I did not know the password. I explained my situation to him. I had no place to go, I had been looking for a job all day but I could not find a job. I explained to him that I did not know where I was and I had no family.

The man took me to his house and told his wife about me. She was very kind to me. She gave me some food and some hot tea to drink. They allowed me to sleep in their house that night. He explained to me that the next day a truck would be coming to the village. He was going to put me on that truck. He told me that there would be other people on the truck. All the people were going to Nonsan. There were a lot of American soldiers stationed in Nonsan. They had money and they needed people to work for them. The man told me that I should try to get a job washing their clothes or something like that. He told me that I should be able to find some work there. I was very hopeful to go to Nonsan and wash the American's clothes.

# 11
## Nonsan
### Camptown

18 years old

The next morning we got up and left the house. We walked to the main intersection of the village. Just as the man had said, a truck drove up to the corner and stopped. The man put me on the back of the truck and wished me well. I was surprised that there were so many people on the back of the truck already. We were all headed towards Nonsan.

Many of the people already had jobs lined up to wash the soldiers' clothes, sew for the soldiers or shine their shoes. We soon arrived at the 76th Engineer Construction Battalion. I was hoping to get some kind of work, but all of the jobs were filled. I did not speak any English so it was difficult for me to ask the American soldiers to give me some work to do. I did not find any work that day.

I looked around and I could see that there were houses in small clusters one or two miles apart. I could see one house here and maybe two or three there. I was hungry and cold. I started to walk from house to house asking for a job or something to eat. I think I went to about five houses and it got dark. I had no place to go and no hope for a job. I came upon an old outhouse near one of the houses. I decided to go inside the outhouse and try to stay warm and sleep in there. The temperatures were freezing and I could not stop shivering. It was very difficult to fall asleep. The bitter cold and shivering were keeping me awake.

During the night, a woman came out of the house to use the outhouse. I had been unable to fall asleep so I heard her coming. I hurried up to get out of the outhouse before she got there. While I was standing outside, I noticed a big pile of straw. I remembered years ago when I slept in the shed with that old cow and how the cow and the straw kept me warm. As soon as the woman went back into her house, I pulled some straw out of the hay pile and I made myself a little nest. I crawled inside the nest and sat down.  At first it was really very cold and still impossible to sleep.  I sat there freezing and shivering.  But the longer I sat in that pile of hay, the warmer it got.  Finally I was able to fall asleep in that little nest.

Dawn arrived and I was still sleeping soundly.  The woman came out again to use the outhouse.  This time, she must have seen me sleeping in the hay.  She woke me up and asked me, "What are you doing sleeping out here?"  Once again, I explained my situation to her.  She felt sorry for me and invited me to come into her house.  Her house was very comfortable.  Her mother and her husband were very surprised that she had found me in their haystack.  The woman gave me some hot water to warm my feet and hands.  She was kind and gave me a bowl of rice and a cup of hot tea.  Although she was not a wealthy woman, she gave me a room to sleep in.

That day I did everything I could to show them how grateful I was.  I got the water and started the fire for them.  I cooked and washed up all the dishes.  I told them I could wash their clothes and help them with their animals.  I was so thankful that these people were letting me sleep in the extra room.  I really wanted them to know just how grateful I was and tried very hard to work for them.

I had been staying with her for about two weeks when she told me I could not stay there for free.  She told me I had to get a job and start paying for my room.  I told her that I had tried to get a job many times and there were no jobs available.  The woman told me to go get a job or start sleeping with American soldiers to get some money.  Her husband could not work anymore and they were taking care of his mother.  I had to get a job or find some soldiers to pay for me.  In other words, I should become a prostitute.

I was about 18 years old and I was terrified of American soldiers.  They looked so big and I had heard stories about them.  When she told me that I should start to sell my body for money, I started to cry.  I pleaded with her to let me stay and I would try to find some other work.  I told her I could not be a prostitute.  She told me that I had no choice. I would have to leave or I should go out and bring American soldiers back. She said I could use the room she had given to me to sleep in. I told her I could not do that.

I would not go out to get a soldier. I just sat there on the porch and kept crying. She tried hard to drag me out to the street but I would not go. There were many soldiers always walking around the streets because they had nothing else to do. There were not any stores or entertainment. Many women in the town had turned to prostitution for survival. Now the woman I was staying with wanted me to make some money for her and her family. She fixed up my hair and she put lipstick on me. She tried to tell me that I looked just fine and that I needed to go out and find a soldier. I still wouldn't go.

Finally she got tired of trying to push me out onto the street and she decided to fix herself up and bring a soldier back for me. She put her own hair up and put her lipstick on and went out into the street. I could hear her shouting in her broken English, "Who wantsa wife? Who wantsa wife?" I had no idea what she was saying. I just sat on the porch, scared and not sure what was going to happen.

The next thing I knew, the woman came back to the house with three soldiers. I was sitting there, terrified. I was shivering, not because I was cold but because I was so scared. Tears were streaming down my face. The lipstick she had put on me was smeared across my chin. I was just a mess.

The big soldier was speaking some English and some Korean to the woman. I sat there shaking and crying while this woman tried to sell me to the soldier. I did not know what was going on.

The soldiers were talking back and forth while the woman kept telling them that I was a good girl and she continued to try to get some money for me. I did not know what they were saying, but eventually she became very angry and told me to leave.

She told me to leave her house and to follow the soldiers. I was terrified. I just got up and followed them onto the road. I had no idea where I was going.  They walked in front of me talking and laughing as they went along.  I did not understand anything they were saying.  I felt like a little lost dog following some people around.  I was trying not to cry anymore but I was still shaking because I was so afraid.

The big soldier must have thought I was cold and he gave me his coat.  It was huge.  I knew the coat was dragging on the ground.  I just kept it on and followed behind the three American soldiers not knowing what was going to happen to me next.

# PART TWO

## The Big Soldier

# 12
## The Big Soldier
### Frank Crimbchin

September 25, 1951

I could not believe it when I got the notice that I was being inducted into the U.S. Army. Yeah, I was old enough, 23 years old, but I was classified as 4F – Not Qualified for Military Service due to Medical Reasons. I thought since I was injured on the job and almost lost my leg; that got me out of the draft. I was sure they had made a mistake. I even called them to remind them of my 4F Classification but it didn't matter. I was told they were aware of my classification and I was going anyway. They needed soldiers and I was to report for active duty just as the letter outlined. What! I couldn't believe it. I was being drafted!

I had been working as a machinist since I was fourteen years old. I had quit school in the eighth grade, well, I didn't really quit. The nuns at St. Mary's told my parents that if they promised not to send me back, they would pass me out of the eighth grade. So the deal was made and I never went back. Yeah, I guess I did give them a hard time.

My Uncle John Rennekamp got me an apprenticeship down at Taylor and Wilson's Machine Shop in McKees Rocks. I had started out as an apprentice and just worked my way up to a machinist. I was as good as any of those college educated engineers as a matter of fact, I doubt if any one of them knew how to run a machine. Those draftsmen were just as bad. I always had to correct their drawings. They sent their drawings out to me and I would make the piece exactly as it was designed only to find out *their* dimensions were wrong. I got tired of that nonsense real quick. I learned to check all their work before I even started the job and if it didn't add up right; it went back to them for corrections. I had no intention of making the same piece over and over again because they didn't know what they were doing. But I was just one of the mill boys and had to sweat in the shop every day, while they walked around in their clean button down shirts telling me what to do.

Yeah. They put me on an old flat belt planer to operate on my own when I was underage. Those planers were designed to shave steel. The old ones would push the steel through a column and the bed would automatically reverse direction. The bed constantly changed back and forth. In between changes, I was able set the machine in neutral. Once the planer was set on neutral, I could climb up to get measurements or mike the piece.

Well, I set the machine in neutral and climbed up to get the measurements. The machine was so old and worn out, it automatically flipped itself into action and my leg got caught in the machine. Instead of shaving steel, it shaved a huge piece of flesh off my thigh. I was only sixteen years old when I almost lost my leg in that machine.

Blood was everywhere. The nightmare was - I was literally stuck on the machine screaming for help. To top it all off, no one could hear me since all the machines in the shop were running full throttle. Finally, my cousin John heard me hollering and came running. John almost passed out when he saw all the blood. He quickly shut off the machine. The pain was incredible. I was screaming and begging him to punch me and knock me out. I just couldn't take the excruciating pain. At first John didn't want to punch me, but I kept begging him to do it. Finally he punched me in the face several times, but it did not knock me out. I kept telling him. "Punch me harder! Punch me harder!" John was screaming that he was punching me as hard as he could. By the time the ambulance arrived and took me to the hospital, my head hurt worse than my leg.

The nurses kept asking me what happened to my face since I was all beat up! John never did knock me out that day. I guess that only happens in the movies.

I didn't walk for six months. The pain was tremendous but I got up and got walking again. We should have sued that bunch. Well, we did talk about it but my Uncle John had got me the job and he was a big shot there. If we sued them it would look bad for him, so we didn't sue. We should have. The only good thing that came out of it was that my injuries kept me out of the draft. I was classified as a 4F – Not Qualified for Military Service due to Medical Reasons. Yeah, right.

4F or not, I was drafted. They said they needed soldiers; well they needed to go find another soldier - not this one. I had my parents to take care of. They had a mortgage they couldn't pay and bills piled up. I had been helping them for the past nine years. My father was a bartender at the Eagles Club in McKees Rocks. He sure didn't make enough money to keep the family. My mother tried to help out by washing the beer glasses down at the club. That brought in a few extra dollars; but it wasn't enough.

I had heard the stories about how they used to take me with them to the club while my mother washed the glasses. They would sit me up on the bar and give me whiskey corks to suck on like pacifiers just to keep me quiet. I must have liked it because I sure do like my whiskey now.

The house they bought was really more expensive than what they could afford. I had been helping them out since I was just a kid. I really didn't know how they were going to make it when I entered the Service. They would be without my paycheck. None of that mattered now. I was drafted into the Army on November 1, 1950, and sent to Maryland to learn how to be a soldier. That was the quickest lesson I ever got. After basic training I moved on to Fort Lawton in Seattle, Washington.

I continued to send as much money as I could home to help my parents with their bills. Unfortunately, my soldier's pay wasn't near what I was making as a civilian so they were getting a lot less money. My parents never asked me for money but I knew they would be struggling and I couldn't let them lose their house.

Now after almost eleven months in Seattle, I just couldn't believe I was headed for Korea of all places. I had never been on a ship in my life and had never seen the ocean. Actually I had never been too far from Pennsylvania. A lot of the guys had already been shipped overseas. I was held back because they wanted me to lose a lot of weight before they would send me. I had been losing weight since I got drafted last November. The food was terrible and the portions were nothing like what I was used to eating at home. One thing about my German parents; they sure knew how to cook good food!

Since I had lost the weight and reached the goal the Army had set for me, I was assigned to a ship headed for Korea. Well the guys on that ship, they just didn't know me. I had been on my own since I was 14 years old and I had always done just what I wanted to do. If those guys thought they were going to tell *me* what to do, they just didn't know who they were dealing with.

# 13
## Trans-Pacific Nightmare
### Journey to Sasebo
September 25, 1951

USNS Marine Phoenix (T-AP-195)

Source: http://www.navsource.org/archives/09/22/22195.htm

I had to admit, the ocean was impressive. I had never seen anything like it before in my life. I had been up to Lake Erie several times, but the Pacific Ocean was amazing. They told us we would be on the ship for about 5,000 miles. I couldn't even imagine it. We were told the trip would take about two weeks to get to Japan. Once we got there, we would have to transfer to another ship to get to Korea.

I went aboard the U.S. Naval Ship Marine Phoenix. The ship was only six years old and in great shape. It even had some recreational facilities for the troops. They warned us that some people would get seasick. I had a strong stomach and didn't expect to get sick at all. I was actually kind of looking forward to the recreational facilities and checking out the Phoenix.

That never happened. The trip was a nightmare. I was seasick the whole time. I actually thought I was going to die before I got over there.  Not everyone was sick.  I didn't know how they did it.  I was downstairs but the guys had been vomiting all over the place and I couldn't take it anymore.  I moved upstairs to get some fresh air.  I could hardly find a place to sit or lay down.

Eventually I did find a place to lie down on the deck.  I was dizzy and nauseated with a pounding headache when some young punk officer came over and kicked me, telling me to move over. He pointed to the rope and said I had crossed the line over to where only officers were permitted.  I told the jerk to get away from me or I would throw him overboard.  He said he would be back and I would be disciplined.  I was so sick I really didn't care. If he laid even one hand on me, I swear I would have thrown him overboard.  He never did come back.

Those were two of the worst weeks of my life.  I had never been sick like that before and all I could think about was that once I got there, I would have to make this awful trip all over again to get back home.  It was a horrible thought.  After two miserable weeks, we finally arrived in Japan.  I was never so happy to get off a ship.

Soldiers arriving at Sasebo Port, Japan

We landed at the Sasebo Port near Kyushu, Japan. I remember what was written on that portal. *"Thru This Port Pass The Best Damned Fighting Men In The World".* Well I had never seen any combat before so I would just have to wait to see if we were the best damned fighting men in the world.

USNS Sgt. George D. Keathley (T-AGS-35)

We didn't stay in Sasebo very long. We were only about 165 miles from Korea. I was hoping that the next leg of the trip might be bearable. We boarded an older WWII ship, *The Sgt George D. Keathley.* We were headed for the port in Inchon (Incheon), Korea. That was the same port that General MacArthur had landed his troops in the previous year. That military operation actually changed the course of the war.

On June 25, 1950, after the Communists invaded South Korea and captured Seoul, the United Nations troops were being pushed further and further south. After three months of fighting, the U.S. and UN were able to hold off the enemy at the Pusan Perimeter. It was General MacArthur's brilliant plan to counterstrike the enemy through Inchon. Due to the incredible currents and dangerous tides, no one had even considered an invasion at this port. The enemy had concentrated their efforts further south at the Pusan Perimeter, also failing to consider an invasion at this port. General MacArthur found confidence in the element of surprise.

On September 15, 1950, General MacArthur launched an amphibious assault at Inchon which included more than 320 warships, 4 aircraft carriers and nearly 70,000 men. The U.S. Marines rode the dangerous tides into the harbor and would continue to fight their way into Seoul where they would recapture the city.

I found it amazing that we would be using the same port and battling the same currents and incredible high tides. Inchon was famous for tides as high as 20 feet but on the day of the invasion, General MacArthur knew the moon's position would cause a rise and fall of 32 feet. The moon and the stars lined up and the General was able to implement the surprise attack.

We sailed on the *The Sgt George D. Keathley* into Inchon on a 20 foot wave. (If the timing was off, a ship would be grounded.) We rode the tide into Inchon and stayed in an abandoned school house for a couple of days.

We were all pretty surprised when we got our first view of Inchon. It was really depressing. If this was one of their biggest cities, it was unbelievable. Where was the city? I just wanted to get this over with and get back to Pittsburgh. There was not a decent thing anywhere. Inchon was a dirty old town with a bunch of bombed out buildings. We stayed a couple days in the school house and eventually a truck came to pick some of us up and take us to Gwangju, (Kwangju).

I could not believe this country. The people were dirt poor. There was nothing here. I could not believe people had engaged in a war over this country. What were they fighting over this for? I could almost see fighting over a country that had something but these people couldn't even feed their own families. And the Communists wanted this place! I just didn't get it. And now Americans were over here dying for this. I really didn't get it. I never saw so many people living in tents and shacks. We didn't pass one decent house the entire trip to Gwangju. What a country.

# 14
# 76<sup>th</sup> Engineer Construction Battalion
## Gwangju, Korea

### October 1951

I was assigned to the 76<sup>th</sup> Engineer Construction Battalion, Headquarters Company, (HQ), which was stationed in a village south of Seoul called Gwangju. Our military camp was known as Camp Sykes.

Each battalion had about 1,000 men. Our battalion was divided into one Head Quarters, and three Companies; Company A, Company B and Company C. The guys were working on a military training camp for the Republic of Korean (ROK) Army. I had heard that the ROK Army was untrained and unequipped but it was really amazing that they didn't even have a decent training camp until the U.S. came over to build it. Here they were in the middle of this disastrous war and they were just now getting a training camp! The 76th had been there for quite a while and had already built about 1,000 Quonset huts and tropical shell buildings for the ROK Army.

I was assigned to a tent with about twelve other guys. The tents were relatively big and designed to hold up to sixteen soldiers. I could tell living in this tent was going to be hell. It was already getting cold and all we had was a small heater in the middle of the tent. We each had a cot and a sleeping bag. I was really going to miss my bed in McKees Rocks.

I was glad to be assigned to the 76<sup>th</sup> Engineers Battalion; at least that kept me out of the front lines. When they found out I was a master machinist, they assigned me to Headquarters, (HQ).

HQ had two "machine shop" trucks that we worked out of. Each truck carried machine equipment so we could travel anywhere and fix or construct anything. The larger truck pretty much stayed at the base. Large projects were brought to the base for repair. The smaller machine shop truck could be driven directly to the job site. If some heavy equipment broke down in the quarry or they needed parts to repair equipment on the bridge, we got the job.

The 76<sup>th</sup> had some pretty heavy equipment to build roads, bridges and landing strips. The machine operators did a lot of busting up rock to use on the projects. There was always something breaking down on the equipment so we stayed pretty busy.

All the guys in my tent were nice fellows. One of the guys, Bob Willem, would eventually become a really good friend to me while I was over there. Bob had grown up in Indianapolis, Indiana. His family was not rich but they taught him to work hard and save his money. Bob had a decent job at RCA before he was drafted. The guy had already served the country in the Marine Reserves, so he was still a reservist when he got called up for duty.

When I met Bob, he had recently learned that his best friend from home died after being severely wounded in battle. Bob was always trying to be the tough guy but you could tell he still wasn't over it. Apparently he and his best friend, Charles Tyler Haslet, were drafted about the same time. Charlie was drafted into the Infantry 7th Division 28 days before Bob was drafted. When Bob arrived in Korea, he continued to write to his good friend. Bob had felt so lucky that he did not have to go to the Infantry like Charlie. Shortly after arriving in Gwangju, Bob's letters to Charlie were being returned to him. It was then he found out his friend had been severely wounded. Later he would find out, Charlie died on July 23, 1951.

Bob never wanted to appear weak and he didn't talk much about losing his best friend but it shook him up pretty bad. Decades would pass before Bob would tell me of the guilt he carried that he had survived the war and his best friend did not.

The guys in HQ all worked together pretty good since we all had some machine work background. Bob had arrived in Korea in April of 1951 so he had about five months under his belt by the time I got there. When he first arrived, he had been in Inchon working on the Cum River Bridge and then was moved to Taejon. Eventually he ended up in Gwangju at Camp Sykes. Bob was our demolition guy. He was really good at blowing things up. Bob would set the dynamite in the mountains and blast the rock out of it to be used to build air strips and roads. Bob was a good hearted guy who would eventually make Sergeant which worked out really good for me.

I made a lot of good friends in the 76th. Another good buddy was Roger Van Winkle. All the guys called him Rip. Rip was a great guy who had a girlfriend back home who he planned on marrying. Somehow he had taken up with a Korean girl in town. Her name was Rose and boy did she fall for Rip. She would hang out by the fence at the base for hours waiting for Rip to get back. I don't think Rose knew that Rip was engaged to someone at home and she was really in love with the guy. Well, I guess it was love. A lot of the women just wanted a ticket to America.

I had another good friend, Thomas Victory. Everyone called him Victor or Vic. Sometimes Roger, Vic and I would go out and find some Korean rice wine known as *nongju.* We would just sit and pass the bottle around but those times were few and far between. Most times we all worked hard on the equipment and trucks. We learned to help each other and always watched out for each other. I didn't know just how important their friendships would be to me for many months to come.

When I first arrived at Camp Sykes, Sergeant Stout was in charge. He was decent, fair to the guys and pitched in whenever he could. He, just like the rest of us, was counting the days until he could return home to his family. No one wanted to be there. It was just too primitive and far too dangerous.

The war had been going on now for over a year and we had lost tens of thousands of men. The South Koreans had lost twice as many people as the U.S. It was madness and it had to end.

Rumors about a peace treaty were talked about all the time but nothing ever seemed to change. We could still hear the battles in the distance and the guys were still dying. As part of the 76th Construction Engineer Battalion, we were not to be within

500 yards of the front line. Although I was glad for that, we still had to be on guard.

Camp Sykes was huge. There were rows and rows of sixteen-man tents, and tent halls for meals. A lot of the Korean people had moved close to the camp trying to find work. Anywhere the Americans set up a camp, the Korean people would follow. These groups became known as camptowns[10]. Soldiers needed help with laundry and alterations. The Koreans were more than happy to work for the soldiers who found their services both convenient and cheap! We even had a Korean tailor on base that could fix or sew anything. He was fast too. All the guys took their repairs to him. Some of the men used the locals to do their wash. That worked out great. A few cents to us was like a hundred dollars to them.

The sign reads "Tailor Shop"; picture of shoe shine boy and tailor.

South Korea was a very dangerous place with enemy guerillas in the towns and villages. We didn't know who we could trust since the Communists looked no different than the South

---

[10] *Camptowns are towns which spring up near military bases. The economy is supported by the presence of the base and some local civilians are fortunate enough to be employed on the base. Part of every Camptown is the presence of prostitution catering to soldiers.*

Koreans. We would eventually lose several guys to enemy guerillas who were dressed in civilian clothes. As part of our responsibilities, we rotated guard duty both around the camp and on the bridges, every night.

The people in the country were starving. War had destroyed their homes and their land. Many of the children had been orphaned and were living on the streets. Most of the men had been killed or sent to fight. The 76th had "adopted" a really great little kid who had been orphaned early in the war. I guess it made us all feel good like we were saving at least one kid. His name was Kim and he always had a smile on his face, even after everything he had lost.

Kim lived in the tent with Sergeant First Class Anderson. Kim did a lot of chores, kept the tent clean, and ran errands – anything you asked him. Sarge was a good ole southern boy from Nashville who sure did love his country music. He had a violin with him and many a night he would play country music for the guys. He really took a liking to Kim. Years later I heard that he

Bob Willem and Kim

tried his best to adopt Kim and take him to America. I'm not sure how that ever worked out.

The people were dirt poor and hungry. Everywhere you looked, people were scavenging for food. I saw mostly women and children trying to survive. Apparently their husbands were either dead or fighting in the war. Women would gather at the well to wash clothes or vegetables. Life was always hard for these women but war made it hand to mouth survival. Everyone worked. The little girls were there to help their mothers and many times they could be seen carrying a younger brother or sister on their back.

I never knew people in the world lived like this. Americans had it so good. If Americans could see how these people lived, then maybe they would learn to appreciate everything they had.

Korean women and children at the wells, washing clothes and vegetables.

Young boys sliding on the ice with boards and ice picks.

It was amazing that even in wartime kids found ways to have fun. When the rice paddies froze over, I would see groups of little boys sliding around the ice on boards with ice picks in their hands. Some things in life are just universal, like finding ways to play.

During the war, a lot of children were orphaned and just roaming the streets on their own. Every night children would climb the fence and crawl through the barbed wire at the top of the fence to get inside the camp. They would sneak in to steal food and scraps from the trash bins. I never understood how they could get through the barbed wire but they were masters at it. We all looked the other way when it came to those starving children. We would let them run in and run out with the scraps of food. Of course the official orders were to shoot *anyone* illegally entering the camp, but no one had the heart to do that.

One night, about a month after I arrived at Camp Sykes, shots rang out when one of the guys from Company A decided not to turn his back and went ahead and shot the boy. The boy looked about eight or nine years old and had just found some scraps from our trash can. He had gotten about half way up the fence, when the soldier took aim. I could never figure out what possessed that soldier to shoot that child. Well after that no one wanted anything to do with the guy. Eventually they had to transfer him out of Camp Sykes for his own safety.

Some things stay in a soldiers head forever. I will never get the sight of that dead boy, lying on the ground with chunks of old bread in his hand, out of my mind.

# 15
## The Girl
### Nonsan, Korea

#### January 1952

We finished the work in Gwangju in January 1952 and we were ordered to move our camp north to Nonsan. We packed up our tents, trucks, equipment, and tools and started heading north. It was cold in Korea in January. There was not a decent thing between Gwangju and Nonsan, nothing but mountains and rows and rows of rice paddies. We traveled about 75 miles on those dirt roads.

We finally arrived in Nonsan and found it was just another poor village. Like Gwangju, people lived in small houses with grass roofs. The town was located between Inchon and Seoul. A lot of fighting had taken place there and all of the bridges heading towards Seoul had been blown up at one time or another. The 76th was sent there to work on a huge bridge over the Han River.

Picture of 76th Enroute from Gwangju to Nonsan, Korea.

The lieutenant ordered us to set up camp in the dry river bed. Well we did just as we were told and set everything up, tents, cots, bedding everything right in the dry river bed. The rocks everywhere made living there really uncomfortable. The whole camp was set up in just a few days.

Bob, Victor and I were working twelve hour days making machine parts for broken equipment. We finally got a day off and decided to go out and see what was happening in "downtown" Nonsan. Of course there was no downtown, just a small village where the houses looked like they were about to fall down. Poverty was everywhere. The people lived in shacks or mud houses with thatched roofs. There was literally nothing to do in these villages.

While in Gwangju, Bob had met a girl whose name was Sunja. They became good friends and she asked him to take her with him to Nonsan. Sunja did come to Nonsan with Bob and she quickly found a room to rent. One thing that was really cheap in these villages was the rent. People were happy to take in boarders for the extra money.

Typical Street in Nonsan.

Soldier posing with village children
next to house with a straw thatched roof.

We were finally granted some free time to go off base.
Bob was heading over to Sunja's place with some coffee and
cereal, so Victor and I joined him for a walk to the village. We
were on our way when we heard a commotion on the street and
decided to go over to see what was going on.

Well there was this old Korean woman, walking down the
road, shouting in some kind of broken English, "Who wantsa wife?
Who wantsa wife?" We thought we had seen just about
everything but we decided to follow her to find out what she was
shouting about. We were laughing and joking as we followed the
old woman into her yard not knowing what to expect.

We arrived at her house and sitting on the porch was the
most pitiful looking girl I had ever seen in my life. The poor thing
was sitting there crying and shaking like a leaf. The girl looked like
she was about 18 or 19 years old. The old woman was trying to
sell her to us for sex. I could tell the girl was terrified. She
obviously did not want to prostitute herself. Many of the Korean

women had done just that, turned to prostitution in order to survive. But this kid, well it was clear, she did not want to be a prostitute. I really felt sorry for her and felt like I couldn't just leave her there for some idiot to take advantage of her. I don't know why I did it, I sure didn't have the money to help her but I just decided to get her away from that woman and try to help the girl.

Bob and Victor thought I was nuts. Victor said, "What are you doing? You can't take her with you. What are you going to do for her? You should just leave her here. Come on, let's go." Bob agreed with Victor and told me to leave the kid there and just move on. There was something about the girl that got under my skin. I don't know if it was her obvious fear or the bad situation she was in. I don't know what possessed me to do anything for her but I just couldn't walk away. I felt like I had to help her.

Well we talked about it. I asked Bob if he thought Sunja would let her stay with her until I could find a place for the girl to live. I would help pay Sunja's rent if she would let the girl share the room with her. Bob didn't think Sunja would like the idea but decided we could ask her about it. The girl didn't speak any English and my Korean was limited to just a few words. We told the old woman to tell the girl to follow us and we would find a place for her. She said something to the girl who then got up, still shaking like a leaf, but she did follow behind us.

The girl continued to follow behind us as we went on to Sunja's place. It was January in Korea and freezing cold. The girl was still shaking so much, I gave her my coat. It was way too big for her but she put it on and continued to trail behind us.

Eventually we arrived at Sunja's place. Sunja was living in one room and was definitely not happy to have another person stay with her. Bob spoke to Sunja and explained that I was going to help pay her rent so then she decided to go along with it. Sunja was great since she could interpret a little for us. We found out the girl's name was Lee Ock Soon and she had no family nearby. I couldn't figure out what happened to her family but I guessed they were killed in the war. I asked Sunja to explain to Ock Soon that I would pay for her to stay here. I had to get back to camp but I would bring some clothes for her next week.

I gave Sunja the six bucks I had on me. I asked Sunja to give her some food and help her out. I left her with Sunja, not sure if she would still be there the next week when I returned. No matter what happened, I did feel good about getting the girl away from the old woman.

I went back to the camp but I couldn't stop thinking about the girl, Lee Ock Soon. I didn't see her smile the whole time we were there but I think she understood we were trying to help her.

I did my job all week, fixing trucks with broken rods, making new bearings and bolts - but every day I woke up wondering if the girl was still at Sunja's place. I couldn't wait to go back and see if she was there. I was broke until pay day. I had sent $75.00 home last month to help my parents. The girl really needed some clothes. I found an extra pair of long underwear and an extra jacket. It was so cold outside; I thought I would take those over to her. I really hoped that everything was working out between Sunja and Ock Soon and the girl would still be there when I went back.

I didn't know why but I just couldn't get her off my mind.

# 16
## The Language of Love
### Frank and Ock Soon

January 1952

So much had happened to Ock Soon throughout her life. Now she found herself living with a stranger in the town of Nonsan. She had tried to find work since being sent there several months ago. Nothing had worked out; but she was glad that the big soldier had brought her here and then went away. She was really afraid of the soldiers and so glad to be with a young woman, Sunja, who was about her age. Sunja was very kind to Ock Soon.

The first thing Sunja did when the soldiers left was to call her landlord to get some hot water for Ock Soon to get a bath. The landlord did just that. Between the two of them they got Ock Soon bathed and scrubbed. Sunja took all of Ock Soon's clothing and burned them since they were full of lice. Sunja did not want lice in her room! She then loaned Ock Soon some of her very own clothing. They were comfortable and Ock Soon was so very happy to be here. Sunja explained to Ock Soon that the big soldier was going to bring her some new clothes next week.

The next thing Sunja did was to take Ock Soon to the hair shop down the road. She used some of the money the big soldier had given her to get Ock Soon a perm. The main purpose was to kill the lice in her hair. Ock Soon had never had a perm and she felt so happy and so pretty by the end of the day. It was like a miracle. The girls became fast friends and each tried to help the other.

A week passed quickly and one day the big soldier came back. Bob, Sunja's American friend was with him. They would talk to Sunja who translated to Ock Soon. Sunja told Ock Soon the big soldier's name was Frank. He had brought some of his own clothes for her. He would not get paid until the end of the month. When he got paid, he would buy her some new dresses but for now, all he had were some extra long johns and a jacket. The clothes were huge and Ock Soon could wrap them around her three times. She laughed but took them anyway. She was glad to have anything at that point.

Frank was so kind to her. They went for a walk into the town. He smiled and touched her hair. She knew he liked her new perm. He smiled and touched her dress, although it belonged to Sunja, she was happy that Frank liked the dress on her. They could not communicate a lot but somehow she had touched his heart and now he was touching hers. They spent the day together. Sunja and Ock Soon built a fire and cooked dinner for the soldiers. The two couples sat down together and enjoyed the rice and vegetables. When the meal was over, the soldiers had to return to Camp Sykes. Frank asked Sunja to explain to Ock Soon that she should stay there and he would be back the next week with some new clothes for her. Ock Soon was no longer afraid of the big soldier; but instead, she would really look forward to seeing him again.

The day ended and Ock Soon felt so wonderful. The big soldier was as kind as he was big and she started to trust him and not fear him. She had never felt so happy before in her life.

A week passed and Frank returned. He brought with him a box and handed the box to Ock Soon. In the box was the most beautiful hanbok, Ock Soon had ever seen. It was made of black satin. The *jeogori* (jacket) was a beautiful soft satin with a beautiful white trimmed collar. The collar was known as a *gi* and when attached to the jacket looked like a piece of jewelry around her neck. The *chima* (skirt) was made of the same fabric and just as beautiful.

In all her life, Ock Soon had only seen the rich women of the town wear a dress like this. She herself had never had one on before. Ock Soon put the hanbok on and it fit perfectly. The satin was so soft on her skin Ock Soon began to cry. She had never had a dress like this in all her life. She could not believe it. She felt so beautiful with her new perm and her new dress, it was like a dream. She had never been so happy in all of her life on this earth. Frank was happy too. He looked at her and just kept staring.  Ock Soon was very shy but when Frank reached down to kiss her, she kissed him back.

Her heart jumped and she knew she had found someone very special.  She did not know how she could have been so lucky but somehow she had found or been found by this man who really did care about her.  She would do anything to thank him and show him how much she cared for him.  She knew she was falling in love.

Ock Soon in her first hanbok in January 1952.

# 17
## Love Unspoken
### Nonsan, South Korea

January 1952

Frank and Ock Soon were falling in love, even though they could not speak the same language there are some things in life that are universal, things like a smile, laughter, passion and love. Although non-spoken, people of all nations and all ages understand these things.

Frank spent every free moment he had available with Ock Soon. Many times he would leave the camp in the middle of the night and break curfew to go off limits just to see Ock Soon. Frank was a big, strong guy who took no gruff from anyone, not even the company commander. Most of the guys didn't mess with him and as long as he was back before wake up call, they turned their heads the other way. No one wanted to mess with Frank or get into a battle with him.

Frank continued to work hard as a machinist in the 76th. Their motto was, "To Work Is to Conquer". He was probably one of the best machinists the company ever had. Most of the guys were young guys that had been on assembly lines and were good at what they did but they had limited skills. Frank on the other hand had been working in a machine shop since he was fourteen years old. He knew how to run every piece of equipment in the shop and could make any part that was needed. Frank was not only a master machinist but he could build just about anything. Before being drafted, even though he worked full time at Taylor and Wilson's Manufacturing Company, he was also building a summer home for the family.

Frank spent every free minute working to build a cottage in Slippery Rock, Pennsylvania. He and his younger brother Donald as well as his parents, would drive 90 miles on winding roads heading north from McKees Rocks to Slippery Rock every weekend. They had put all of their money together and bought a heavily wooded lot along the Slippery Rock Creek. Frank recognized that the lot had potential and he had a dream. He wanted a place in the woods to go on weekends and vacations. He wanted a place where he could go to hunt and fish. This lot was perfect for his dream to build the family a second home along that creek.

Every weekend, the Crimbchins' worked day and night cutting down trees and clearing the lot. The trees were huge; some of the giant oaks were forty feet tall. The guys would climb those trees and tie bull ropes around them. They would get the six foot long two man saw and cut into the base of that tree. They would each take turns pulling on that saw manually, sweat pouring off their backs, while others pulled on the rope guiding the tree in the desired direction. Finally someone would shout the urgent, "Timber!" and all heads went up to make sure they were not in the way of the giant oak falling to the ground. There is a science involved in cutting down huge trees. Many a man has been killed or injured trying to take those giants down. But somehow, Frank always knew where to cut into the base of the tree and how to angle the cut in order to have that tree fall exactly where he wanted it to fall.

Felling the tree was just the beginning. After it hit the ground, the hard work continued. The next step would be to manually saw each of the branches off the giant and from there saw the branches and the giant trunk into manageable logs. Of course after that you had to split each of the logs in order to get them into a good burnable size. It would take days and days to get one tree down and sawed into the final product. Over and over again, the men worked to saw down those giant oaks in order to clear a spot to build that dream cottage.

Pulling out stumps was also part of the hard labor. Frank would dig and dig removing the dirt from around the giant roots, digging as far down as possible. Those roots were like monsters to work on. It would take hours of digging before he would reach a point where he could take the big ax and cut the root. After he freed the giant roots from the earth, he would tie a rope onto the huge root and pull it out of the ground with his car. He would drag that root into the fire area in order to burn it. The work was unimaginable. Clearing the lot and preparing it for the cottage would take months and months. There was just so much to do.

One of the first things they had to do was to clear a place for the driveway in order to pull their vehicles off of the dirt road. There were only two other houses along the country road. Frank's would be the third cottage built deep in the woods on that lovely country lane.

In addition to clearing the lot, they would also need to dig a well for water since there were no public water or sewer lines in the area. He would have to build a septic system for the house including digging out for a septic tank and drain field. In the meantime, he built an outhouse across the road and it was to be used by everyone.

One of the most massive jobs Frank would undertake was building the huge stone fireplace. He would drive up to the old strip mine where once there had been coal. He would find huge fieldstone and haul them back to the lot. As with many skills, although never formally trained in stone masonry, Frank was able to construct the most beautiful stone fireplace in all of Slippery Rock.

It was the kind of project that Frank would become known for since nothing was insurmountable and nothing was impossible. He could build or make anything with his hands and he really enjoyed doing it. Some might call him a workaholic but to Frank, it was a hobby, albeit a very big hobby.

Sometimes his buddies would travel to Slippery Rock to lend a hand. Of course after all the things Frank had done for them over the years, fixing plumbing, finishing rooms, replacing roofs, they really owed him. They would come up to help and they all worked hard. By Sunday night, the guys would always end up celebrating their progress by drinking far too much alcohol. The weekend would end with a lot of the men who partied too hard. Since Frank had been drafted, the work had come to a major halt. Frank really missed those weekends and couldn't wait to get back to his favorite project, the Slippery Rock cottage.

Before meeting Ock Soon, Frank had been thinking a lot about his summer home. But now all of his thoughts were focused on Ock Soon. He had never felt like this about anyone before.

Over the next several months, Frank and Ock Soon became very close. Ock Soon had never been happier. Although with every paycheck, Frank continued to send money home to his parents, he also continued to pick up new clothes for Ock Soon. She was always surprised and delighted to get a new outfit. Everything he bought her was just beautiful. Every night, Ock Soon would take out each new hanbok and gaze at it. After a while she would refold it carefully, piece by piece, and put it back into the drawer. She now had several jeorgoris and several chimas. She took great care not to get anything dirty on them. She had never owned anything like these before and she could hardly contain her joy.

Every day as she dressed in her new clothing, she would go outside and she didn't even feel like she knew who she was. Everything was so different now. She wasn't starving and scrambling for food. She wasn't freezing in the cold searching for a warm stack of hay to sleep in. She wasn't infested with lice anymore. She was so afraid this was going to end someday, but she wouldn't allow herself to think about that now. She was just going to pretend this would go on forever. Frank had come into her life and rescued her. She had fallen in love with him. No one had ever treated her like this. She had always been an abused slave or needy servant. Sometimes she felt more like an animal than a human being. And suddenly all of that had changed. She couldn't wait to see him again and hoped he would stay safe while he was away from her.

Ock Soon really cared deeply for Frank but she also knew her relationship with him had become outside of what she found appropriate or acceptable. She always carried the guilt of having an intimate relationship with Frank while they were not married. It really tore at her heart and soul. Sometimes she felt so ashamed. Although she loved Frank deeply, she could not shake the feeling that everyone knew what she had done and they were talking about her. When she walked down the street and people looked at her, she always felt deep shame.

Throughout Korea, anywhere American soldiers set up military bases, desperately poor Koreans gathered to find work. Some were fortunate enough to find legitimate work as tailors, launderers, cab drivers, beauty salon workers or cooks. Some very fortunate people (usually those that knew some English) found jobs on the base as clerical staff. Unfortunately, there were many women, who were uneducated and without family or husbands, who out of desperation had turned to prostitution. These women became known as *yang gongju* (Western Princess), or *yang galbo* (Western Whore). Ock Soon did not want to be a yang gongju. In Korean society, once a girl became a yang gongju, she would never be considered acceptable again. She was considered "dirty" and would not be able to find decent employment or lead a respectable life. A Korean man would never marry a yang gongju. Many young girls would find themselves trapped in an ongoing existence of prostitution and abuse after becoming involved with American soldiers.

Ock Soon carried the burden of her inappropriate relationship with Frank in her heart. One day Ock Soon decided that if she left the town and moved on to another village, no one there would know about the soldier. So, she packed up all the clothes Frank had given to her. She took the money Frank had given her and went to the train station. Although Ock Soon was very sad to leave the comfortable apartment and security of Frank's provisions, she felt she had to get away from the shame she was carrying. She wanted to go somewhere new, where people did not know she had been living with an American soldier.

Ock Soon walked to the train station and bought a ticket to go to Taejon. While she was waiting for the next train, Sunja came running to get her. Sunja was frantic. Frank had come to see Ock Soon and found out she was leaving Nonsan. He was out of control. He started overturning tables, busting through doors, screaming and calling for her. Sunja asked Ock Soon to come back quickly, Frank was tearing up the town looking for her.

The girls ran back to the house and Frank was in tears. He told her he loved her and he wanted to marry her. He asked her not to leave and he would do everything he could to make her his wife. Ock Soon was crying; she could not believe that he really wanted to marry her. She was a peasant, why would this American soldier tell her that he was going to marry her? Somehow, she believed in him. Thus far, everything he had said he would do for her, he actually did. She really did love him but she had never believed that she would ever be his wife. Now he was promising her that they would be married. Ock Soon wept with joy and promised that she would never leave him again. Frank took her train ticket and ripped it up. Ock Soon returned to stay with Sunja until she and Frank could be together forever.

Frank knew it was very difficult for an American soldier to marry a Korean woman. The Company Commander discouraged the men from getting involved with the Korean woman over and over again. The Commander was dead set against any soldier marrying any Korean girl. He did not believe the relationship would work out and he did not believe Americans should bring Koreans into the United States. It was only problematic for everyone involved. American's should marry their own. But Frank was determined. The more the Company Commander told the men to stay away from the Korean girls and don't think about marrying one, the more determined Frank was to do just that. No one was going to tell him he could not marry Ock Soon. No matter what he had to do to marry this girl, he would do it.

Frank went to the Chaplain and told him he was in love with a Korean girl and wanted to marry her. The Chaplain told him it was not advisable and he could not help him. The Chaplain told Frank he should end the relationship since marriage to an Asian was very difficult and immigration laws were very complicated. Soldiers had been warned about getting involved with the locals. Presently it was against military regulations for any soldier to marry a Korean.

Frank decided to go to the missionary to see if anything could be done. The minister at the missionary advised him the same – he really could not help him. Frank then went to the local Catholic priest in Seoul hoping that he would understand and marry them in the church. The priest told Frank the same thing. Marriage was not possible and he was not willing to perform any ceremonies.

Frank eventually explained to Ock Soon that they could not get married at that time, but he would find out what they needed to do and someday they would be married. Ock Soon believed what Frank was saying to her. She just needed to be patient and wait.

Ock Soon in Nonsan.

# 18
# Building Bridges and Friendships
## Yongdongpo, South Korea

### February 1952

Frank was in Nonsan about six weeks when the riverbed flooded. The men woke up in the middle of the night and found everything was soaked. A flash flood had washed through the riverbed. The soldiers jumped up and grabbed anything they could, threw it on rubber mats and tried to drag or float the stuff out. What a mess! Everything was soaked and it was bitter cold in the night. They salvaged what they could and were ordered to move the company out of Nonsan and on to Yongdongpo. The town was also the company headquarters and hundreds of soldiers were already there.

Yongdongpo was located south of Seoul, situated along the Han River. The Han River Bridge had been blown up several times since the war started. Now the 76th Construction Engineers were needed to rebuild the bridge once again. Yongdongpo was more "developed", if you could call it that, than Nonsan. Many of the homes were made of wood instead of straw roofs. They actually had trolleys and buses running through the town.

By now, Frank and Ock Soon had been together for almost ten months. Their love had grown much deeper and there was no way Frank was going to move without her. As the battalion packed the trucks for the move, Frank told Ock Soon to pack her things. He would find a place for them in the new town.

She packed her clothing and personal items. Frank gave her money for a bus ticket to Yongdongpo. He would meet her there and get her from the bus station. As soon as Frank arrived in the town and was able to get away, he found a room, paid the rent and had Ock Soon move into it. This is where they would be together until Frank's tour of duty was completed.

Ock Soon's time in Yongdongpo was to be the happiest time in her life. Frank and Ock Soon were able to see each other regularly and spend a lot of time getting to know each other.

Unlike courtship in the United States, there were few restaurants or dance halls.  There would be no nights out dancing or bowling.  But the town did offer some places for soldiers and friends to get together.

Many of the soldiers were "dating" or had become friends with the Korean girls.  Frank and Ock Soon would spend time with their good friends like Bob and Sunja or Roger and Rose.  Many of the Korean girls had taken on American names because they thought the names to be more "acceptable" and it was just easier for the soldier.  Bob called Sunja, Judy.  And Roger had nicknamed Min Ji, Rose.

Frank had been thinking of an American name for Ock Soon but every woman's name he thought of just didn't seem to fit.  Ock Soon was so very special to him.  He had never met anyone like her in all of his life.  Every woman's name he thought of reminded him of someone he knew and Frank just felt the name wasn't good enough for this beautiful woman.  She was so kind and gentle and only thought the best of other people.  She would do anything for him; cook, clean, wash his clothes.  She was so grateful for the simplest things in life, vegetables or a new blouse.  She never lost her temper or asked for anything.  She was always so happy to see him and always broken hearted when he had to return to Camp Sykes.  Coming up with an American name for this woman was very difficult.

When Frank was just a young boy, he remembered hearing his aunt, Sister Mary Perpetua, tell the story of one of her favorite saints in the church.  Sister Mary Perpetua was his mother's sister who had taken the vows of a Catholic nun when she was only 16 years old.  Sister Perpetua was everyone's favorite person in the family.  She was nothing like the nuns who taught him in the Catholic school.  She wasn't mean or stern like the nuns at St. Mary's Catholic School.  Sister Perpetua was actually a very kind person and was always so happy to see her nieces and nephews.  She was probably the only Catholic nun Frank truly liked.

One day, the family was having a dinner party on Sister Perpetua's birthday, January 8.  When they were cutting the cake,

Sister shared with the family that her birthday fell on St. Pega's feast day. She told them the story of St. Pega who was an anchoress in the ancient Anglo-Saxon kingdom of Mercia. Sister Perpetua had learned that St. Pega loved the Lord and had become a hermit in order to spend time alone with God. When St. Pega's brother died, she traveled to his funeral and it was said that she healed a blind man enroute to her destination.

Frank had never heard of St. Pega before the story and he certainly wasn't impressed by her sainthood, but always thought the name very unusual. He knew of no other person named Pega.

When the Korean girls were taking on English names like Judy or Rose, Frank changed Ock Soon's name to Pega, (pronounced 'peeja'). Ock Soon had no problem with that. Some of the soldiers had been calling her Lee, others called her Ock Soon, and it really did not matter to her. Frank thought Ock Soon was so different than any other woman he had ever encountered; he chose to call her Pega. From that day forward, Pega would be her name.

Pega (on right) washing vegetables.

Rows of kimchi crocks behind the women.

Lee Ock Soon (Pega) in Yongdongpo.

Frank in Yongdongpo.

Although on occasion the men did have some free time, the work the 76th did was remarkable. The 76th had the dubious honor of being the first Engineer Construction Battalion to arrive in Korea (July 1950) immediately after the start of the Korean Conflict. During the war, the 76th constructed roads, built bridges, and laid airfields. One of the major projects during 1952 was rebuilding the Han River Bridge. The equipment was not the best and the work environment was extremely difficult. None the less, the 76th completed the project and would later receive commendations for this huge achievement.[11]

The writing on the trestle reads:
"This Bridge Rebuilt By 76th Engineer Construction Battalion.
Started 17 Feb 51   Completed _____.

---

[11] Source: Chief of Military History, SSUSA Organizational History & Honors Branch. 19, May 1953.

In addition to their daylight "machine shop" responsibilities, the men had to take turns standing guard on the Han River Bridge. The enemy was known to float down the river late at night, attempting to set up dynamite to blow up the bridge. It was the guard's responsibility to watch the river and shoot anyone they saw floating towards the bridge. None of the men liked this post, but someone had to do it. They had too many incidents with this type of enemy action and could not risk their work and their men.

Every day members of the 76<sup>th</sup> Company A worked on welding the bridge. One day one of the soldiers fell from the bridge to his death. For days, the soldiers dredged the river, trying to retrieve Private Webber's body. Although they never found him, what they did find would haunt many of the men for the rest of their lives. Many bodies were dredged from the river. Some were families who had tied themselves together and taken their last brave jump to their death in the river in order to escape the guns of the Communists approaching them. None of the men had ever seen anything so disturbing as the bodies of young children tied to their parents, lying dead at the bottom of that river. The tragedy of war in this "land of morning calm" was profoundly evident in the dead remains of the children of Korea.

Besides rebuilding the Han River Bridge, the 76<sup>th</sup> Construction Battalion would work on many major projects during the war. Kimpo was an Air Force Base north of Seoul. The 76<sup>th</sup> worked tirelessly building the air landing strip. Building the air strip required heavy equipment to clear the land and then move the gravel and stone to build the base. Throughout the Korean War, the 76<sup>th</sup> would be called upon to build or rebuild bridges, roads and airstrips. Even when the war ended, the work was just beginning for the 76<sup>th</sup>. The H and S Company would be sent to a new location just south of the 38<sup>th</sup> Parallel. On July 29, 1953, the 76<sup>th</sup> would be called upon to begin leveling the hills for the prisoner compounds which would be part of Operation Big Switch, the prisoner exchange. For nearly two months, the men worked twelve hours on and twelve hours off preparing the ground for the prisoner compounds and Freedom Village. The 76th would battle severe heat, monsoon rains, and long hours helping to build that monumental site.

Shortly after the 76th moved north to Yongdongpo, a new soldier, Ed Kenny arrived in the camp and was assigned to Frank's tent. Ed was a big guy who was born and raised in Cleveland, Ohio. During WWII, Ed had tried to enlist in the Navy but he was rejected due to a knee injury. Ed had been classified 4F, Not Fit for Active Duty due to Medical Reasons, just like Frank. At the time Ed was rejected by the Navy, he was very disappointed but moved on with his life. He ended up working for General Motors in a Tool and Die Apprenticeship program. Although he was a journeyman, Ed was making decent money, had a sweet girlfriend and was heading towards a permanent job in the car industry. He was just as surprised as Frank was when he got a draft notice in the mail. That was the last thing he wanted to do – go to Korea. There was nothing he could do about it. He would have to serve because just like the letter said, "His neighbors and his friends were counting on him." It was April 26, 1951 when he was sent to Fort Meade, Maryland for basic training. He went to a machine shop school there for six months.

His journey to Korea would start in Pittsburgh, Pennsylvania. From Pittsburgh, he flew to California where he boarded a ship to Japan. Like all the transpacific journeys, it would be two weeks before his feet touched soil again. He would never forget the day he was sent to Korea. It was the day after Thanksgiving when he embarked on a ship and left for Japan. His mother was so upset. Why did he have to go to Korea? Everyone wanted him to go to Germany. That was the place to be – certainly *not* Korea.

Of course there was no opportunity to tell the government what you wanted to do. The draft meant he had to leave his job and his girl and hope he would make it back alive.

Ed crossed the ocean like so many before him. He stayed in Japan a couple days and then took a ship to Busan and from there would go to Inchon. Ed arrived in Inchon in the middle of the night on the 40 foot tidal wave. He stayed in the old school house for several days until he was finally on a truck to Yongdongpo. Ed joined the 76<sup>th</sup> in Yongdongpo where he would meet Frank. Ed and Frank would become very good friends before the war ended.

Ed was a very good looking man and soon found that many of the Korean girls took a strong liking to him. Ed realized that these girls wanted to go to America and were hoping that he would be their "passport" out of Korea. Like so many soldiers, he really had to let the girls know up front, he was not planning on getting married any time soon.

Ed was a skilled machinist and he and Frank completed many projects together. The men enjoyed working with each other since they could depend on each other to get the job done right. Ed would turn out to be another great friend to Frank when he needed someone he could count on.

Glenard Crabtree, Roger Van Winkle, Lionel White, Ed Kenny,
Frank Crimbchin, Tom Victory, Robert Willem.

# 19
# A Korean Bride
## Korean Marriage Banned

### Spring/Summer 1952

Frank had been slow to reveal to his parents his new found love. He was not sure how they would take to having a Korean daughter-in-law. His father, Frank Sr., didn't think too much about it, never believing his son would ever bring the girl home. His mother, Kathryn, was more concerned.

Kathryn was a devout Catholic and above all else, her boys *had* to marry a Catholic girl. She simply would not have any other religion in her family. All of her children and grandchildren must be Catholic and must be raised in the Catholic Church. There was no other real church and nothing else would be acceptable. Anytime Kathryn would try to raise her concerns to her husband, he would always remind her not to worry about it saying, "All the soldiers think they are in love when they go to war. That's just because they are so lonely. There would be little chance of this girl ever coming to America."

Kathryn was able to accept this explanation for a while but as Frank continued to write home about this Ock Soon Lee, "Pega", her concerns deepened. Frank had written many letters home and all of them mentioned this girl. By March of 1952, Frank wrote his parents and told them that he wanted to marry the girl and bring her home.

Kathryn was so upset. This girl was not a Catholic. Kathryn immediately wrote to her son and told him, he could not bring the girl home unless she was baptized Catholic and they were married in the Catholic Church. She would have it no other way. Kathryn reminded Frank of all the virtues of being a Catholic. He could not turn his back on his religion. She had raised him differently. He needed to remember that being a Catholic was special and there was no other way to get to heaven. She could not bear the thought of her son and his family going to hell. The girl must convert and they must raise their children as Catholics!

Now that was going to be a challenge. Although Frank was raised Catholic and had gone to a Catholic elementary school, he certainly was not a devout Catholic like his mother. He could hardly express his love to Pega let alone explain a religion. But Frank also knew his mother meant business. There would be no way she would allow Pega into her home unless these guidelines were met.

Kathryn, herself, had been raised by strict German parents who went to church every Sunday and ensured everyone made their weekly confession of all their sins, both committed and omitted. No sin would be unmentioned and no sin would be un-forgiven. They must do their penance and be prepared to enter the gates of heaven at any given time. Although there never was a priest out of the bunch, at least one of the girls became a Catholic nun and that surely earned them some points with their Heavenly Father. Thank goodness for Sister Mary Perpetua. Her constant prayers would surely get them all out of purgatory.

Pega had never heard of God or any other spiritual being. She had never been to a church or a temple. Her entire life had been working as a servant for others and no one in her life had ever told her about any gods. She knew she had to take care of herself in order to survive. Life had always been very difficult – at least until now. She had never depended on any "god" to help her.

Frank didn't know how he was going to convert Pega into a Catholic. Pega had never indicated or demonstrated that she believed in any religion. Actually, religion was the least of his worries. But he knew it would have to happen to keep peace in the family. It would just have to wait. Frank didn't mention his mother's wishes to Pega because he knew she was not able to understand. He would have to deal with first things first. He had to figure out a way to marry this girl and then he would deal with religion.

Frank was aware that the Naturalization and Immigration statutes indicated that Asians were banned from permanent residency in the United States. It had been that way forever. But during the early years of the Korean War, the statute banning Asian immigration was lifted and Asian brides of service personnel were permitted to immigrate to the U.S. Unfortunately, the exception to the law expired on March 18, 1952 and servicemen were once again not permitted to marry Korean women, nor were Koreans permitted to immigrate to the U.S.A. The doors had closed and the window of opportunity had passed. Frank was unable to get any further information from his superiors in regard to permission to marry Pega. He wrote his mother asking her to get some information related to the ban on Asian immigration. Frank needed to know if and when the ban would be lifted.

In early May, Kathryn began corresponding with her Congressman, James G. Fulton requesting his assistance. On May 21, 1952, the Congressman wrote Kathryn advising her that he was forwarding her request to the Department of the Army in Washington D.C. to see if anything could be done to assist her son. On June 6, 1952, Congressman Fulton sent Kathryn a copy of a letter from the Lt. Colonel, Artillery Liaison Division of the Army which explained the current regulations. Lt. Colonel M.T. Tilghman confirmed to Congressman Fulton that as of March 18, 1952, the immigration laws banning the admission of Asians into the United States for permanent residency was in effect. Lt. Colonel Tilghman went on to write the following:

"I am unable to determine whether legislation will be enacted to permit the entrance of Oriental brides of service personnel and therefore, I cannot hazard a guess as to when such statutes might be effective if enacted. You may be assured, however, that any such legislation will receive wide publicity in the press and other public information media, and will be disseminated through the Army's information channels to individual soldiers who might be interested."

Kathryn was very disappointed.  She knew there was legislation before Congress regarding changes to the Immigration and Naturalization laws which would once again open the doors, allowing Asians to immigrate to the U.S.  She had hoped the Congressman would give her some idea as to where that legislation stood.  Did he have a time frame in regard to when it would be presented for a vote?  Did he think the legislation would pass?  Would he be able to assist her son in obtaining special permission to marry Ock Soon and bring her to the U.S.?  Instead, she received a letter advising her to read the newspaper for updated information.

Kathryn wrote to her son and gave him the information.  They would have to wait for the laws to change and watch for updates in the news.

Frank knew his tour of duty would be coming to a close in September.  It was already June and he was running out of time.  What was going to happen when he had to leave in the fall?  Frank was very worried that he would lose contact with Pega when he left Korea.  Did she really understand just how much he loved her?  Did she really believe him when he told her he would have to leave but he would be back for her?  Would she wait for him or would she end up getting involved with another GI?  He had never forgotten her attempt to leave Nonsan and he knew she could do it again.  He had to come up with a plan to ensure Pega would be safe and she would have a place to live while she waited for him to return.

By the end of June, Frank heard rumors that the U.S. immigration laws were changing.  Frank learned that on June 11, Congress had passed the McCarran-Walter Act[12], also known as

---

[12] "The 1952 Act created symbolic opportunities for Asian immigration, though in reality it continued to discriminate against them.  The law repealed the last of the existing measures to exclude Asian immigration, allotted each Asian nation a minimum quota of 100 visas each year, and eliminated laws preventing Asians from becoming naturalized American citizens.  The new law allotted new Asian quotas based on race, instead of nationality.  An individual with one or more Asian parents, born anywhere in the world and possessing the citizenship of any nation, would be counted under the national quota of the Asian nation of his or her ethnicity..."
http://www.state.gov

the Immigration and Nationality Act; Public Law 414, which repealed the blanket exclusion laws against the immigration and naturalization of Asians. President Harry Truman thought the new law was still too discriminatory and vetoed the bill on June 25. Within two days Truman's veto was overridden by Congress. Although the laws had been changed, it would take some time before the new guidelines would be implemented.

Frank could not believe it! It looked like he might be able to marry Ock Soon and take her with him when he returned to the States. Over the next several weeks, Frank would visit Chaplain Hart several times to discuss his desire to marry Ock Soon.

Frank was hoping that the Chaplain would assist him or provide him some direction. The Chaplain explained to Frank that although the McCarren-Walter Act had passed through Congress, presently soldiers were still not permitted to marry Koreans. Neither the U.S. Army nor the Korean government permitted it. Although Chaplain Hart understood his strong desire to marry the girl, in his heart he believed it would not happen. Frank found little comfort in speaking to the Chaplain.

Frank wrote to his mother again and asked for her assistance in obtaining further information about the new laws. He had heard the McCarren-Walter Act had passed through Congress but he was finding he still could not marry Ock Soon. On July 24, 1952, Kathryn wrote to the Immigration and Naturalization Service, (INS), explaining her son's desire to marry a Korean girl and bring her to the U.S. She requested further information regarding the procedure and what Frank needed to do to marry Ock Soon and bring her home with him when his tour of duty was over. Unfortunately, it would be many, many months before Kathryn would receive a reply from the INS.

July and August passed by quickly with no change in regulations regarding servicemen marrying Korean women. September arrived and Frank's tour of duty was coming to an end. Frank remained determined to find a way to bring Pega to America. He could not leave this girl behind. He loved her deeply and could not live without her. By September, Frank was beginning to realize there would be no way to marry Pega before he left Korea. This meant there was no way to get a visa for her to go to the United States. Frank knew that if he could not marry her and take her with him, he would have to find someplace for her to stay until he could return for her.

Again he visited the Catholic priest at the Myeongdong Cathedral in Seoul who recommended that Frank go to see Father Houng at the Babies Home in Sodemun Ku, Seoul. Maybe Father Houng would be able to help him. The priest told Frank that sometimes Father would accept adult women at the orphanage. Time was closing in on him and Frank knew he would have to go to the orphanage as soon as possible and meet with this Father Houng.

He had no other plan. He would have to make this proposal work.

# 20

# The Arrangement
## Collumba Babies Home

### September 1952

Father Houng was a stern, old, Catholic priest, who had been assigned to The Collumba Babies Home in Seoul. He had been there far too long now and had become frustrated at the lack of support he was receiving from the diocese. He had become a priest because he had faith in God. But now the old priest had seen too much. The war had destroyed his country and many of his friends and family had been killed. He still believed in God; but what happened? Didn't God care about Korea and all the killing? Didn't God see all the suffering of the people and the children? When would the suffering come to an end?

If there had been some way for Father Houng to escape from all of this, he would have done so. All he wanted was a small church and to perform Holy Mass every day. Yes, he would still hear their confessions and give them their penance, but that was it. He was just too old to deal with the unending needs of these people anymore.

His hope to save the children was fading, it was just too difficult. They did not have enough money, the health care was deplorable, the Korean government was corrupt, he was getting older and the war had taken a toll on the old priest. He was tired.

Now this American soldier comes and wanted to tell him the same story he had heard so many times before. Yes, yes, yes. This was just another American soldier who wanted a Korean bride. They all said the same thing - but they never came back. He had been burned so many times after he agreed to take in the girls. The soldiers never returned and then he was stuck with them. After the soldiers returned home to the United States, Father would never hear from them again. He was not interested in taking in any other women. This was an orphanage for children, not a boarding house for loose women.

But Eunah, his Director, was standing in front of him asking him to see the solider.  Eunah told Father that the soldier was standing outside the mission and he would not leave until he saw the priest.  He was a very stubborn man and very persistent.  He wouldn't take 'no' for an answer.  Eunah asked Father Houng to please see the soldier briefly and then send him away.  She had tried to tell him to go away but the American would not leave.

Disgustingly, Father Houng said; "Okay, I will give him ten minutes of my time and tell him the house is full.  No new women are being accepted.  There simply is not enough room to take in any more adults."

Eunah returned and told the soldier that Father Houng agreed to meet with him briefly.  Frank was excited and hurried up the steps and into the office to meet the priest.  Frank sat down across from the priest's desk and explained that he was in love with a Korean girl by the name of Lee Ock Soon.  Frank explained that he wanted to marry the girl but could not find anyone who would marry them.  His tour of duty was coming to an end and he had to find a safe place for the girl.

Frank went on to tell the priest that he was born and raised a Catholic.  He was baptized and made his Confirmation in the Church.  He even went to Catholic school.  His Aunt Mary Perpetua was a Catholic nun in the United States.  He wanted Pega to become a Catholic and wanted to marry her someday.  Father listened to the story with no change of heart.  He was a busy man and really needed to get on with his duties.  It was late in the morning and the women would be returning from lunch for prayers.  He had to go to the chapel and lead the prayers.  He was about to end the meeting when the soldier actually said something of real interest to the priest.

Frank told Father that he wanted to send him money every month in order for him to keep the girl.  He was offering to send $25.00 a month to the priest for the room and board and in addition, he promised to send another $50.00 a month for the girl's personal expenses.  Anything the girl needed for herself, she would be able to get with the $50.00 every month.  She would be able to buy her own food and clothes. The priest would not have to give her anything.

Frank also requested that Ock Soon learn all about becoming a Catholic while she was staying there. Frank wanted her to be baptized in the Catholic Church. In addition, Frank would like Ock Soon to attend school with the other students in order to learn to read and write. She needed to learn how to speak English so she would be ready to go to the United States.

The only thing the priest heard was $75.00 a month. That was more than the diocese was sending him. He really needed the money to keep the orphanage running. Many times they were low on food and if it wasn't for the Americans giving them oatmeal and cheese, the kids would be starving.

But how did this soldier intend to get the money over here? Father knew that if the soldier sent the money directly to the mission, Father would never see it. Money never made it to the recipient in Korea. Someone would always steal it from the envelope. Father was very interested but told Frank he could not send the money directly to him. Frank would have to make other arrangements to ensure the money arrived.

In exchange for the money, Father would allow Ock Soon to live at the orphanage and attend catechism. Father would also send Ock Soon to school with the other students so that she could learn to read and write in English. Frank explained that he would set up a bank account in the United States and make the deposits into that account. Frank would send the account information to Father and Father would be able to withdraw the funds. Everyone was happy. Father would get the money he needed and Frank could be certain, Ock Soon would be safe. He would be back for her as soon as the laws allowed. In the meantime he would have to save enough money to come back for her. Frank was hoping that within three months, the laws would be changed and he would be able to return to Korea and marry Ock Soon.

Frank was truly happy and very relieved. Yes, he knew that $75.00 a month was going to be very difficult for him, but he would do whatever he needed to do to get the money and make sure Pega would have this safe place to stay. It was actually a perfect plan. Pega could learn all about becoming a Catholic, so that should make his mother happy. In addition, Pega would be able to attend school and learn English. He knew life in the United States would be difficult enough; she needed to study hard and learn how to read and write. He could not have asked for anything better. This arrangement was just perfect.

Frank and Pega met with Roger and Rose at Rose's apartment. Frank explained the arrangements he was able to make with Father Houng to everyone. Rose did her best to translate everything to Pega. She explained to her that she was to stay at the Collumba Babies Home until Frank came back for her. It would be several months, but he promised to return. While she was at the orphanage, she was going to go to school. Frank asked that she study very hard and do her best to learn English. She would need this when she gets to America.

Now even as Rose was translating for Frank, it was very difficult for her. She wanted to go to America too. Roger had not made any promises to her and she was getting very angry. Rose once had a baby girl but when she met Roger, she let the child die. She just stopped feeding the baby. She knew that Roger would not take her to America with someone else's child. She had given up her baby in order to go to America with Roger. But Roger would not talk to her about this. As time went on, Rose had become angrier with the situation. At least she could read and write in Korean. The peasant girl couldn't even do that. Rose had a house to live in. The peasant girl didn't have anything to offer. But Frank was promising to take Pega to America. Rose did her best to hide her feelings from everyone. She did not want to upset Roger. He was her only chance to get out of the country. She had to quit thinking about it and act like she cared about the peasant.

Rose continued to explain to Pega what was going to happen. Pega hated that Frank was not going to take her with him when he left. That had been her dream. She had always thought she would simply leave this country with Frank. Frank had moved her from Nonsan to Yongdongpo.  Why couldn't she just move to the United States with him?  She never once thought she would be left behind in Korea without him.  He had promised to marry her and take her to America.

She did not want to go to the orphanage.  She could learn English in America.  Rose tried to explain to Pega why she was unable to go, but it was difficult.  Pega did not understand all the legal implications.  Pega did not understand why they couldn't be married and why the United States would not allow Asians in the country.  All she knew was that she did not want to be alone again in this country.  She did not have a job, she was uneducated and could not get a job anywhere in the town.  She did not understand how this was going to work out.  She really wanted to go with Frank when he left Korea.

It was a very sad day when she realized she was not going to America when Frank left.  She finally came to terms with the arrangements.  She was comforted by the fact that he had found a place for her to live.  She tried to keep her thoughts on going to school.  She was excited to finally be able to learn to read and write.  She would study very hard.  Frank would be so proud of her when he came back for her and she spoke very good English.  She would surprise him with her English.  That is what she would focus on while she waited for him, she would learn how to be an American.

She trusted Frank and once again, he was taking care of her and made sure she would be safe until his return.  Every time she thought about his leaving her, she would become very sad, but she always believed in him and knew that someday they would be together.

September came and Pega knew the days were closing in.  She knew her time with Frank was coming to an end.  Fear was overtaking her even though she believed in him.  Frank would remind her to use this time to learn everything she could about God and becoming a Catholic.  He always reminded her that she would be going to school with the other students and she should work hard at learning English, reading and writing.  Everything would work out. Frank told her no matter what happened she was not to leave the orphanage. Frank knew that if Pega were to leave the orphanage, he might never find her in Korea. It was very difficult to locate people in this country. There were few telephones and no mail delivery. Above all else, she had to stay at the orphanage so he could find her.

It was so hard. She wept. Frank insisted she put on her favorite dress and they go to the photographer. He wanted a picture of the two of them together before he left. It would be their "goodbye" picture and anytime she thought he was not coming back for her, she was to look at that picture and remember just how much he loved her. Pega went to the hairdresser and had her hair done. She dressed up in her favorite hanbok. Together they would go to the photographer and sit for a picture. Pega would come to cherish the photograph. Every day during her stay at the orphanage, Pega would start her day looking at her love and remembering the time they had together. It would be a picture she would keep for the rest of her life.

Leaving Pega in Korea would be the hardest thing Frank would ever have to do. His orders had been received and he was to leave Korea on September 5. Frank had tried everything he could to marry the girl and bring her back to the states with him. There was just no way to make it happen. The laws and restrictions would not allow for it. It was final. Pega would have to stay behind and Frank would have to come back for her at a later time.

Lee Ock Soon and Frank Crimbchin. The "Goodbye Picture".

Before Frank left Korea, he asked Victor and Roger to continue to check on Pega while she was at the Babies Home. He explained to his good friends that Pega was illiterate; she could not read or write even in Korean. Frank knew she would not be able to write to him. He didn't think Father Houng would be the kind of man to give him updates either. Victor and Roger might be the only contact Frank would have with Pega. He asked them to check on her frequently and write to him as often as possible and let him know what was happening. Both Victor and Roger proved to be loyal friends to Frank. Both of his good friends would go to the orphanage regularly until they too would leave Korea. They were to become some of the best friends Frank would ever know.

Now there was one thing Frank was aware of but neglected to mention to the priest. He did not want to mention it because he was afraid the priest would not accept the girl. Frank was concerned that Pega could be pregnant. It was unbelievable to Frank, but it appeared that Pega did not understand the basics of conception and pregnancy. How could this woman not understand how babies were made? Frank had become aware that Pega was late in getting her period and might be pregnant. Hopefully his concerns were unfounded and there was nothing to worry about. Pregnancy would be a disaster for Pega in Korea without him. He had to be certain that Pega was not expecting and everything would be okay.

Pega on the other hand did not have any idea what the implications of missing a period were. She had missed her period many times in her life due to malnutrition and starvation. No one had ever explained to Pega anything about conception, pregnancy or birth. Even though she was almost twenty years old, she was not only uneducated, she was truly naive.

Now Frank was embarrassed to ask his buddies to keep an eye on Pega to make sure she wasn't expecting a baby but he had no choice. Pega could not write and she could not call him on a telephone. Frank certainly did not want to mention this to the priest, it could ruin his arrangements. He would have to depend on his buddies. Boy he hated to bring the subject up to them. Hopefully, this would be resolved before he left and he would not have to mention it to anyone.

Unfortunately, things did not "resolve" and he had to talk to Victor and Roger. Well when he finally asked them about this, the soldiers found the whole thing quite funny. They were going to have to go and see this woman and ask her if she got her period! What next? Maybe Frank would want them to stick around to help deliver the baby! They had a good laugh at Frank's expense but told him they would do it for him.

Frank told them he was probably wrong and she was probably not pregnant but he had to make sure. All he wanted them to do was check on her weekly and let him know. Hopefully he was just being overly cautious and everything would resolve itself. Only time would tell.

# 21
## Tour of Duty Ends
### Return to U.S.A.

September 1952

Frank had hated to go to Korea and now he hated to leave. It was on the 5<sup>th</sup> of September that Frank would board a U.S. Navy Supply ship on a return voyage to the United States. He could not contain his tears as the boat left the peninsula. He tried not to think about all of the great fears he held inside. His greatest fear was that Pega would not stay in the orphanage and he would never be able to find her if she chose to leave. He had to keep reminding himself that she promised to stay and study. He would just have to believe in her.

The week had been so difficult. He had taken Pega to the orphanage earlier in the week. They were both broken hearted and scared. Frank kept reassuring Pega that he would return for her. They had gone to the photographer the day before and had their picture taken. He gave her a copy of the photograph. She looked so solemn. She did not want him to leave her there in Korea. Even though she trusted him, so many bad things had happened to her in her lifetime. Frank knew nothing about how difficult life had truly been for her. What if he never came back? What would she do? How would she survive? She never wanted to live the way she had lived before. She tried not to think about it. It only made her afraid. She had always been a strong and brave girl. She had to be in order to survive. She would have to be strong and brave again.

On Thursday, September 4, Frank was so sad. He was leaving Korea the next day and although he had visited Pega with his buddies on Wednesday, the visit was just too brief. It was difficult to say goodbye with everyone right there. He did not have an opportunity to tell Pega just how much he loved her and how important she was to him. It didn't feel right. He had to see her one last time before he left.

He tried but was unable to get the jeep so he decided to walk back to the orphanage. Frank walked about seven miles to the Babies Home. He saw Father Houng and asked him to find Ock Soon. Father took Frank to the nursery and called Ock Soon to come out. Ock Soon came out the back door and sat on the steps with Frank. Father Houng stood nearby overseeing the couple. They wept together and found it so difficult to leave each other. Frank kept telling her how much he loved her. He promised to return for her as soon as possible. She should study English and Catechism while she was at the orphanage and above all else - she should not leave the orphanage. He would be back.

Finally, the time had come for Frank to leave. He would be on the next truck out of Yongdongpo in the morning. He had to get back to camp. Father Houng had been standing off to the side watching the couple say their goodbyes. It was time to go and Frank asked Father if he could kiss Ock Soon goodbye. Father said, "No." With that, they hugged each other and Frank left.

Ock Soon wept bitterly as she watched him walk away. She sat on the steps of the orphanage watching him walk away until she could no longer see him. Her heart was broken unlike anything before. She got up and quietly returned to the nursery.

When Ock Soon walked into the room she was unaware that all of the little children had been watching the couple from inside the window. They were giggling and teasing with each other. They did not understand what was happening. In their little childish voices, they chanted to her, singing *"Ajumma ga ulgo issda, Ajumma ga ulgo issda."* which means: "Auntie is crying", Auntie is crying." Their giggles made Ock Soon smile. How young and silly and innocent these little children were. At least they had found a place where they could laugh once again.

Ock Soon went back to the room that Eunah had assigned to her. It was a room that she would share with one of the older woman who was living in the orphanage. She went back to the room and sat on the mat, staring at the picture of her love, hoping she would see him again soon. Tears soaked her cheeks. She knew she had to get control of herself. Eunah had wanted to meet with her today in her office. Ock Soon wiped her tears away and made her way through the orphanage to see Eunah.

# PART THREE

Ock Soon-"Pega"

# 22
# Collumba Babies Home
## Seoul, Korea

### September 1952

Frank was gone now. He had taken Pega to the orphanage earlier in the week and went to see her one last time yesterday. He would be leaving South Korea in the morning. Pega did not know when she would ever see him again but she truly believed he would return for her. She knew she had to stay in the orphanage and study hard. That was what Frank had arranged for her to do. She would do just as he asked. She wanted him to be proud of her when he came back. She wanted to be a good American.

Eunah had asked Pega to come to see her as soon as possible. Although Eunah was not a Catholic nun she was in charge of the day to day operations of the Catholic orphanage. Pega did not know exactly what she did but she was the boss and gave orders to everyone else. Pega had been crying all morning but she wiped away her tears and went to see Eunah. She was anxious to find out more about the orphanage and when she would be able to start to go to school.

Eunah took Pega to an office and sat her down. They talked. This was the first time Eunah had ever met Pega and she was shocked at how poorly the girl spoke. Her language was like that of an uneducated peasant girl. Pega was talking about going to school. Eunah asked her to read from the book on her desk. Of course, Pega was unable to read. When Eunah realized the girl was illiterate, well, there was no way anyone had time to deal with this.

It might have been different if the girl knew how to read and write in Hangul[13]. Teaching this girl English, well, that was next to impossible if she was unable to read and write in her own language. It was difficult enough to learn English if you were able

---

[13]Hangul: Korean alphabet sometimes spelled Hanguel.

to read Hangul but it was impossible to teach this girl any English if she could not read or write in her own language. Of course, there was never really any true consideration that the girl would be educated while she was at Collumba. There was a war going on! They needed her to help with the daily chores and to care for the children. It was unreasonable to think that anyone had time to educate this peasant.

Eunah told Pega that the nursery needed help with the babies and Pega would be assigned to work there. Many of the children were very sick and the staff needed more assistance. An infection was going through the nursery and some of the children had diarrhea and vomiting. She would be assigned to assist in this area. Pega would be taught how to care for the babies and help with the housekeeping and laundry. She would also be asked to help feed the babies since the staff always needed help during mealtimes. Mi Chi, another young woman living at the orphanage, would show Pega what to do and what chores needed done.

Pega asked Eunah when she would be able to go to school. Eunah told Pega she would not be going to school. She was too old to go to school. School was just for the younger children. Furthermore, Pega was illiterate even in her own Korean language. How did she expect to learn a foreign language? Frank had been mistaken. She would not be attending school.

Pega did not understand. Of course she could not read or write. She had never attended a school before. That was why Frank was paying for her to stay here. She was supposed to learn to read and write. Frank told her that he would pay them to keep her and teach her how to speak English. Everything was very confusing now.

Eunah told Pega that she was to start her day every morning by attending Mass with the other women. Everyone goes to Mass in the morning. After Mass, she would report to the nursery. She would assist the women there and help feed the babies their morning meal. After all the children were fed, she was to assist the staff with caring for the children's needs. After the midday meal, there is prayer time in the chapel. She was expected to attend prayer. When prayer time was over, she would report back to the nursery. There were many children to care for and everyone had to carry their load. In the evening, everyone ended their day with prayer in the chapel. Pega was expected to join with the others for worship and prayer.

Pega tried once again to explain that Frank told her she had to go to school and learn English. Frank would be coming for her and expects her to know how to read and write so she will be ready to become an American. Eunah just laughed at her. YOU, become an American. That is impossible. She laughed again. Pega did not understand what was so funny. Yes, she was going to become an American. Frank would be back, he promised. Pega told Eunah that she must have time to go to school. That is what she had promised to Frank. If she did not learn English, he might not take her back to America. She must learn English.

Eunah told her to stop talking about it. They needed her in the nursery. She couldn't even read or write Hangul, how did she expect to read or write in English?

Pega could not believe what she was hearing. This could not be happening. She *had* to go to school. She *had* to learn English. She *had* to learn to read and write. Frank was counting on it. Frank had been very clear with her. He told her she was to go to school! This was the reason she was there.

Pega did not know what to do. She went to her room and sat on the mat and wept. She missed Frank so much and needed him to tell her what to do. When he returned for her and she had not studied, he would be so disappointed in her. Maybe he would be so disappointed he would not take her to America. Somehow she was going to have to go somewhere and learn these things. She would never be ready to go to America if she could not speak the language. She wanted so much to ask him what to do. Did he want her to stay here? Maybe he could find a different place for her to go and learn English. Should she leave? While she was sitting on the mat crying, Eunah came to her room and asked her to join the other staff and assist with the children.

Pega went to the nursery. She could not believe her eyes. There were so many young babies, some newborns. They ranged in age from newborns to about four years old. She did not know how they all ended up here. Many of the babies were biracial, Korean and Caucasian or Korean and Black. Apparently, their mothers had abandoned them here at this church. Korea was a single race country and there was no tolerance for biracial children. Pega knew the Korean people would mistreat these children. Koreans did not accept children who were of mixed race. It was very important to keep their race pure. Koreans married Koreans! Families would be shamed if a son or daughter married a person from China or Japan – let alone an American!

Pega saw that many of the children were very sick and had severe diarrhea. She would tend to the children and try to comfort them. Some could not keep any food down and everything she fed them would come back up. She spent the rest of the day cleaning up after the sick babies.

Pega saw that many of the children had very big stomachs. Their arms and legs were like twigs but their stomachs were huge. She did not know why but they were the sickest. Some were so sick they just lay there, no more tears, just wide eyed and barely moving. She would do her best to try to help them but these children did not respond to her touch or smile when she held them.

At noon everyone gathered for the midday prayer service. Pega had never been to a church before. She followed Mi Chi and imitated all of her actions. The chapel was very quiet and there was a statue of a man hanging on a cross. Pega had seen a picture of the man before but she did not know who he was or why he was in the chapel on a cross. Pega saw a statue of a woman dressed in a blue hanbok. Mi Chi said that was the man's mother. Pega did not understand why everyone was coming into the chapel and saying prayers to these statues. She had heard of Buddha but had never heard anything about this man or his mother. But she was going to listen to what they had to say because Frank told her she should learn all about them. Frank's

Mother wanted her to be a Christian so Frank could be married to her.  If Frank and his Mother believed in these statues, then it had to be true.

The first day in the chapel, Pega sat there looking around at all the strange things.  Sometimes Mi Chi would stand up and sing songs. Sometimes Mi Chi would kneel down and say prayers. Sometimes she sat on the bench.  Pega just followed along and did everything Mi Chi did.  This was a very unusual place but Frank wanted her to learn all about this.  She would do her best to understand.

After Chapel, the women ate some rice and kimchi and then went back to the nursery.  Mi Chi showed Pega where all the dirty clothes were placed.  Her job every day would be to do the washing. They had piles of clothes and diapers that needed washed.  It seemed that no one else wanted this job, so now it would be hers to do.

Pega spent the rest of the day washing the clothes, rubbing them against the rocks like she had done so many times before. Father Houng had taken in an older woman from the village, Ho Sook.  Ho Sook was Pega's roommate and together they would have the job of washing all the clothes.  Father paid Ho Sook one dollar per month.  Everyone at the orphanage was paid the same, one dollar per month.  Ho Sook was glad to have Pega help her wash the clothes every day.  Pega was determined to do a good job and maybe they would see how hard she worked and allow her to go to school.  She would try to make this work. Frank had told her not to leave this place. For now she would stay and hope they would teach her to read and write, just like Frank said they would.

All afternoon, Pega worked on the wash.  Every time she thought about Frank, the tears would run down her cheeks.  She missed him so much already.  How she wished she could let him know what was happening.  If only she could talk to him.  He would know what to do.  She was so angry at herself for not knowing how to write a letter to him.  If she could write a letter and send it, he would tell her what to do. She had promised to stay here, so she would stay until she figures out how she should handle the situation.

The pile of dirty diapers and clothes never seemed to end. The more she washed, the more they appeared. Fortunately, there was a natural spring in the courtyard of the orphanage. Pega would fill the jug with the fresh spring water and carry it back to the wash area. She would rinse the dirty diapers in the cool fresh water. Together Ho Sook and Pega would boil some of the water and add the lye soap. They would wash the dirty clothes in the warm water and rinse again in the fresh cool spring water. All the clothing was wrung out by hand and hung out to dry. The work was grueling and by evening, Pega was exhausted. It had been a very long day. Frank had left Korea only this morning but somehow it seemed like days ago. Pega was told to clean herself up and go to the chapel. She washed her face, her hands and went back to the chapel for evening prayers.

Again everyone was gathered in the chapel. Again Pega followed along and did whatever everyone else was doing. It had been a long day. She was exhausted and sitting on the bench, she felt like she could fall asleep. She managed to stay awake during prayer time, went to the kitchen for some rice and kimchi and finally went to her room for sleep.

Exhausted she fell into a deep sleep and dreamed of her love. She dreamed that Frank had come back for her. He had arrived in America and missed her so much that he immediately turned around and came back for her. She felt him shaking her to wake her up. She was so happy to see him again. As she opened her eyes, her heart broke. It was not Frank waking her. She remembered now. She was in the orphanage and her roommate, Ho Sook, was shaking her and asking her to get up. It was time to go to Mass. Her heart sank as she started day two of her new journey in this Catholic orphanage.

Pega got up and joined the others for morning Mass. The first thing she noticed was that Father Houng was presiding over the Mass. Pega was so happy to see him. She wanted to speak to him about going to school. Surely he would understand that

Frank was sending him money every month to make certain Pega was able to attend school. She would have to catch him after Mass and tell him that she had to attend classes. Pega again followed Mi Chi and knelt when she knelt, stood up when she stood up and sat down when she sat down. Father was saying the prayers and everyone was responding in unison. Pega could not concentrate on what was going on around her. All she could think about was getting to see Father Houng as soon as this was over. The Mass went on for about one hour. As soon as it ended, Pega ran up to the altar and asked Father Houng to please speak to her for a few minutes. Pega tried to tell him that she had to attend classes but Father Houng brushed her aside, telling her that if she had any problems, she would have to speak to Eunah. He did not have time to discuss these problems and Eunah would speak to her about these things.

Pega was devastated. Now who could she turn to? Father Houng had no time for her and was angry that she even approached him. He was not going to help her. And Eunah thought it was nothing but a joke. She had no intention of helping Pega learn to read or write or learn to speak English. Pega knew she had to get a message to Frank and let him know what was happening. He would be able to tell her if she should stay here or go somewhere else. The last thing she wanted to do was disappoint him. If he came back in March and she did not know anymore English than when he left, what would happen to them?

Eunah saw Pega speaking to Father Houng and became quite disturbed. What did she think she was doing, going up to bother the priest! She immediately went to Pega and told her to follow her to the nursery. Eunah asked Pega; "What were you talking to Father Houng about?" Pega told Eunah that she was asking Father about going to school. Eunah became very angry. She told Pega that she was never to discuss that with Father Houng again. Father Houng was a very busy man and he did not have time to get involved with her petty problems. She had already told her that she was not going to school and now she needed to stop talking about it. She told Pega to report to the nursery immediately and begin her work. Pega was devastated but did as she was told.

Pega went to the nursery and helped to feed the babies the American oatmeal. It tasted odd to her and she preferred rice but the babies didn't seem to mind. After the morning meal, she helped to change the babies. Her heart was pounding in her chest and tears were welling up in her eyes but she did everything she could not to cry. She could not stop thinking about how she was going to get a message to Frank. She had to let him know what was happening.

Pega spent another day washing dirty diapers and dirty clothes. She went to noon time prayer, ate the rice and kimchi and returned to wash the clothes. By evening, she was again exhausted. She tried to stay awake while the others prayed in Chapel. She ate supper and went to bed, crying herself to sleep. She could not believe this was happening to her. She had been so excited to finally be able to go to school but her big dream was just that – a big dream. Maybe her wish to go to America was nothing but another big dream. Maybe Frank was not going to come back for her. That is what Eunah believed. Eunah did not believe the soldier would return for the peasant. That is why she didn't care about the things Frank had asked them to do for Pega. Eunah thought Pega was just another girl left behind after the soldiers left. There were several other girls waiting at the orphanage for soldiers to return. Some have not heard from their boyfriends for over a year. Eunah believed Pega was just another one of these foolish women.

For Pega, everything was wrong. Nothing had worked out as planned. She had been so sad to see Frank leave but so happy that she would be able to learn to read and write and study English. Now all she was going to do was wash the dirty diapers. The other girls said they gagged and couldn't do it. It would become Pega's full time job. She had to let Frank know of this. She had to find someone to write a letter to him as soon as possible.

Morning came early. The women got up very early to start cooking and caring for the babies. Some of the babies needed to be fed before Mass. Some of the other women were in charge of cooking and feeding the babies. They got up extra early to start their day. Pega woke up in time for chapel at 6:00 a.m. She joined the others and again Father Houng was presiding over the Mass. Pega knew she was not permitted to go to him so she sat quietly and mimicked her friend Mi Chi. Pega learned to go through the motions of Mass every morning. She wondered why these people would spend all this time in the church praying to that man on that cross. She just didn't get it. He was dead. What could he do for them; all this praying and for what? She needed real help not something pretend. She needed someone to help her now.

A week passed and Pega realized there was no way Eunah was going to help her. It was final. She would not be going to school. Every day the routine was the same. Rise early, go to Mass, help feed and change the babies, gather the dirty diapers and clothes and begin washing them. At noon, go to prayer, eat a midday meal, and wash the dirty diapers and dirty clothes. At 5:00 p.m., feed the babies, go to prayer, and assist in the nursery until time for sleep. Pega's hands were once again beginning to become chapped. She did not mind the work, nor did she mind taking care of the babies. If only she was able to be pleasing to Frank and learn to speak English, then she wouldn't mind working even twenty hours a day, if only she was permitted to attend school.

The weeks passed slowly and on Sunday, September 22, Eunah came and found Pega to tell her she had guests. Pega was so happy. Maybe Frank was back already and she could go with him. Pega ran out to the main gate and found Victor and Roger. Of course Frank was not with them. It was so strange for her to see Frank's soldier friends but not Frank.

Roger did his best to communicate with Pega. He asked her how she was doing but Pega did not want to complain. She did tell Roger that she was washing clothes and showed him her dry hands. Roger asked her about school and Pega shook her head, no. She tried to explain to them that she was not permitted to go to school. She started to cry. She really just wanted to see Frank.

Roger felt really bad for her and reminded her that Frank said he would be back in March. He told her not to leave Collumba; she should wait there for Frank. Roger tried to encourage Pega not to give up hope; Frank would be back just as he promised. Pega did calm down and tried to find comfort in Roger's words.

Roger remembered he had to ask her about her period. Rose had told him to say *wolgyeong jugi* (monthly cycle) and Pega would understand. So Roger asked her, "Wolgyeong jugi?" What! Why was Roger asking her such a personal question? Embarrassed, Pega answered, "No." What an odd thing for Roger to bring up! Pega was very confused and embarrassed. She really was upset, seeing the soldiers made her yearn for Frank so much more. She only wanted to see Frank. She could not believe Roger would ask her such a question!

Roger and Victor did not stay very long; they had to return the jeep back to camp. She desperately wanted to go with them - but how? She couldn't pay anyone to let her stay with them. She felt so all alone. Rose was so lucky. She still had Roger with her. Pega knew she was feeling angry and jealous of Rose. Rose could read and write Hangul, she had her own room and Roger came to see her all the time. They would never understand what was happening to her now. She had to find someone to help her.

For the next several weeks Roger and Victor would borrow the Army jeep and ride over to see Pega. She was always happy to see them, since their visit reminded her that Frank would be back for her. Somehow seeing Frank's friends kept her strong. She liked the fact that they was still checking on her and would let Frank know how she was doing. They were such nice men and they were always laughing and joking and their laughter would lift her spirits. Their visits made her feel special since none of the other girls had American visitors like she did. Pega grew fond of both Roger and Victor.

She did find it embarrassing that they always asked the same question, "Wolgyeong jugi?" Every week, Pega had the same answer, "No wolgyeong jugi." She still did not understand why they would inquire about something so personal. The questioning was always very awkward. Finally after about the fourth visit, Roger asked her again and got the same response. "No wolgyeong jugi."

Roger smiled a huge smile and gave Pega a great big hug, laughing and said, "Congratulations, you are pregnant! You are going to have a baby!" He touched her belly and demonstrated rocking a baby back and forth. Pega was shocked. The soldiers were happy and smiling but she was not happy. Could this really be true? Was she really going to have a baby? Pega was startled and confused. She could hardly believe that she was pregnant. Roger seemed genuinely happy but Pega was numb with fear. How could she ever take care of a baby? Now she knew she had to leave this place as soon as possible and somehow get a message to Frank.

# 23
## Discharged
### Frank Returns to the U.S.A.

September 1952

Frank arrived back in California on September 19, 1952. Immediately, both he and his mother continued to pursue the Immigration and Naturalization Service, (INS), through telephone calls and letters, attempting to gather information on how to bring Pega to America. Kathryn had written to the INS back in July but had never heard back. It would not be until the middle of October when Kathryn would finally receive a response from the United States Government.

Kathryn received a letter dated October 15, 1952 from Mr. Edward S. Maney, Chief, Visa Division, of the Department of State in Washington, D.C. The letter read as follows:

My Dear Mrs. Crimbchin:

I have by reference from the Immigration and Naturalization Service your letter of July 24, 1952 concerning your desire to obtain information regarding the entry of aliens into the United States for permanent residence.

Under the provisions of the Immigration and Nationality Act (Public Law 414) which was passed on June 27, 1952 and which becomes effective on December 24, 1952, persons of the Korean race are eligible for citizenship and are admissible into this country for permanent residence. It is therefore suggested that the alien in whom you are interested be advised to communicate immediately with the American Consular Officer in the district of his residence with a view to registering as an intending immigrant. However, no visas can be issued pursuant to the Public Law 414 prior to December 24, 1952 the date on which it becomes effective.

Sincerely yours,
Edward S. Maney,
Chief, Visa Division

Upon receipt of the letter, Kathryn immediately contacted her son stationed in California. She sent the government letter directly to him. Frank realized that Pega would not be able to pursue the American consular on her own. She would need assistance to accomplish this. Frank wrote to his buddy, Victor, and asked him to please take Pega to the United States Embassy in Seoul and register with the consulate there. Victor would have to assist Pega to register as an intending immigrant. Hopefully he would have the time and willingness to do this.

As soon as Frank was able to get off the base, he set up a checking account with the Hibernia Bank in San Francisco, California. Frank was able to deposit money into this account and Father Houng would be able to withdraw the payments. He quickly forwarded the account information to Father Houng. He wanted Father to know he intended to keep up his end of the bargain.

On October 25, 1952, Frank was formally discharged from the Army. He never made it past Corporal and that was just fine with him. He returned to his home in Pennsylvania with his mother and father who were so glad to have their son back. It had been a very long two years. It was good to be home again. Frank had hated the country of South Korea but he had found the most important thing in his life over there, Pega. He knew he would have to work hard and save his money in order to return and bring Pega to the United States.

Frank wasted no time contacting the airlines to get a price for the tickets. He would need to estimate what his travel and living expenses would be when he returned to Korea. He learned that he would have to stay in Korea for about ninety days. That should be enough time to process Pega's visa. After researching the costs, Frank estimated he would need about $2,000 to return to Korea to get Pega. Two thousand dollars! He had never been able to save that kind of money before. It was a huge amount of money but he knew he had to do it.

He soon learned that his parents were very behind in all of their bills. Even though he had tried to keep them afloat by sending money to them every month, it just wasn't enough. Frank could not wait to get back to his job at Taylor and Wilson's Manufacturing Company. The problem was that the job did not pay enough to cover all his parent's bills as well as save enough to go back to Korea. He soon realized he would need to work two jobs in order to save that kind of money.

Frank found a second job, replacing manhole covers, with the City of Pittsburgh. The covers weighed up to 250 pounds each and not everyone could lift that much weight. Frank was a big strong guy and lifting 250 pounds was manageable for him. He was hired immediately. Monday through Friday, Frank would work at Taylor and Wilson's from 7:30 a.m. - 4:00 p.m. He would eat his packed lunch on his way to his second job. By 5:00 p.m., Frank was in downtown Pittsburgh to pick up the truck and begin loading manhole covers. After loading the truck he would take them to their assigned location and switch out the old damaged cover for the new one. It wasn't steady work but it did bring in some extra money. He planned on saving all the money he earned from his second job for his trip back to Korea.

Frank was very worried about Pega. He had written many letters and sent them off but he had not heard anything from Victor or Roger. They promised to write to him and keep him informed about how Pega was doing at the orphanage. It had been several weeks and he had not heard a single word from them. Of course communication halfway around the world was difficult and very slow in 1952. Mail was sent by boat and could take up to six weeks to get from the writer to the recipient. In addition, there were other major problems. Pega was illiterate and could not write to him. Even if she could write in Hangul, Frank would not be able to translate the letters written to him. He was totally dependent on Victor and Roger to help him. He really needed their friendship and loyalty now.

Since he had not received any news, he could only hope that Pega had remained at the orphanage. He did everything he could to set things up before he left. Father Houng agreed to accept the $75.00 a month and Pega would be able to go to school to learn how to read and write. In addition, he had asked Father Houng to make sure she learned to speak English.

He couldn't wait to hear from Victor or Roger and checked the mail box every day. He had written to Roger again and asked him to give him an update on Pega. How was she? Was she staying at the orphanage? Did she get her period? Frank was still worried about the possibility of pregnancy – even though he really did not believe Pega was pregnant – at least he didn't want to believe that.

He also sent several letters to Father Houng but had not received anything back. He was trying not to panic but he really wanted to hear something about how things were going at Collumba Babies Home. He made sure he deposited the money into the account which he had set up for Father Houng at the Hibernia Bank. Frank was faithful and made sure the money was deposited just as he had promised. He would not want to upset Father and have him ask Pega to leave the orphanage.

Frank worked seven days a week. Monday through Friday he worked as a machinist at Taylor and Wilson's. In the evening he worked for the City of Pittsburgh. Every Saturday and Sunday he traveled to Slippery Rock to work on the cottage. He could not let that property go unattended any longer. There was so much upkeep with the cottage and his time out of the country did not help. He had to finish the interior of the house since they had just put up the frame and outer walls before he left for Korea. Now that he was home, he had to get back to finishing that project.

Frank missed Pega so much but there was nothing he could do except to wait until after December 24, 1952 at which time the new law would become effective allowing him to pursue marriage to a Korean woman and bring her to America.

He only wished he knew for sure that Pega was safe and waiting for his return. He needed to know that she would not leave the Collumba Babies Home. If Pega were to leave the orphanage, Frank knew he might never find her again in that war torn country.

# 24
## Pega leaves Orphanage
### Collumba Babies Home

#### October 1952

Monday, October 13, 1952 was a crisp fall day in Seoul. That was the day Pega decided to leave the orphanage and return to Yongdongpo. Roger had been there on Sunday and told her she was going to have a baby. Pega panicked. What should she do now? She had not heard from Frank. It had been weeks. She was not learning any new English and she was not going to school as Frank arranged for her to do. And then she learned she was pregnant. She had to get a message to him as soon as possible.

Pega took the money Frank had given her before he left for America. She had a plan. She would go back to see Rose. Although Rose could not write a letter in English, she would be able to help Pega communicate with Roger or find someone to write a letter to Frank. She had Frank's address in the United States and she had to find someone outside of the orphanage to write the letter for her. She did not trust anyone in the orphanage to help her. They had lied to Frank about allowing her to go to school and nothing they told him was coming true. She could not trust any of them. Pega left with her money and walked to the bus station. She got on a bus that would take her back to Yongdongpo.

Pega went to Rose's. Rose was so surprised to see Pega at her house; "What are you doing here? Frank told you to stay at the orphanage. Why did you leave?" Pega told Rose everything that was happening at the orphanage.

Pega told Rose that Eunah would not allow her to study. She told her about the sick babies and how all she did every day was wash dirty diapers and dirty clothes. She must learn to read and write and speak English. Then Pega told Rose that she was pregnant and scared. She did not know what Frank would want her to do. She had to learn English. She had to learn to read and write. She wanted to go to America. Rose listened to her story well into the evening.  After talking for several hours, the girls finally fell asleep.

The next morning Rose took Pega to a *Papa-san* (elderly man) who could read and write in English.  Pega offered the papa-san five won to write a letter for her.  He immediately agreed to do this.  Pega began to explain to the old man what had happened but she was crying so hard, the papa-san could hardly understand what she was trying to say.  He listened to her story as best he could, took the money and wrote the following letter – much of which was not accurate!

October 14, 1952
Seoul, Korea
To: Frank
From: Pega

My Dearest Frank,

I guess you had returned your home where you have been yearn for without any trouble and met your family.  I tasted waves of hardship and difficulty since you left me.

I still remember that you told me to work for the orphanage and study.  I think you had great big hope on me they let me do that.

However, unfortunately I could not study.  Therefore I came to Seoul to see my mother. Due to the poor condition of my mother's living I sold everything you presented me and I am living with that.

And my body is getting heavier day after day since you left, therefore I can't work for the orphanage.  I will wait for your answer at my mother's house.  Please write to me through your good friend Ray.

At the end of the letter I pray for your health from the place far away from you.

By the way, I'd like to send my regard to your parents directly however due to the different custom, and my poor knowledge of English, I could not write your parents directly. Please have noble and wide understanding of me and forgive me.

138

After writing the letter, the papa-san folded it over and handed it back to Pega. She was so relieved to be able to tell Frank what was happening. Of course Pega was not at her mother's house and she had not sold anything Frank had given to her as was written in the letter. Between her crying and sobbing as she spoke to the papa-san, the accuracy of her circumstances was lost. In addition, Pega was unable to read what the papa-san had written so she had no idea of the misinformation being sent to Frank.

Pega did not have an envelope or any knowledge of how to mail the letter to Frank. She would have to see Roger and ask him to mail it for her. She would have to wait until Saturday. That was when the soldiers had time to see their girlfriends. Pega returned to Rose's home and stayed there until Saturday morning. As fate would have it, Roger did not come to see Rose that Saturday in October. The girls came up with another plan.

The next morning, Sunday, October 19, Rose encouraged Pega to go to the mission in Youngsan and speak to the minister there. Maybe Frank could arrange for her to stay at that mission and go to school there. Pega decided to do just that. She would go to the mission today.

She left Rose's house and headed towards Youngsan. When she came to the Yongdongpo Bridge, she would need her pass to cross the bridge to get to the mission. She reached into her pocket to get her pass but could not find it. It was only then that she realized when she was on the bus, the young boy who bumped into her and almost knocked her over, must have stolen her pass. Now she could not cross the bridge.

She was so distraught walking back to Rose's and crying. A truck full of missionaries stopped to ask her what was wrong; "Why are you crying? Can we help you?" Pega explained she had to speak to the minister, it was very important but she could not get across the bridge. When the missionaries realized she was headed to their very own mission, they decided to give her a ride with them. The missionaries put Pega on the back of the truck and hid her. She crouched down while they all sat around her.

The missionaries successfully hid her from the crossing guards as they rode over the bridge. The missionaries knew they would be in trouble with the authorities if they were caught sneaking the girl across the bridge but they felt sorry for her and decided to go ahead and take the chance.

They drove directly to the mission and dropped Pega off. When Pega went to see the minister, to her dismay, he was not there. He had gone away for the week and would not be back for days. Pega knew she had no choice. She could not stay there an entire week. She did not know anyone. She would have to return to Yongdongpo. The missionaries allowed her to sleep in the house with them for one night and they would take her across the bridge in the morning.

The next morning, the missionaries put her back on the truck and took her over the bridge. When she arrived on the other side, she decided to go directly to Camp Sykes. She would look for Frank's good friend Roger and maybe he could help her. She walked several miles to the camp. She was so heartbroken to see all the soldiers on the other side of the fence. How she missed Frank. Maybe if she stood there long enough, he would magically appear, just like he did on the first day they met. She was standing outside the fence crying when Corporal Ray Liddencoat saw her.

Ray recognized her as Frank Crimbchin's girlfriend. Now anytime Ray saw Pega with Frank, she was always so happy and cheerful, he had never seen her like this before. She was almost hysterical. She was crying so hard and trying to explain to him something about the orphanage and going to school. She had not heard from Frank and she didn't know what to do. Ray tried to calm her down but the girl would not stop crying. He could not understand one word of what was being said. Ray called one of the ROK soldiers into the office and asked him to interpret the conversation. The Chaplain heard the commotion and stopped over to see what he could do. In the meantime, Lieutenant Hittaker wanted to know what the heck was going on. Hittaker started on his soap box about the soldiers getting involved with these Korean girls.  This was such a problem.  This was why they all need to stay away from these women.

Corporal Liddencoat explained that Frank had been discharged but apparently intended to return for the woman.  In addition, they were still receiving packages from him at the mail desk addressed for Collumba Babies Home.  Now the Lieutenant was really angry.  If Frank was sending boxes to the orphanage, he would need to report that.  It was against military rules for the soldiers who had been discharged to be sending packages through the Army like that.  Lieutenant Hittaker wanted to know exactly what Frank had sent and how many boxes had been received.

Furthermore, if he intends to marry this woman, has he even started on the paperwork?  If so, the Lieutenant wants a copy of the paperwork sent over.  If Frank has not started on the paperwork he needs to let this woman know because he will not stand for his soldiers leading these women along with false hopes and dreams.

There was so much confusion with Pega near hysteria, the ROK soldier trying to interpret, the Chaplain and Hittaker going on and on about Korean women, Ray felt like he was in the middle of a huge mess. In the meantime, Pega was telling the ROK soldier that she didn't know what to do.  Someone had stolen her bus pass.  She was stuck in the town and could not travel anywhere.

Oh, so apparently in addition to everything else, the woman had lost her bus pass.  Well, Ray knew he could work on that for her. Pega was going on and on about the orphanage and the babies.  He knew Frank did not want her to leave the orphanage.  He asked the ROK soldier to advise her to return to the orphanage and he would stop over sometime this week to see her and straighten things out for her.  Pega wanted someone to write a letter to Frank and let him know she missed him and needed to know what to do.

Ray said he would write a letter to Frank for her and he would ask Frank to write back and let her know what to do. The following letter was written by Corporal Ray Liddencoat to Frank.

October 20, 1952

To: Frank Crimbchin
      McKees Rocks, PA

From:  Corporal Harold R Liddicoat
          HS Company 76th Engineer Construction Battalion
          C/O PM San Francisco, CA

Hello Frank,

I have been asked to write this letter to you from your girlfriend, Pega. I hope I can make myself understood and I hope you will answer me as soon as possible. I leave here about the 8th of November, so would you please hurry?

First, would you have a photo static copy made of the papers you have for marriage? Also let me know how many packages you have sent, clothes – and if you sent any money? You see Pega is worried because she hasn't heard from you. She sends her love and wishes you were here and she misses you very much.

A few days ago when Pega was on a bus traveling to Yongdongpo, someone stole her pass and she is very blue. But I have talked to the Chaplain, he is new, but he is going to help her. Also I have talked to the Company Executive Officer HS Lieutenant Hittaker. He will help her too so she will have her pass in a few days, so don't worry Frank.

Now I will pay a visit to the mission where she is staying and I will let you know what and how everything is going. Okay. Well I will close for now but I will write again in a couple of days. So, please answer this letter as quick as possible Frank so she will be able to know everything is alright.

Yours truly,

Ray
Corporal Harold Liddicoat

Pega was so happy that Ray wrote the letter for her. Now she knew Frank would get the letter. Ray told her that everything was going to be okay. Ray offered to drive her back to the orphanage but Pega did not want to go back yet.

She wanted to go to see Rose. Rose had her clothes and the letter from the papa-san. She had to return to Rose's and she needed time to think about whether she should return to the orphanage. She wanted to wait until Frank told her what to do. Above all else, she had to learn to read and write English.

Pega returned to Rose's to wait for Frank's direction. On Saturday, Roger and Victor stopped over to see Rose. Pega and Rose told them everything about the orphanage. Pega did not know how she would learn to read or write. The men didn't know what Frank would want her to do. They knew Frank was so glad to have found the orphanage and the priest who was going to help them. Victor knew that Frank was paying the priest to educate Pega. He really did not know how to advise her. Victor told Pega that he would try to write to Frank as soon as possible.

October 29, 1952

To: Frank Crimbchin
    McKees Rocks, PA 15136

From: Victor

Sorry I haven't written sooner but I have been really busy. Will (Bob Willem) and Whizzer left today. I am the head hauncho now. We have really been working our heads off. Well I know you don't want to hear about that.

Well I have some bad news to tell you. Pega took off from the orphanage a couple of weeks ago. She is out at the house with Rose. I have been out to see her couple of times. Rose sees her every day. She hasn't decided whether to go back to school or not. She wants you to write and tell her what to do. I also have a letter here from her that a Korean papa-san wrote for her. I will hold onto the letter you sent me to give to the priest until I hear from you and Pega decides what to do.

At first she was talking about going to the mission out by the 121 Evacuation Hospital. But now she is talking about going back to the orphanage. Don't send any money to the priest's bank account until everything is straightened out. Pega told me that all she is doing at the orphanage is taking care of the kids and not going to school.

By the way Frank, she said she is going to have a baby. I thought it best to tell you. It's no use holding anything back from you. I don't know what is going to happen when Rip (Roger) and I leave. You won't have anyone to keep in contact with her.

By the way, you talk about hard luck, you know it was only about two weeks after you left, a circular came down from Headquarters that GI's are allowed to marry Koreans again. It's a shame you couldn't have stayed here a little longer.

Well I am keeping my end of the bargain up so far Frank, so as you know, I will be leaving in about two months. So after me you will have to depend on Rip but that will only be for a short while too. Well I guess I'll close for now, and am going on guard.

Until I hear from you,
Your Buddy,
Victor

PS The clothes from Sears and Roebuck haven't arrived yet.


**With that, the letter was sent off to America.**

# 25
# All News is Bad News
## Frank

### October 1952

By October, Frank was working day and night seven days a week. He didn't mind it; he had a goal. He wanted to bring Pega to the United States and he wanted to finish the cottage in Slippery Rock. He was willing to work as much as necessary to make it happen. He had to save $2,000 in order to bring Pega to America. Frank continued to write to his buddies as well as Father Houng but he had not heard anything back. He was beginning to worry more and more every day. How was Pega? Was she okay? Did she need anything? Why didn't the priest answer his letters?

He finally received a letter from Korea, it was from Ray Liddencoat. That was strange. Frank opened the letter and began to read it. He was confused. Pega was at Camp Sykes and apparently had told Ray that she lost her bus pass. Frank had told Pega to stay at the orphanage; what was she doing at Camp Sykes? If she had stayed where he arranged for her to stay, she would not have had her bus pass stolen. He could not believe that she was at Camp Sykes! In addition, Ray wanted to know how many packages he had sent to the orphanage. Why? What does that have to do with anything? Frank began to worry about what exactly was going on. He knew sending money and packages to the orphanage through the camp was against import regulations. The recipient was avoiding the import tax but Frank knew the orphanage could not pay the tax and he wanted to help Pega and the orphanage. Now Liddencoat was involved and questioning him.

He could understand if Pega was upset and missing him. He was upset and missing her too. But nothing else made any sense. He sat down to write a letter to Ray Liddencoat and also sent one to Roger. He had to know why Pega was at Camp Sykes. Frank was worried sick.

Another week passed and on November 5, Frank received a letter from his buddy, Roger. The letter was dated October 29. He couldn't believe what he was reading. Pega had really left the orphanage. She had lost her bus pass when she was traveling to Yongdongpo. Roger wrote that the priest was not teaching her any English or sending her to school. On top of that Roger wrote that two weeks after Frank left Korea, the laws changed and he could have married Pega! And the most shocking news of all – Pega was pregnant. Now what was he going to do? He *had* to get back there as soon as possible.

Frank could not believe all the bad news he was getting. How could Pega have left the orphanage? He might never find her again. This was the worst news Frank could ever receive. Frank was at the end of his rope. He handled things the only way he knew how. He went to work that day knowing he had to go to his second job at 5:00 p.m. As soon as he was done with his second job, he drove to the Eagles Club where his father used to work and ordered some shots. He sat there drinking whiskey and beer until he was overly intoxicated. Frank downed shots with anyone and everyone. Yeah, he was going to be a father but he didn't even know where the heck the mother of his baby was. Nothing could have hit him harder.

Frank staggered out of the bar and went to his car. He fumbled for his keys and struggled to get the key into the door. He couldn't get it in. He was so angry that he smashed the window open with his elbow and proceeded to unlock the car door. With blood running down his arm, he got into the car. Again he struggled to start it up but while he was sitting in the driver's seat, two policemen came up to him with their guns drawn. "What are you doing?" the cop asked him. "I'm trying to get home." Frank slurred. "Why are you stealing a car to get home?" they asked him. "I'm not stealing a car." Frank replied. "This is my car."

"No." the policeman said. "This car belongs to this guy. You just broke into his car and now you're going to jail." Frank got out of the car and as they were handcuffing him, he looked across the street.  There sat his Chevy; same make, same model, same color.  He couldn't believe it.  He had just broken into some other guy's car!

The policemen took him down to the jail in McKees Rocks, where he was kept overnight to sober up.  He had never been in jail before in his life and this was a first.  Yeah, he had gotten a ticket for speeding before, but never anything like this.  The next day after he paid a huge fine his father came to pick him up.  Between repairs and fines the whole thing would end up costing him over $300.  That was about all the money he had saved towards his return to Korea.  He wrote a check to the officer and left the building.  His life was becoming a disaster.

Frank's Mother, Kathryn, was so upset she spent the entire day crying.  She called on her sister, Sister Mary Perpetua, and asked her to write another letter to Congressman Fulton.  They really needed someone to help Frank get Pega out of that country; now there was a baby involved.  Nothing could have been worse.  Kathryn was already worried sick about this girl and now to think she was going to have Frank's child.  Kathryn was scared for the girl.  She had trusted the priest in Korea.  She was so disappointed to learn that he was not teaching the girl how to read or write or speak English.  Surely this was a mistake and the priest was doing everything as it was arranged.  Frank was paying him to help her.  Sister Mary Perpetua might be able to get them some help.

Sister Perpetua agreed to write the Congressman again and plead for help.  In the meantime, she encouraged Kathryn to have Frank go to see Father Joe from St. Mary's Church.  Maybe if Father Joe wrote a letter to Father Houng in Korea, the Korean priest would respond.

Kathryn encouraged her son to go to the priest at their church, and tell Father Joe his problem. Father would certainly be able to do something for the family.  Maybe he could contact the Catholic orphanage in Korea and find out what was happening.  Kathryn's family had a long history with St. Mary's Catholic Church.   Kathryn's parents, Frederick Sonnett and Margaret

(Yonkas) Sonnett, were both from Germany and had immigrated to the United States in 1882. They along with five of their siblings had all settled in McKees Rocks in a predominately German Catholic settlement. Kathryn's parents were a big part of the German community and helped to build the first Catholic Church along Chartiers Creek in McKees Rocks. The community had spent $800 to build that first church. Unfortunately, the church was built right along the creek bank and was at many times inaccessible except by boat.

Several years later the German community built their second Catholic Church but this time on higher ground. From 1886 to 1905, this would serve as the place of worship for the community. On May 28, 1905, a third church was dedicated. It was an awesome edifice of Flemish-gothic style and had been patterned after a cathedral in Cologne, Germany. The building was unique in that it had no interior columns. The strength of the building was in the heavy walls and steel construction. Free from the usual obstruction of pillars the sloping floor permitted an unbroken view of the sanctuary and alter from all parts of the nave. The church was magnificent.

The Sonnett family helped to build that church and worshiped there for many decades. Kathryn's sister, Elizabeth, was raised in this church and had become a Divine Providence nun and eventually taught school for many years. Kathryn had been baptized, attended school, and was confirmed in this church. She had sent her own sons, Frank and Donald to the same Catholic Church built and supported by the German community of which she and her decedents were a very big part, both financially as well as in service to the community. Now Kathryn needed her church. She encouraged her son to go to see Father Joe.

Father Joe performed Mass every morning and Kathryn had been attending every day while her boys were overseas. Every night, Kathryn prayed the rosary and asked Mother Mary to watch over her boys. So far God had been very good to her. Frank had survived the war and Donald was now serving in

Germany. Many young men had been killed. Kathryn was so grateful to God for watching over both of her sons.

Frank was desperate so he placed a call to Father Joe and asked the priest to see him as soon as possible. On Saturday morning, Frank met with Father Joe at the beautiful church in McKees Rocks. Frank entered the church through the massive front doors and immediately went to the confessional. Father Joe listened to Frank confess his sins, his recent bouts of drinking, his lack of confession and communion, his lack of attendance to Mass while in Korea and even since he returned to the U.S. Frank confessed to Father Joe his relationship with Ock Soon and how much he loved her and wanted to marry her. Frank explained to Father that no one would marry them and now she was over there alone and pregnant. Could Father Joe please help him by writing a letter to Father Houng and finding out if Ock Soon was still at the orphanage? Frank explained that Ock Soon was illiterate and had no family. She could not read or write letters to him. In addition, there were no telephones or any other way to communicate. Frank explained the payment arrangement he made with Father Houng and his concern that Father Houng had not been answering any of his letters. Frank had become worried sick that something was wrong and he had no way to find out.

Father Joe listened patiently while Frank went on about how hard it has been to be over here and not being able to know what was happening to Ock Soon in Korea. When Frank finished, Father sat quietly for a short time. Then he told Frank that he needed to forget about that girl and move on with his life. God would forgive him his sins. Many soldiers met women during wartime but they did not have to marry them. He did not have to go back for her. His life would be a lot easier if he just learned to forget about her and find himself an American girl.

Furthermore, Asians were not welcome in this country and he would certainly be better off without her. Father Joe told Frank that if the girl could not read or write English she did not belong in this country. She would only be a burden to him and to the rest of society. Father Joe told Frank that he, himself, did not

149

believe that Americans should marry Koreans. He did not believe Congress was right in changing the laws. He would not marry them either. He did not feel in good conscious that he could assist him in bringing a Korean girl to America. He was sorry but he simply could not help him.

Frank could not believe his ears. What was this priest saying to him? Frank had been attending Mass here in this very church his entire life. He was baptized in this church. It was here at this very altar that he made his first Holy Communion and later was confirmed into the Catholic faith. He sat in these pews week after boring week listening to the priests preach to him about love and forgiveness. And now he sat in this confessional across from Father Joe, shocked at what he was hearing.

It was at that point in his life that Frank made the decision that he was finished with the Catholic Church. As long as he lived he would never come back to this church. All the preaching he sat and listened to all his life in this very church and for the first time in his life he reaches out to Father Joe for help and this is what he gets.

Frank was furious. He had really believed that Father Joe was actually going to help him. The disappointment and rage he felt could not be explained. He walked out of the church and vowed that he would never again set foot in St. Mary's Catholic Church.

# 26
## Pega's Decision
### Return to Collumba

#### November 1952

Pega was staying with Rose and she thought about all the things that had happened since Frank left. She knew she needed her bus pass in order to get back to the orphanage. She had been desperate to get in touch with Frank and tell him about their baby. She was so glad she was able to get a letter to him. Maybe she would hear from him any day now.

Pega stopped back at Camp Sykes to see Soldier Ray and find out if he had a new bus pass for her. She again met with Soldier Ray and the interpreter. Soldier Ray gave Pega her new bus pass and told her to go back to the orphanage and wait for Frank there. Although he did not get a letter from Frank yet, that is the best thing for her to do. Pega decided to take his advice and return to the orphanage.

She went back to Rose's, packed her clothes and took the bus back to Collumba Babies Home in Seoul. She was so happy to have a bus pass again. When she arrived at the Babies Home, Eunah was furious with her for having left. Pega had not told anyone that she was leaving and they were all worried about her. Eunah told her that although she could come back this time, if she ever left again, they would not accept her back. She reminded Ock Soon that they were doing her a big favor by allowing her live there. She was so ungrateful for all they had done for her. She ought to show more respect and gratefulness to both Father Houng and herself.

Pega listened to Eunah rant on and on and said nothing. She would stay and work for them. Soldier Ray had told her that he would write to Frank and let him know that she planned on staying at the orphanage until his return.

Pega was not fond of Eunah. Eunah did not care about anything that Pega was going through. Pega decided that she would keep her pregnancy a secret from them. She was ashamed and afraid to let them know that she was going to have a baby. She would just hide it for as long as possible. Maybe when Frank learned that she was going to have a baby, he would come back immediately. If Frank came back for her right away, she would not have to tell any of them. It would be her secret.

Pega resumed her schedule. She was still responsible for all the dirty clothes and dirty diapers, since none of the other girls wanted to do it. The other girls were more educated and had come from homes with both a mother and a father. They had not known the kind of hardships that Pega had faced her entire life. They were educated and they knew how to read and write. Their lives had been relatively comfortable until the war broke out. They would do anything they could to get out of washing those dirty diapers by hand. Ho Sook and Pega worked together every day to wash the clothes. Ho Sook was thankful for the work. Her entire family was killed during the Second Battle of Seoul and she had found refuge in the church. Father allowed her to stay at the orphanage and for this she would be forever grateful.

Every day Pega and Ho Sook went to the spring and captured the water in the jugs. Every day they washed the diapers by rubbing them against the stones. They would rinse them thoroughly in fresh spring water and hand them to dry. There were dozens and dozens of diapers to wash every day.

Pega's favorite time of the day was when she helped feed the babies. She always found time to spend time with them. She grew to love those babies and found comfort in rocking them and playing with them. Anytime she thought about her own baby, she was both happy and sad. She could hardly believe that someday she would have her own little baby, just like the ones in the nursery.

Pega had grown attached to a little boy named, Hyo. Hyo was not even one year old but he was always so happy to see her. Anytime she came to his crib, his little face lit up with joy. Pega always chose him to feed at mealtime and she always rocked him to sleep after his lunch. Pega noticed he was becoming more and more listless. Even though she was feeding him she thought he was starving to death. His belly was chubby but his arms and legs looked like twigs. One morning, Pega went to get him out of bed but was told the baby had died through the night. Pega was shocked. She could not believe that little Hyo had died. She was rocking him and trying to feed him just yesterday and now he was dead! Pega was crying and crying. How could this be? Little Hyo had been her new little friend. Somehow she had found comfort in holding that little baby boy. She could not believe the child had died. No one else seemed bothered or upset by this. Pega could not understand. The baby was dead and no one cared.

Later that night as Pega walked across the porch, she let out a loud scream when she saw Hyo's cold lifeless body lying outside near the wall. Someone had moved the child from the nursery and just set him on the porch. His body laid there frozen in time, eyes wide open, staring at her. The sight caught her by surprise, she ran across the porch and into her room. She did not know that they had moved the dead child out on the porch and just laid him there! She could not believe it. This was a Catholic orphanage and they just threw the child outside like garbage. She hated this place. How could they do that to her little friend? She cried herself to sleep that night wishing she could tell Frank what had happened.

The next day Hyo's little body was gone. She was so glad someone had moved him. She hurried to the Chapel and after prayers; she went into the kitchen to help prepare food for breakfast. She asked Mi Chi what happened to Hyo's body.

Mi Chi explained that the old man, whom they called *Halabeoji* (Grandfather), always buried the children. Eunah would notify Halabeoji whenever a child died. Halabeoji was the old man who shared a room at the orphanage with his granddaughter Cho Hee. Pega had seen the old man working in the garden every day. He struggled to hoe the ground with his broken body. Apparently he had suffered a stroke some years before and only had use of his left side. He dragged his right leg along the dirt as he worked in the garden.

Pega remembered several weeks ago, Eunah had sent the old man to sell the harvested vegetables at the market. The old man was gone all day. It was a very long walk to the market. He dragged his dead right leg along the road with the vegetables tied on his broken back. He was very angry when he returned with the money. He had walked miles and miles to earn just a few won for Eunah. Pega overheard Eunah complaining about the old man; "Can you believe he just threw the money at me?" Pega felt sorry for the old man with the broken body who worked so hard.

Apparently anytime a child died, Eunah would call on him to bury the body in the woods. Although Halabeoji tried, he could hardly dig with only one good arm. Now that the ground was hard, it was far more difficult for him to dig a deep grave site.

Later Pega heard the students talking about Halabeoji. They said that he was not digging the graves deep enough. Pega had heard that the animals had dug up the bodies of some of the children and were eating them. Pega did not want to think about any of this anymore. She was so sad that Hyo was dead. She did not like this place at all. She wished she had learned to read and write and then she could write to Frank and tell him all about this.

One Sunday, November 9, Eunah was looking for Pega to tell her she had visitors. When Pega learned she had visitors, she was so excited. She went outside and found Roger and Victor with a large box. Victor told Pega that Frank had sent the box for her. Pega was so glad to see her old friends. Pega couldn't wait to open the package and see what was inside. She opened the box and found all the special treasures from America.

On top was a very beautiful little box and it was wrapped in the most colorful paper Pega had ever seen. She opened it and inside was a gold bracelet. Victor told her it was a wrist watch. All the American women wore these. It would show them what time of day it was, just like a clock. Pega was so proud that her boyfriend had sent her such an expensive gift. Pega asked Victor to help her put the watch on. Even though she did not know how to use it, nor could she read it to determine the time of day, she wore the watch with great pride.

Also in the box was a wooden cross with that man hanging on it. It was from Frank's mother. Pega thought about Frank's mother and how wonderful it was that she would send Pega a gift. She was so surprised that Frank's mother was so kind to her. Americans were so kind and so very rich. Pega opened another small package and found some brown candy. She immediately ate one piece. It tasted like the candy Frank had given her when he was in Korea. He knew how much she liked the brown candy and sent her some. She was the luckiest girl in the whole orphanage.

After she opened her presents, she dug down into the box and found some women's clothing. Frank had sent her some beautiful dresses and several winter coats. She was very happy and excited as she was going through the clothing. At the bottom of the box was a pair of shoes. Pega tried them on and they fit her perfectly. She was so thankful for all the things Frank had sent to her.

After she had finished going through the box, Pega and the soldiers talked about the orphanage. Pega told them about all the work she was doing. She explained again that she was not permitted to attend school. She was feeling very tired because of the baby growing inside of her. Pega told Victor that no one else there knew she was expecting a baby. She did not tell them. She was hoping Frank would return soon and come for her before the baby was born. The soldiers stayed for a short time and encouraged Pega to stay there until Frank returned. After a brief visit they had to leave.

Pega was so happy to know that Frank was still caring for her. He sent all of these wonderful gifts to her and some money too. He was such a good man. Roger said that Frank would be coming in the spring. Pega could hardly wait. She thought the baby will be born in the summer. Frank should be here before the baby comes and then they could leave this place. No one would have to know that she was going to have a baby. It was still her secret.

When Pega carried the box into the nursery, all of the other women came running over to see her treasures. They were all very excited and anxious to see what was inside. Eunah had watched Pega in the yard with the American soldiers and the big box. She followed Pega into the nursery as she was very curious to see what the soldiers had brought to her.

Eunah stood next to Pega and watched over her as she opened the box. She noticed the gold watch that Pega had on her wrist and thought how silly it was that this peasant was wearing such a precious thing.

Eunah saw the cross and immediately said they would hang the cross in the nursery, that way everyone could see it. Pega didn't mind since she spent a lot of time in the nursery and she would be able to enjoy it there also. Eunah took the cross out of Pega's hands and said she would have it put on the wall.

Pega dug down into the box and found some beautiful dresses. She had never seen such beautiful things. They were very colorful and nothing like the hanboks the women in Korea wore. Pega found a heavy coat, pulled it out and tried it on. It was a perfect fit. As she dug deeper, there was another coat. Mi Chi saw it and loved it. She asked Pega if she could have the other coat. Mi Chi's coat was very old and thin and all the buttons were missing. Pega handed the coat to Mi Chi who was delighted to receive such a beautiful item. But before she could even put it in her hands, Eunah grabbed the coat. She began ranting at Pega telling her that these items are not for her to give away. Frank had sent them to the orphanage and they did not belong to her, they belonged to the orphanage. She told Pega to go ahead and keep one coat and one dress for herself. Pega picked out one coat and one dress. Eunah grabbed the box and left the area.

Pega felt very badly that Mi Chi did not get that beautiful coat. She really needed a new one and Pega would have been so happy to give Mi Chi a coat. Mi Chi had become one of her best friends and always helped her during Mass. Mi Chi was always talking to Pega about Jesus and Mother Mary. Mi Chi loved Jesus and his Mother Mary. She was always telling Pega to pray to

156

Mother Mary and Jesus would help her. Mi Chi always told Pega to have faith because God loved her very much and had sent his only son to die for her. Pega would have loved to give Mi Chi that coat. She felt sad that she herself had a new coat but Mi Chi did not. Sometimes Pega really did not like Eunah at all.

Several weeks passed and one day Pega saw Eunah meeting with a strange woman in the courtyard. The woman came to the orphanage once every couple of weeks. Pega had seen her there before but did not really understand who she was or what she did. Pega was surprised to see Eunah give the woman, the big box of clothes that Frank had sent to her. Pega asked Mi Chi why Eunah would give the clothing to that woman. Mi Chi told Pega that the woman stopped by the orphanage regularly. Eunah saved items to give to her to sell on the black market. Anytime Eunah received nice things from donations, she always gave them to the woman and they would split the money. That would not be the last time Pega saw the woman. The woman would come by anytime Frank sent boxes to her. Most of the boxes that Frank sent would end up with the woman in the courtyard.

Pega looked at her beautiful watch and felt so glad that Eunah did not take it from her. Pega would have to find someone to write a letter to Frank. She wanted to let him know how much she missed him and to thank him for the beautiful watch. She would not tell Frank about the woman and the black market. She did not want to upset him.

Mi Chi was always so busy. It was December now and they were preparing for the Christmas holiday. There were special Masses and everyone had to learn new songs about Jesus. Father Houng arranged for the children to sing for the soldiers at Camp Sykes. There was so much to do to prepare for their Christmas music.

Every time Pega asked Mi Chi to write a letter for her, Mi Chi would agree to do so. But by evening, Mi Chi was so exhausted from working hard all day and choir practice in the evening that she was just too tired to write a letter for Pega.

Writing a letter in English was a very big project. Mi Chi was learning some English but it took a long time for her to put a letter together.

Every night she promised Pega that she would write a letter tomorrow. Every day Pega dreamed of all the things she would want Mi Chi to write on paper. First she would tell Frank how much she missed him and loved him. Then she would thank him for all the beautiful gifts he sent. Then she would tell him about the nursery and all the babies. Every day Pega would think of these things and every night she would ask Mi Chi to write a letter for her. But every night Mi Chi fell fast asleep, simply too exhausted to concentrate on writing a letter in English.

♥

Photo: Some of the woman and orphans living at
Collumba Babies Home Orphanage during the Korean War. 1952.

♥ Ock Soon is the young woman in the back row
(slightly left of center) gazing downwards at the baby in her arms.

The three little children in the front row:
Hyewon, Minju and Yeonsang all passed away in 1952-1953.

# 27
# Hoping and Saving
## Frank

### November 1952

It was already November. Frank continued to work hard to save his money. He knew he had to get back to Korea. It was so difficult to get enough money together. He would need money for a round trip flight to Seoul for himself. In additional he would need a one way ticket for Pega and the baby. Frank had been pricing tickets and they were outrageous. He had set his goal of $2,000 before he could return to Korea. That was more than the cost of a new car! He could buy a brand new car for $1,700. None of that mattered. He knew he would have to come up with the money.

Every time he turned around there was something else to fix or replace. He was still trying to get caught up on all the late bills his parents had. In addition, he had the property taxes to pay on the cottage. His car needed brakes and the hot water tank broke. He could not give up his second job. He had to save as much money as possible.

Frank knew that Father Houng did not read English and any letters sent to Father would have to be translated into Hangul. Maybe that was the reason why he had never heard anything back from the priest. Frank thought that if he could write the letters in Hangul, maybe Father Houng would be able to answer him more quickly. Of course Frank could not write Hangul and he could not find anyone else who was able to do so either.

Sister Mary Perpetua had encouraged Frank to look for a Korean student at the University of Pittsburgh. She knew that some young Koreans had come to the U.S. to study. Frank had called the University Admissions Department when he first got back to Pittsburgh, but they would not give him any information about the students. They did give him permission to post a job on their billboard. Frank had gone to the University and posted an advertisement for a Korean translator.  Weeks had past and he had not heard from anyone.

Frank always looked for mail but it seemed he rarely got any letters from Korea.  Ray had written him again and told him that Pega returned to the orphanage.  He wrote Father Houng several letters but never received a reply.  Frank continued to deposit the $75.00 a month into the Hibernea bank account.  The money was being withdrawn so he knew that Father was receiving it.

Frank continued to send boxes of clothing to Pega.  His cousin, Roberta Rennekamp, worked at Hornes Department Store in downtown Pittsburgh.  Roberta was a kind hearted and beautiful woman who was happy to give Frank coats and dresses to send to the orphanage.  In addition, Roberta had organized their neighbors and church friends to donate clothing for Pega and the others at the orphanage.  Frank was afraid Pega might be cold now that winter had set in.  He could only hope that Pega was getting all the packages he had been sending to her. He knew it was risky but he had also sent some special gifts to Pega. Several months ago, Frank had found a beautiful watch when he was downtown.  It was a lot of money but Christmas was coming and he had wanted to give Pega something very special.  He had bought the watch and sent it over with the clothing.  He could only hope that it got there safely.

# 28
# Finding a Translator
## Frank

### December 1952

Christmas was coming and Frank was both worried and depressed. He had been sending packages to Camp Sykes hoping Roger would take them to Pega. He had not heard from Pega in a very long time. Communication was extremely difficult since he returned to the U.S. The mail was very slow, some never arrived. In addition, his buddies did not speak Korean very well. Pega spoke very little English. Frank knew they would be having a difficult time communicating with each other.

Also since Pega could not read or write, even in Hangul, she needed someone to write the letters for her. If Frank received a letter written in Hangul, he would need an interpreter to translate the letter. Frank had been sending letters to Father Houng in English. Father Houng could not read English very well and he would have to have them translated into Hangul. Frank wasn't sure if Father Houng was doing that or even if he was taking the time to read his letters. Everything was extremely difficult and with the holidays approaching, Frank found himself becoming more and more discouraged.

Finally during the first week in December, Frank received a call from a young man, Kim In Sun. Kim told Frank he would be able to translate the Korean letters for him. Frank could pay him for each letter he writes or translates. Kim was happy to make a few extra dollars and since he was studying English, he thought it would be good for him to have an American friend. Frank invited Kim to his home for Sunday dinner. From then on, every Sunday, Frank's Mother would cook a big dinner and Kim would come to the house. Every Sunday, Kim would write a letter for Frank in Hangul. If Frank had any letters from Korea, Kim would take them with him and return them later, translated into English. It was a good arrangement and Frank was happy to have someone to help him.

Kim, In Sum and his wife-Translators from University of Pittsburgh.

Kim and his wife came for dinner on Sunday, December 7, 1952. Kathryn had cooked a big traditional Sunday dinner of roast pork, whipped potatoes, sauerkraut and applesauce. Kathryn had been baking all day on Saturday, dinner rolls and homemade apple pie. She really wanted Mr. Kim to enjoy coming for Sunday dinner since her son greatly needed this friendship.

Frank drove out to Oakland on Sunday and picked up Mr. Kim and his wife and brought them back to his home for dinner. The couple arrived and truly enjoyed the American menu. This was going to be a new experience for them, having American friends like this. Both were anxious to build this new friendship. After dinner, Mr. Kim wrote a letter to Pega from Frank. The letter follows below:

December 7, 1952, Sunday

My Dear Ock Soon,

162

I tried to write a letter to you several times, but I couldn't because of the language problems. Finally I was able to find a Korean man from the University of Pittsburgh. His name is Kim, In Sum. He is a very nice man and he will be able to translate the letters. His wife is also very nice; they are both studying at the University. I think they will be good friends for you when you come to America.

I have not stopped thinking about you since I left Yongdongpo. I think about you constantly and I was working to find out how we could be married. I just received a letter from our Congressman saying the United States Congress just passed the laws granting permission for Americans to marry Koreans. The law goes into effect on December 24, 1952. I can't tell you just how much I love you. My plan is to return to Seoul in April or May. We can be married and then if everything goes okay, you can come to live in America.

Please write to me as soon as possible and let me know if you received the wristwatch that I sent you five weeks ago. It was an expensive wristwatch and I want you to keep it with you to remind you of me. Also please let me know if the shoes I sent to you fit you. I also sent you $40.00. Please don't be disappointed that it is not a lot of money. I have to save everything I earn for our marriage expense which will be about $2,000.

I heard you went back to the orphanage. I want you to stay there and wait for me. Study hard and learn English. When you learn English then we can tell each other how much we love each other. When you come to America, you can go to a good school and learn more.

I was so glad to find In Sum Kim. I was looking for a Korean student for a long time. Finally I found this young man who is studying English at the University. He said he will translate all the letters you send to me. So next time you send a letter in Korean, I will have no problem finding someone to translate it.

I think of you all the time Ock Soon. I can't wait to make you my wife. Please take care of yourself. I love you and send you my hugs and kisses.

All my Love,
Frank.

P.S. Do not worry about applying for immigration to the United States. I will help you when I get there. Just be healthy and take care of yourself.

Frank was truly happy to have met Kim. He was so anxious to mail the letter and so anxious to hear back from Ock Soon. Frank mailed the letter to Father Houng the next morning. Every day Frank checked the mail box for news from Korea. He was so eager to hear from anyone, Ock Soon, Roger, Victor, Father Houng – anyone. But each day, Frank was disappointed – no letters from Korea in the mail box.

The following Sunday, Frank drove to Oakland and again picked up Kim and his wife. The couple came for dinner and once again sat down to write a letter to Ock Soon.

Sunday, December 14, 1952

Dear Ock Soon,

I keep worrying and I am concerned about how you are doing with winter coming. Do not worry about me; I am fine living with my parents and my brother. I hope you are doing well and enjoy studying. I didn't mention the baby in the last letter.

Do not worry about the baby. When you feel uncomfortable, you must go to the doctor and do not worry about paying him. I have already asked Father Houng to find a good doctor for you. Please write and tell me the expected due date for delivery. How wonderful if we had a son! Don't you think so? But it is not up to us, whether it is a son or daughter, both are God's beautiful creations.

Now I am changing the topic. On December 9, I sent two packages of clothes that I thought you might need. Pick out whatever you want from the clothes and give what you do not want to others. Also, you will receive three more packages by airmail. One is candy and gum, some soap. I tried to think of

164

what you would need, but please send me a list and I will get it. I also sent Father Houng $75.00 for your December expenses.

You might be curious as to who is writing this letter, so the next sentence is from him.

> 'My name is Kim In Sun. I am the same person who wrote Frank's last letter. Before the liberation, I had taught English at Kyog-Bok Middle School and had worked as the Director of Education of De-Sung English Institute. It is my understanding Ock Soon should be the happiest woman in the world. I have met many young Americans but I have never met a good man like Frank before. I too have a friend who is working at the U.S. Army Hospital in Busan. She moved from Seoul and is waiting to come to America. I have met several Americans who married Korean woman around here. I am an outsider but I hope you and Frank have a very happy marriage.'

Back to my letter:

I (Frank) love you very much Ock Soon and I think very highly of you. Until I come to marry you, please be happy and be strong.

I miss you, my love, Ock Soon!

Love,
Frank

Again Frank mailed the letter and could only hope to hear from Ock Soon someday soon. Frank missed Ock Soon desperately. When he did not hear from her, he could only imagine terrible things. Maybe Ock Soon had left the orphanage. Maybe she was ill or something was wrong with the baby. Maybe she found someone else. Frank's mind would not stop worrying about all the possibilities that could go wrong during this time in

Korea. How he wished he would get a letter from Ock Soon. He just needed to know that she remained safe in a country destroyed by an ongoing war.

# 29
## Finding Faith
### Pega

Christmas 1952

Another month had passed and although Pega was getting packages and every once in a while a letter, she was still finding it very difficult if not impossible to find someone who would write a letter to Frank for her.   She thought about going back to Yongdongpo and finding the old papa-san; but she herself was so busy she could not get away. Pega desperately wanted someone to write a letter for her, but everyone was working long hours. Only a few girls were able to write a little English.  Writing a letter in English would be a very big project for any one of them.  Asking Father Houng to help her was simply out of the question.  He had no time for her and she didn't even know for certain if he was able write a letter in English.

Pega had been listening to Mi Chi tell her all about Jesus. Mi Chi told Pega that God loved her very much and He knew of all of her pain and suffering.  God knew just how much she loved Frank and how she desperately missed him. God wanted to help her now.  Mi Chi explained to Pega that God had sent his only son, Jesus, to this earth to live a perfect life.  When Jesus was a young man he would suffer and die on a cross.  Because he was a perfect sacrifice he would take all the sins of the world onto himself.  But Pega had to recognize that Jesus was the son of God and acknowledge him as her Savior.  If she recognized Jesus as her Savior from sin, and asked him to take all of her sins unto himself, Pega would be pure before God.  Pega need only ask God to forgive her and she would be forgiven and become a child of God. When she died, she too would go to heaven to be with Jesus.  Mi Chi told her that Mary was Jesus' mother and she would ask Jesus to help her.

Pega needed help.  She needed a Savior.  She needed a mother and she needed someone to go to Jesus and ask him to bring Frank back to her.  Pega began praying to Jesus and his

Mother Mary. She began to ask God to help her, forgive her of her sins and bring her Frank back to her. She wept at the foot of the statue and prayed earnestly all day and especially when she went to Chapel.

In the church yard was a tall statue of Mother Mary. Every day Pega went to the statue before Mass and prayed to Mother Mary. "Mother Mary, please help me. Please ask Jesus to send Frank back to me". Pega believed that Mother Mary and Jesus could help her in her time of need. She did not have a mother, but she found one in Holy Mary. She did not have a Savior but she found one in Jesus.

One morning Pega saw Father Houng in the courtyard. She asked him directly, "Father, do you believe Frank will be coming back to get me and take me to America?" The priest stared at her for quite some time before answering. Finally, Father Houng answered her saying, "No. I do not believe the soldier will be coming back for you. Soldiers do not come back." Pega was stunned. She could not believe that Father Houng did not understand that Frank was coming back for her. Now she understood why Father Houng did not feel the need to send her to school or to follow up on any of the promises he had made to Frank. He never believed that Frank would return.

Pega wept for days and days after hearing those words from Father Houng, but she herself did not stop believing. Frank had promised to come back for her and Jesus had given her hope. Although shaken by what Father Houng had said to her, she would not stop believing in Frank and having faith in Jesus to help her.

As the days turned into weeks and the weeks into months, still Pega believed. If Frank believed in Mother Mary and Jesus, he would know all about these things. Furthermore, Frank's own Mother believed. They must be right. She would believe also.

On some days in the early morning hours, Pega would awaken and hear the women praying in the Chapel. She would run to the Chapel, thinking she was late for Mass. She would open the door of the Chapel, but no one was there. Pega was certain she heard their prayers. On mornings like this, Pega knew it was God who awakened her to come and meet with Him. She never found it odd that she heard prayers coming from the Chapel, yet no one was there. She believed it was God calling to her to come and pray. God would fill her with the hope and the peace she needed to go on. Pega had faith and no one else's disbelief would take that away from her.

Christmas was coming and everyone was excited to talk about how Jesus was born. They said it was a miracle. Jesus was the Son of God born to a virgin. Pega listened to all the teachings and embraced them. She needed Jesus, Mother Mary and God more than ever before in her life. She thought about everything she had been through and believed that God Himself had spared her life. So many times she should have been killed and yet she had survived. She did not understand why God would protect her but she knew that He had done just that. She thought about the death of her parents, the abuse she had suffered, the battles in Seoul, and the long journey on foot to Taejon. She knew in her heart that it was God who kept her safe. She believed that God had sent Frank to her to love her and help her. She knew in her heart that Frank would come back for her. God had always loved her and watched over her all the days of her life. Even before she knew God, He knew her and loved her. She believed in Frank and now she believed in Jesus, her Savior.

On Christmas Eve, everyone wanted to go to Camp Sykes for the Christmas Party. Pega said she would stay back and take care of the babies. All the women and children loaded up in the trucks and headed towards the camp. Pega went into the nursery and cared for the babies. She sat in the chair rocking one of the babies in her arms. As she sat there, she could hear the beautiful singing from the students and the children as they drove by in the trucks. They sounded like angels voices in the night. She sat there alone with the babies, enjoying the most beautiful music she had ever heard.

Later when they returned from the party, everyone was very excited. They had received tea and cookies from the soldiers while they were at the event.  Someone had dressed up in a red suit and passed out gifts and candy to all of the children from the orphanage.  Each child received packages from the man in the red suit.  Pega was looking at all the gifts the children brought back. She told Mi Chi and the other women just how beautiful their singing was.  Pega had heard them singing on their way to the party.  They looked at her strangely and told her that no one was singing in the truck.  Pega was bewildered.  She had heard the angel voices so clearly.  Then she realized that it was not the orphanage choir she heard, she really believed that she heard angels singing.  Pega believed that just like the morning prayers, the angel choir was a special gift from God to her as she sat alone in the nursery with the beautiful abandoned babies praying for her Frank to come back for her.

How she wished she knew how to read and write.  If only she could read and write, she would send a letter to Frank and let him know of these miracles.  He would be so surprised about the prayers from the empty chapel and the music she heard from heaven.  She couldn't wait to see him and tell him all about this. Maybe now that Christmas was over, someone would have time to write a letter for her.  She would ask them again.  Her heart was full of Christmas joy since God had been so good to her and she wanted to share her joy with Frank.  She could hardly wait to tell him all about what God was doing for her and how she loved Mother Mary and Jesus.

# 30
# Losing Contact with Ock Soon
## Frank
### January 1953

The holidays had passed and Frank had heard nothing from Ock Soon. Kathryn, Frank's mother, continued to cook the big Sunday dinners for their new Korean friends. Every Sunday, Frank continued to go into Oakland, pick up Kim In-sun and bring him and his wife over for dinner.

On Sunday, January 4, Frank asked Kim to please continue to write to Ock Soon even though he had not heard anything back. By now even Kim was feeling sorry for Frank. He knew how much Frank missed Ock Soon and how desperately he wanted to know how she was doing. Kim could not understand why any Korean woman would not write back. Here was an American man who wanted to bring her to America. She should be writing him every day reminding him of her deep love. Kim was feeling sorrow for Frank as each week passed and no letter from Ock Soon was received.

Uncertain if the letters were being lost in the mail or if Ock Soon was no longer at the orphanage, Frank had Kim write the following letter to Ock Soon that first Sunday in January.


January 4, 1953
Sunday

My Dear Ock Soon,

I have been waiting so anxiously for your letters. Please send me a letter once a week if possible. I want to know that you are okay and how you did through Christmas and the New Year.

In three months, I will fly to Seoul just as I wrote you in December. That will be such a wonderful moment.

I am going to write to the officials in Korea and Father Houng. Maybe he or his friends can help me get approved for a visa. All you need to do is learn about becoming a Catholic and we will be married in the Catholic Church.

Also, please let me know as soon as possible which kind of gold ring you like. Do you like gold rings made in America or gold rings made in Korea?

Also, please let me know if you received the clothing that I sent to you. I took some pictures around my home and of Kim. I will send them to you.

I hope you understand that I would write you in more detail and more often if I could write in Korean. I close this letter with a kiss and I want you to take good care of yourself.

Love, Frank

PS 1) I already sent Father Houng the January expenses so do not worry about that.

2) I need to know your address where you are staying. I cannot send the letters to the military address anymore. I will send my letters to your address at the orphanage.


Frank mailed the letter and continued to hope for a response from Ock Soon. Every day he hurried home to check the mailbox and every day he found nothing from Korea.

It was on a snowy cold day the first week of January when Frank opened the mailbox and there sat a letter from Korea. It was from his good friend Victor. It was written almost eight weeks ago!


November 10, 1952

To:     Frank Crimbchin

From:   Corporal Vic
        HQ Company
        76th Engineer Construction Battalion
        PM San Francisco, CA

Hi Frank,

How are you boy? Well I might as well spread the good news. Lee went back to the orphanage a week and a half ago. She told me to tell you she would stay there and not to worry about her. She also sends her love to you and to your Mother and Dad. She also gave me two pictures to give to you.

Frank, I will try to do everything I can for you but boy I am not kidding you, they are running us ragged. We have been working hard ever since Will and Wizard left. There is a MA Corporal here with us. He has five years in grade. I jumped all over him the other day. I left him go for a while but he just tried my patience a little bit too much. He don't give me no problem either.

By the way, I have the picture of our motley crew, it looks pretty good. I also wanted to tell you your gifts for Lee came at a very opportune moment. They came on Saturday; the watch, the crucifix from your mother and the box of candy.

Sunday, Rose and I went to see her and delivered her your gifts plus the $22.00 you sent her. I received your other money order today and will straighten everything out with the money.

I also forgot to tell you Frank, you asked me to get Lee to the American Consol. Well Frank, the way I understand the American Embassy is in Pusan now. I know I can't get enough time off to take her there. Besides, Captain Dole is now Company Commander of A Company. Otherwise anything I can do for you I will.

I want to say something to you. Listen Frank, you need to straighten up and act your age and stop drinking. That isn't going to help you get Lee back to the states. It isn't right for you to be acting up the way you are. It's not right for you to be that way. You probably have your Mother and Dad worried sick. I know in one of your letters you said your mother was ill. I hope she's well now. Tell your parents I said hello. When the kid from Milwaukee gets back, he will have to stop and straighten the boy from McKees Rocks out.

I was down to play bingo tonight, guess what, I won $92.50 and Berry's gold wristwatch, it's really a beaut. I just noticed above that I forgot to tell you how pleased Lee was with her watch and the other gifts. She really liked them very much.

Well Frank, stop worrying about Lee because everything is number one. So take care of yourself and quit hitting the bottle. Well Frank I think I will close for now. I have to get up at five o'clock tomorrow morning to go out on the rifle range. Until I hear from you, be good.

Your buddy,
Vic
P.S. I am a real short timer now. I only have about 45-60 days left.


Frank was never so glad in all his life to receive a letter. It was good news that Pega did receive the packages he had sent. He was glad to hear that she liked the watch and the other gifts. He did notice that Vic said he received $22.00. He had sent Pega $40.00. He had worried about the inspectors stealing the money. Oh well, at least she got the watch. He felt like crying when he got the letter. He missed her so much. No one could possibly understand what he was going through. The inability to write letters or call her on the telephone made communication next to impossible. Frank had to trust others to help him and the only friends he had over there would be leaving Korea shortly.

He was really worried about what was going to happen when Victor left Korea. On November 10, Victor wrote that he would be leaving Korea in about 45 -60 days. Sixty days had already passed by. Victor might already be back in the United States by now.

How would he ever be able to keep in touch with Pega? Less than four months had passed since he last saw her and it seemed like four years. Not only that, Frank knew that he would not have enough money until at least March. March was a long way off, a very long way off.

The next day, Frank received a letter from his old friend, Bob Willem. Will's tour of duty ended in October. Will had left

174

Korea on October 31, 1952 and was discharged from the Army in early December. Frank had written to him last week just to find out how he was doing. It was good to get a letter from Will.

January 2, 1953

Hi Frank,

How are you? I received your last letter, day before yesterday and sure was glad to hear from you! I got out of the Army the 4th of December at Camp Carson, Colorado. I caught a plane the next day and flew the 1,150 miles in 4 hours and 10 minutes. Man, I sure hate to travel by troop ship. I don't think I felt worse in my life for those 13 days.

Well Frank, I didn't waste much time before going back to work as I started last Monday. I sure got a break there as I was given 90 days to make the grade as set-up man on Brown-Sharp automatic screw machine which will pay me $2.20 an hour on days.

I have my order in for a new 1953 Chevrolet hard top which I should see the 9th of this month.

Frank, you know I was thinking about my friend, Judy. (Sunja). She was such a good woman. Honest to God, she told me something before I left Korea and it was really sad. I got a letter from her after I arrived home. She must have had some Korean write it for her as I don't think she can write any English. If you get back to Korea, please look her up and see how she is doing. She was a good friend and I hope things work out for her.

Well Frank, I'm going to drop up and see you sometime the last of this month or the first of February. I'll let you know before I come. Take it easy "ole buddy" and I'll see you soon!

Hope to hear from you soon.

Your Buddy,
Will

The letter made Frank feel sad. Will had been such a good friend to him. Will's friend Sunja had helped Ock Soon so much in the beginning. Frank would never forget all they had done for both Ock Soon and himself. Sunja had been an angel for Ock Soon. Ock Soon had grown very fond of her and so thankful for all the help cleaning her up that day so many months ago. It was out of her kindness that she allowed Ock Soon to stay with her in Nonsan. She had been so generous, giving Ock Soon some of her own clothing. Frank recalled the some of the evenings they had spent together, having dinner and laughing about silly things. Now Will was gone and no one knew where Sunja was. Frank felt so sad for Sunja. Frank knew that Sunja had wanted Will to take her to America. But although they were good friends, Will had never made that promise to her. Sunja's dream would never happen for her. Will didn't say what Sunja had said to him that broke him up so much. Sunja would probably turn to prostitution to survive. It was all so very sad. Korea was such a broken country. There were so many poor, starving women and children everywhere you looked. So many men had been killed. Poor Sunja, she was such a good woman. She was so kind to Ock Soon when Ock Soon needed her. Frank wondered what would become of her now. Maybe he would be able to look for her when he returned to Korea.

On January 11, Frank wrote to the Passport Office in Washington, D.C. requesting information on how to obtain a passport and visa to travel to Korea. He knew it could take months to get the documents and he wanted to get everything in order as soon as possible.

In the meantime, Frank continued to check the mailbox every day after work. It was the middle of January when he was almost surprised to get a letter from his good friend, Roger. Roger had also been so good to Frank while they worked together. He was a very hard worker and Frank respected him for that. Anytime Frank and Roger worked together on a project, Frank knew that Roger could pull his weight and get the job done correctly. That's what Frank liked in a machinist — competence. He always liked it when he and Roger traveled together to work sites. Roger wasn't like some of the other guys who couldn't even run a lathe. He was a good worker and a good friend. He was also very good to his girlfriend, Rose.

Rose like so many other Korean women was hoping for the American dream. Rose had experienced some of America's material wealth. Roger had brought her so many delicious things she had never seen before. Roger would bring her coffee, Spam and peanut butter. He brought her special things like jam and jelly, Oreo cookies and Hershey's chocolate bars. Rose knew Roger was a very wealthy man. He was so rich, he would even give Hershey's chocolate to the children in the streets. Rose had heard of how rich all the Americans were. She had heard there was so much money in America, it could be found lying out in the streets. How wonderful it would be to live in a country like America where all you had to do was bend over and pick up the money you needed.

Rose had suffered so much since the war came. After her family was killed, Rose was homeless and starving and she had turned to prostitution in order to survive. She had been abused by many soldiers, beaten and raped. She hated to sell her body but there was no other work available. When she met Roger, everything changed for her. Roger loved her and he provided everything she needed.

Of course, she never thought about that little baby girl she once had. She pushed those thoughts out of her mind. She did not allow the picture of that little baby to enter her mind. Never! It was two years ago that she learned she was pregnant. Rose was so upset she did not even know who the father could be. She had been with so many soldiers after her husband was killed.

Rose would never forget that awful day when Seoul was invaded. Her husband, Gang, was dragged out of their home and taken into the streets where he was told to kneel down and then shot in the head by one of the Communist soldiers. She was terrified and did not even let out a scream until after the Communists left the area. She stood there stoic and watched quietly as they shot the man she loved so deeply. She thought of her husband often and missed him so much. They had only been married for a few months when the war broke out. They had loved each other completely and he would never have wanted her to do the things she was doing. But Rose had no choice. She needed to pay for food and she needed somewhere to live. She, like Ock Soon, had looked for work but there were no jobs available. She turned to what so many women had turned to during the war - prostitution. When she found out she was pregnant, she did not want the baby. She could not take care of herself - let alone a child. Rose did not have an abortion and the baby girl was born.

After she met Roger, everything changed for Rose. Roger did not want her to be with other men. He put her up in a room and took care of her. Rose fell in love with Roger. Maybe it was just because he was an American who was rich and so kind to her. No matter what, Rose was dreaming of the day she and Roger would leave this country and she would be his wife.

Rose knew that her biracial baby girl was going to keep her from getting to America. She simply stopped feeding the infant and eventually the baby died. She made herself a promise to never think of the child again and she never did. Her entire focus was winning Roger over so she could get to America. She had to get out of this country and go to America where people had food and clothes. She had heard that the Americans lived in homes that were like palaces. Money was everywhere and no one was poor. Rose knew that somehow she had to get to America.

Frank could not wait to read the letter from Roger. As he opened Roger's letter, he was delighted to find a letter from Ock Soon also enclosed. He would have Kim translate Ock Soon's letter as soon as possible.

In addition, in the mailbox, Frank found a second letter from Ock Soon which had been mailed directly from the Collumba Babies Home. Frank would drive over to Oakland after dinner and give both letters to Kim for translation, that way Kim would be able to bring the translated letters with him next Sunday. But first he had to read what Roger had to say. Roger wrote the following:

January 4, 1953

Corporal Roger Van Winkle
76th Engineer Construction Battalion
San Francisco, CA

Dear Frank,

Guess I better get busy here and write you a few lines. Rose got a letter from Pega the other day and had wanted for me to send to you. So I will send it along with this. Pega looks fine Frank and we took all the clothes over there Sunday just before Christmas. She was really happy to get the box of clothes. She'll never leave the orphanage. I always keep telling her to stay there and you would be over either April or May. Rose keeps telling me that Pega will stay there and wait for you Frank.

Yes Frank I got the two small packages I haven't taken them over as yet but I will probably go over next Sunday. So that Victor can go just before he goes. He should be leaving around the 10th or 15th. I figure I should be leaving around the 10th til the 18th of February. I am still in the house and same room. There are a bunch of papa-sans living in the other room. Kemble is with Holter's old wife.

Well Frank I can't think of much more to write. Hope everything is going fine at home with you. I suppose Victor's told you we've gotten more new guys in the shop now. It is kinda crowded in there sometimes.

We have had pretty good weather so far up to this New Year's Day. We got about three inches of snow that day and it has been pretty cold since then. Well Frank it is getting late so I will close for now. Hope you are in fine health. And take care of yourself. Bye for now.

Your old pal,
Roger

Frank read the letter from Roger. He was so glad to know that Ock Soon was still at the orphanage. He missed her more than anything. He could hardly wait for Kim to translate Ock Soon's letters. He had been waiting to hear from her for so long.

The following Sunday, Frank went to Oakland and picked up Kim and his wife and brought them over for supper. This time the visit would be very special because Kim was bringing the two translated letters back with him. Frank could not wait for Kim to give the letters to him.

Frank laughed out loud when he read the letters. Ock Soon was a very simple country girl and had never talked in flowery poetic language like the words written in the letters. Frank knew immediately that most of the letter was composed by her friend and not Ock Soon herself. Frank didn't care. All he cared about was that Ock Soon still loved him and was waiting for him. That's all that mattered. It was so great to hear from her.

December 28, 1952

My Dearest,

Time seems to flow away as fast as a rapid current. It is already four months since you left this rugged battle field, this waste land!

It is a long time ago when the Jack Frost made at home here. Day after day, the degree of the cold weather shows it's crescendo, and the snow bound scenery around here is certainly beautiful.

I have received your letters several times, and I know that you are all right, but my mind is always dwelling upon you and even now I wonder how you are getting along. When I think of you being afar, afar away across the Pacific Ocean, I fall into a deep nostalgia of our past romance.

We had a wonderful Christmas with the little children and Father Houng. It was the happiest and hilarious moment to me as well as to those youngsters. Yes, I remembered you at that time and your loving parents. I do wish to see you and your parents someday soon.

I have received your letters through your friend in 76th Co. and heard of you from Father Houng, though, this time you made me a great surprise with a Korean letter written by a Korean student for you. I really appreciate his kindness and help for both of us, and I do not hesitate to write my letter to you in Korean language.

I am helping those little children as best as I can, and I always pray for their future will turn out well. Whenever I have time I try to study and learn something new.

I received a watch, a cross, clothing and money which you sent for me. I just can't express how happy I was! Again I say thanks for your sincere love. Whenever I see my watch, it brings me the golden memories of our past, and when it was after sunset, I could not help falling into sentimentality, and couldn't stop my tears of joy, tears of love!

Father Houng always takes care of me and I am living fine. I hope you will not spend too much money for me. Well, that is all for time. I'd like to close this letter with my sincere prayer for your health and your future and for all your family.

I sent a little thing as a token of my love to you. I do hope that you will accept it.

PS I sent two pictures of me in new coat which you sent. As to my address, you may send a letter for me through Father Houng or directly to me. My address is as follows:

Collumba Babies Home
Seoul, Korea
Lee, Ock Soon

Frank then read the second letter from Ock Soon mailed from the Babies Home.  Obviously it too was composed by yet another person.

January 3, 1953

My Dearest Frank,

    I received you letter written last week.  I just can't tell you how I enjoyed your letter and how much I long to see you.  Certainly time seems to fly away so fast.

    It is hard to believe you were here with me a couple of months ago.  I wrote a letter to you last week but your letter didn't seem you got my letter.  I believe you got it by this time.

    Thank you very much for sending me such wonderful things as a watch, a pair of shoes, three packages of clothes.  The shoes fit me just right.  It fits me perfectly.  You are so wonderful.  I feel that you touch my bare feet and you embrace me tightly.  I am so happy Frank.

    Yes, I picked out whatever I wanted and gave the rest to my friends here.  The cross that you sent me and that I love the most, is now on the wall of the children's room.

    Ten dollars, a package of chewing gum, another package of chocolate were all safely delivered to me.  Only two packages were by air mail, you said that you sent three by airmail though.

    I wish I could send you a letter everyday but I can't.  It is very difficult to borrow others hands to get a letter for you.  I am very sorry that I cannot write you as often as I want.  Forgive my ignorance, Frank, I will do my best for you.

    Whenever the happy seasons of the year come around, I fall into a deep sentimentalism and I am very lonesome for you.  Last Christmas was one of the most lonesome seasons.  To whom can I tell my lonely heart, Frank?

    Oh how often and how many times I have dreamed of you.  When I received your letter I could not help crying.  I was so happy that I could not stop crying.  Yes my hungry heart for your love was filled with your warm blood of love and was full of joy and hope.  I felt your handkerchief wiping off my tears on my cheeks tenderly and kindly.  I knelt on my knees and I prayed for you and myself.  Oh what a wonderful day it would be when we meet again.  I kiss you with all my heart.

Three months, it seems to be too long to wait you coming.  I learned that Jesus suffered for us.  I am glad to wait for our happy life.

I feel little pain once in a while but I haven't seen my doctor yet.  I believe I will have a baby sometime in May of this year.  Frank I am already excited to think of our baby.  Oh and I do want to be nearer to you and be with you.

I do appreciate the help of Korean friend for you and me. I hope he will be a good friend for us.  I believe he can help me in learning things when I will be in America.  I do respect him as a friend and as a teacher.

I always want to be nearer to you and to live with you. Please write me soon.

I need $20.00.  If you can send it, I am very glad Frank.


From your love,
Ock Soon


Frank immediately realized that the letters were written by two different people and the letters did not sound anything like Ock Soon's words.  But Frank could read between the lines and see that yes, Ock Soon still loved him, missed him and was waiting for him.  She has been getting the packages and Father Houng has been getting the money. Nothing else mattered to him.  He would have to write a letter to Ock Soon today before Kim left.

On January 11, 1953, Frank wrote another letter to the Passport Department in Washington.  He wanted to know how to apply for a passport in order to return to Korea.  The borders had been open to Asian immigrants as of December 24, 1952.  Frank had been waiting for this date for so long.  He had called the INS office but no one could tell him how to proceed.  He finally decided to write to them in order to get an accurate answer.

In the meantime, Frank's buddy, Victor, kept his promise to Frank and he continued to check on Ock Soon.  It was towards the end of January when Frank received the last letter from Victor while he was still in Yongdongpo. Frank knew the day was coming when his buddies would be leaving Korea and he was very concerned about how he would be able to keep in touch with Ock Soon.

The letter writing had not gone as smoothly as he had hoped. The language barrier, Ock Soon's inability to read or write Korean and English, the lack of response from Father Houng, boat mail, lost mail, everything seemed to be a hindrance.

It was a very sad day in late January when Frank received a letter from Victor. The letter was dated January 13, 1953, sent to Frank Crimbchin from Sergeant Thomas D. Victory from the H &F Company, 76th Engineer Construction Battalion, c/o PM San Francisco, CA. The letter follows:

Hi Frank,

How are you and your folks? I hope everyone is well. Thanks for the ten dollars but you shouldn't have done it. We don't need any bottles. But I guess since you insist. Well I was over to see Pega a little before Christmas. She is fine all except for a slight cold. Well I am leaving here the 16th. When I get to the states I will be out to see you so you better keep your nose clean or I'll rattle you a bit.

I handed over the pliers you gave me to John. We got a bunch of sorry replacements in the machine shop. I finally made Sergeant the 20th of December.

By the way about sending packages, John said he would be happy to help you out. The Chaplain we have here now is a funny bird. He don't believe in GIs marrying Koreans. I wouldn't ask him to accept the packages.

I know Pega is sincere about you and will stay at the orphanage for you, but you don't realize the legal red tape you are going into to get her back. Remember that Sergeant from C Company. He finally got clearance to marry. It took him three — six month extensions. He told me he had a hell of a time getting things straightened out.

I hope if and when you come back, you don't have as much trouble to go through as him. Well Frank, I haven't much more to say for now.

Until I see you,
Your buddy,
Victor

Three – six month extensions! That was eighteen months. There was no way Frank could even consider living in Korea for eighteen months. He would never have enough money saved and in addition, he still had bills to pay here in this country. Frank found himself becoming more worried and depressed. He just couldn't believe it could take eighteen months to get someone out of that country. He was saving enough money for three months. He should be able to get it done in three months. Frank was counting on it; $2,000 would cover his airline tickets and living expenses in Korea for a three month period. If he went to Korea in April, he should be back with Ock Soon and his baby by July. That was the plan.

January 22, 1953
From:   Corporal Roger Van Winkle
        76th Battalion
        San Francisco, CA

Dear Frank,

Well, guess it's about time I write you a few lines and let you know how things have been going. To start off with, I just came back from the hospital the 19th. I was in for almost a week, I was playing basketball one night and chipped a bone and pulled the ligaments in my ankle. So now I am just sitting around in a tent. I've got a cast on my foot, almost up to the knee. I guess I'll be pulling steady CQ pretty soon though.

I am going back to the hospital in about a week though and see if I can't get out of here. The nurse told me when I was there that I could probably fly back, I've only got such a short time left.

If I stay here though I figure I'll leave around the 18th of February. Victor left last Friday the 16th. They said I'd have the cast on for about six or eight weeks. So I will be on my way home by the time it comes off.

I get out March 26th. Sacco is leaving tomorrow the 23rd. Crabs just missed it by one day. Don't know when he'll get to go for sure. We've got Captain Carey for the motor office and H/S Co. He came back in October or November I think.

Yes, Frank, I've gotten the packages. I am going over to Seoul on Sundays and so I will write again Sunday and let you know how things are going. Victor and I were over there the week after Christmas so I haven't been over there since. It's kinda hard to get a jeep now. Carey is more strict now than before. So can't go very often. I try to go as often as possible.

I'm trying to think of a way how we can get Rose over there and they could talk some and maybe it will make Pega feel a little better. I believe Rose told me the baby will be the last of March or April sometime. I don't know for sure though. So I will find out Sunday and then I will let you know.

Yes I have been staying with Rose up until now when I banged up my leg. So I told her I can't come out very much. So I am not going out anymore now. She comes over here by the fence every day at 1500 hours though. I told her you and Pega would be there to see her so she will be around there somewhere. She talked about moving over another street but she didn't know for sure yet. Kemble is staying with Holters, so he's right in back.

Well, Frank I can't think of much more to write. I haven't been doing a darn thing and guess I won't either now til I get out. I'll send you my home address but I will be working down near Chicago and Kenosha, Wisconsin, so I won't be home.

I guess I will be getting married in May or June. So after I get settled down I'll drop you a line. Bye for now Frank and take care of yourself.

Your pal,
Rip
P.S. I'll try to get an answer to those Korean letters Sunday when I go over there.

Time was closing in on Frank. Roger was his only American connection to Ock Soon, and his time in Korea was winding down. All of his other buddies had already left Korea. Frank had to come up with another plan. If only Father Houng would answer his letters. It was so frustrating and infuriating that the priest never wrote back. Frank was faithfully depositing the $75.00 a month. The least he could do was answer one letter.

Victor said John would receive the packages that Frank sent to Pega. Frank knew he couldn't trust John. John was nothing but a drunk. John had re-enlisted in order to go back to Germany. Instead of going back to Germany, they sent him to Korea. John absolutely hated it! Even when Frank was still over there, John did nothing but drink a pint of whiskey every night and pass out on his cot. Frank couldn't trust John to help him with anything.

Victor said he did not ask the Chaplain because the Chaplain didn't believe in GIs marrying Koreans. Frank had no choice. If all else failed and he didn't hear from Ock Soon, he would have to ask the Chaplain to help him. He hated to do it, but there was no other way. He knew of no one else who could receive the mail and the packages and help him to keep in touch with Pega. He could not lose her now.

In late January, Frank finally received a response from the Passport Office in Washington, DC. Mr. R.B. Shipley, Director of the Passport Office, replied indicating Frank was required to apply for permission to enter Korea through Headquarters, Far East Command, APO 500, c/o Postmaster, San Francisco, CA. Frank was mandated to furnish the full details of the purpose of travel, the name of the organization he was going to represent, his expected date of arrival and length of stay, his exact destination and his source of logistic support while in Korea. After submitting all of this information, if permission was granted, Frank would then have to execute a formal application for his passport before a clerk of courts and include a copy of the Far East Command permission with the passport application.

Frank was astounded. The only thing he wanted to do was to go to Korea, get married and bring his wife and child home. He was not representing any organization nor did he know the date of his arrival or exactly how long he would be there. He did not know where he would be staying and had no source of logistic support to identify during his stay there.

His numerous telephone calls to the Passport Office offered no resolution. Kathryn made calls to the Passport Office with the same dismal results. Finally, she decided to reach out to Congressman James G. Fulton once again. After calling the Pittsburgh Office of Congressman Fulton, she was advised to write to the Congressman for his assistance. He was on the Committee of Foreign Affairs and might be able to help them.

On February 17, 1953, Frank wrote to Congressman Fulton explaining the problems they were facing trying to get Ock Soon Lee to America. Congressman Fulton did reply to Frank on February 25. The Congressman indicated that he had forwarded the letter directly to the Liaison Office to Congress, Department of the Army, House Office Building, in Washington requesting their attention and advice.

Congressman Fulton indicated that as soon as he heard back from them, he would contact them.

Frank hoped that maybe, just maybe, someone could actually help him.

# 31
## Surviving the Winter
### Pega

#### January 1953

January was a very cold month in Seoul. Pega's days were the same every day. It was more difficult to do the wash in the freezing temperatures but miraculously the fresh spring water never froze up. The water was certainly cold but Pega was able to get fresh water daily for her duties. She carried the water now since Ho Sook, the older woman, found it difficult to do so. Ho Sook had hurt her back and this did not allow her to carry the jugs on her head anymore. Pega did not mind. The water was nearby, not like when she carried the water for her stepmother so many years ago. Pega thought of those days when she was such a young little girl and carried the jugs on her head. Her life was so difficult then. She was so grateful for the home and the food she now had. Unlike the other girls who came from comfortable families, Pega appreciated everything she had here at the orphanage. She never complained like the other girls— what was there to complain about?

She only missed her Frank. Yes she was alone for now and yes she was going to have his baby, but she never lost faith in her love. Every morning when she prayed to Mother Mary and humbly requested she take her requests to her precious son, Jesus, Pega believed. She left the chapel with peace in her heart, knowing Jesus would answer her prayers.

Sadly, several more babies died during January. Their little bodies lay frozen on the porch, until the old man could come and dig the graves. The snow and frozen ground made burial even more difficult than usual. Sometimes he would not come for days. Pega hated to see those dead babies frozen solid lying on the porch. Anytime she had to walk through the porch, she would run and try not to look at the lifeless bodies of her little friends.

By the end of winter all three of her little friends would die. She remembered the children who in the fall were running around and teasing her about her tears the day Frank was leaving. They had become her little friends, Hyewon, Minju and Yeonsang. Pega remembered how sweetly they played together and sang their little songs. They were always so happy to see Pega and would come running to her for a snack or a hug. One by one, each child became ill that winter and one by one they passed away. The sadness and sorrow of life during this awful war seemed endless.

Every once in a while, Eunah would come and read a letter from Frank to Pega. Eunah told Pega that Father Houng had requested Eunah send an answer to Frank's letters since he was too busy and unable to do so. Eunah told Pega that she would send Frank a thank you. She asked Pega if there was anything she wanted to tell him.

Having Eunah answer Frank's letters was very awkward for Pega. Eunah did not believe Frank was coming back to get Pega and she told Pega that on more than one occasion. Pega did not like to share with her what was truly in her heart. She could not tell Eunah to write to Frank and express her deep love for him or her dreams of their life together in America. She could not tell Eunah to write to Frank about his mother and father and how she was praying for them every day and so happy to meet them someday soon. She could not tell Eunah to write to Frank about her joy at having his baby. She was grateful that Eunah was writing the thank you letters and simply asked her to tell Frank that she missed him very much and was looking forward to his return.

On several occasions, Eunah did take time and wrote a letter to Frank. She was always careful to let him know of all the items they received. Eunah would write and thank him for the clothing and the winter coats. She was certain to let him know that Pega picked out everything she wanted and gave the rest to her friends. Eunah was always careful to mention that Pega received all of the special boxes from America.

Eunah always ended her letters to Frank with a special request for money. She could certainly use the money. Eunah was aware that Frank was depositing $25.00 a month into Father Houng's account and another $50.00 a month to give to Pega. Obviously, the man was rich. Now Father never gave any of the money to Pega because what on earth would she do with it? Pega had no need of money. They fed her and gave her a room to sleep in. She had all the clothing and food she needed. The peasant didn't need anything and she never asked Father for any money. But Eunah needed things. She needed the money far more than the peasant. Eunah would always end her letter asking Frank to send money "to Pega" and the man always sent it. After all, Eunah really needed it.

# 32
# No "Buddies" Left
## Frank

### February 1953

January passed and Frank did receive a few letters from Ock Soon. His dear mother continued to provide Sunday suppers for his new friends. Frank continued to pick up Kim for the Sunday meals in order to write letters to his love, Ock Soon. Somehow even though Kim was a stranger, he had become very special to the Crimbchin family. Even though Kim had never met Ock Soon, there was a deep connection, an understanding of the value Frank placed on her. Kim understood the battle Frank was facing and would do anything to help him.

On Sunday February 1, 1953, Kim wrote the following letter to Ock Soon from Frank.

February 1, 1953

My Dear Ock Soon,

How are you? I love you and miss you. I received your last letter two weeks ago but I have not answered it until now because my Korean translator has been busy. The last letter was very nice and it meant a lot to me. I really enjoyed reading it very much.

I hope you receive the $10.00 I am enclosing in this letter. I am sending you $10.00 for postage. I want you to send me a letter at least once a week if possible.

(Kim inserted the following)

"This part of the letter is from Frank's translator and I hope you understand it, even if Frank doesn't mention it. Most American women send a letter to their lover once a day. I did not send a letter that often when my fiancée was in Busan at first, but then I sent her a letter once a week. Frank's friend is coming back to America this month. I will send you Frank's address and you can send your letter here. Please try to send Frank a letter once a week."

(Frank resumes)

Ock Soon, I have deposited the money for Father Houng in his account. The receipt is enclosed in this letter. Please give it to Father Houng. Tell him that January's expenses; $75.00- has been deposited in the bank.

I wrote to the American government in Washington about my visa. They tell me that I must get permission by the Central Headquarters of Pacific if I want to travel to Korea. I am going to send them a letter.

Also, please continue to study to be a Catholic and please learn the doctrine in the next 2-3 months. It is a Catholic marriage regulation and I want you to be able to follow it so we can be married. Also my mother and I hope you understand the Catholic faith.

Some other news, our dog was fourteen years old and he has died. We buried him in our back yard at our house. He was a good dog, I will miss him.

My brother Don will be entering the military war soon. My mother is sad that he will be leaving for war.

I have become friends with Kim In-sun. He moved closer in Pittsburgh last week. He has been a great help to me.

Love,
Frank


It was a cold February in 1953. Frank was feeling down. Will had left Korea on October 31, 1952. Victor had left on January 16, 1953. His final connection to Ock Soon was Rip and he was leaving in February. Frank had hoped to get to Korea by March but he was not able to get a visa and his trip was pushed back to May. He could easily lose track of Ock Soon if he did not have someone to check on her. Time was running out.

In addition, Frank had concerns about the letters he received. He did not know who was writing the letters for Ock Soon and found it odd that she needed money. She had never asked him for anything, the entire time that he knew her in Korea.

He had been sending money every month to Father Houng's account for Ock Soon. Frank faithfully sent the $75.00 a month for Pega's room and board.

The average income in the United States in 1953 was $3,139 annually; therefore, $75.00 a month was a significant amount of money even in the United States. Frank knew that dollars were of great value in Korea. Before the war, in 1945 the exchange rate was 15 won to $1.00. Since the outbreak of war in 1950, the won was of less and less value.[14] Frank was well aware that $75.00 a month was a lot of money in Korea. Frank was concerned about Ock Soon and what she needed. He would send her anything but he just wasn't certain it was getting to her. Frank wasn't sure why Pega needed money, maybe it was for doctor visits or she could be ill. How he wished he could just talk to her.

In early February, Frank received the following letter from Rip, his last buddy in Korea.

January 29, 1953
From: Roger Van Winkle

Hi Frank.

I guess it's time I get writing you a few lines again. Well today I got the good news, I am leaving February 4th. I just made the shipment, so guess I am finally leaving here.

I received your big package so think I'll try to go over to Seoul tomorrow. I'll give Pega the ten dollars then too. Well, I was over there last week; she is alright but said she has been doing all the washing I guess. So probably you should write a letter to the priest.

She's fine other than doing quite a bit of work. She said the baby will be coming in May. I told her to keep the paper Victor had and the watch too. So then she showed me the watch, she had it on her wrist. I always keep reminding her

---

[14] By the end of 1953, the won had become so devalued that the exchange rate was 6,000 won to $1.00.

you'll be here the last of March or April sometime. I'll send you the Chaplain's address on the end of this letter.

There's really not too awful much to write about. You know Captain Carey is in the Motor Office now. He came back in December. Frank and Sacco made Sergeant. Crabs left the 27$^{th}$ of January. Almost all the old men are gone now. I guess John will be going around the 20$^{th}$ or 25$^{th}$ of February.

Well I guess when I get home it won't be long before I get married. I am going to try and wait till May or June. I'll wait to get into the swing of working.

Yes Frank, I sure remember last year at our birthday. In a way I'd like to make a special trip to Coatesville. Boy every time I think of him, it makes me mad. He was sure a son of a gun.

Well Frank, guess I'll sign off for now. I'll write again tomorrow or the next day after I get back from Seoul.

Good night Frank,
Your buddy,
Rip
Oh Yes, Happy Birthday Frank

So it was over. Rip was already out of the country. He had thought that Rip would be there until the middle of February but just as fate would have it, Rip got out early. Nothing was working out. Although Frank had set everything up with Father Houng before he left; the priest was still not writing back to him. He wasn't sure that Ock Soon was getting any of the money he was depositing. Frank was confused that Ock Soon needed money since she never said what she needed it for. He would never want her to be hungry or cold. She was having his baby. Maybe she was sick and needed to see the doctor. Somehow he had to find out what was going on.

Kim came for dinner on Sunday and wrote the following letter.

15 February
Sunday

My Dear Ock Soon,

I received your letter yesterday and my friend Kim In-sun translated it. It was a very nice letter. The first letter was together with Rip's letter and the second one was directly from you. I only received these two letters.

I no longer have my friends over there so I do not know how I can send the money you need. I will have to find out how I can do this. The problem with sending cash to Korea is that it is considered illegal. While my friends were still living over there, it was easy to send money. Now that all of my friends have left Korea, I will have to find another way to send money to you.

I sent a letter to Father Houng about your financial needs a couple of months ago. He has not answered yet. I will need him to agree that I can deposit more money in his name in the American bank for you. Anyway, I am going to send him another letter. Although I appreciate him very much but I want him to be more responsible for you.

Also, Ock Soon, if you are having any problems physically in your condition, you must see the doctor right away. I have written to Father Houng to let him know that this is what I want. After you read this letter, please go to see Father Houng and see what he has to say. Please write again soon.

I also want to know who is writing your letters to me. I am very glad that you are receiving everything I send. Also, please let me know how your studies are coming along. I love you very much Ock Soon. I wish today's problems would be over very soon.

Love,
Frank


Frank did not have anyone to send the letter to. Roger had already returned to the states. Father Houng had not been answering his letters. Push had come to shove and Frank decided to reach out to Chaplain Hart.  He would send the next set of letters to the Chaplain.

Frank was becoming more and more concerned that Ock Soon's letters always indicated she needed money.  Frank could not understand what she needed the money for.  In the last letter, she said she needed $30.00.  Thirty dollars was a day and a half pay for Frank.  His money was very tight.  He was sending $75.00 a month to Father Houng, trying to save $300.00 a month for his trip to Korea and still helping his parents out.  In addition, Frank had his own bills, his car payment, supplies for the cottage.

He loved Ock Soon so much, nothing she would ask him for would be denied but she never spent that much money – even when they were together.  He was not certain that Ock Soon was getting the money.  But if she needed it; he certainly wanted her to have it.  He would do his best to get the money to her as soon as possible.

Frank had $23.00 cash in his wallet.  He sent Ock Soon the $20.00 and wrote a check for the other $10.00.  Tomorrow was payday so the check would be covered.  Frank decided that if he could teach Ock Soon how to cash the check at the bank, he could be more certain that the money was getting to her.  He did not believe cash would make it from the United States into her hands through the mail.  On Thursday night, Frank wrote the following letter to Ock Soon.


19 February, 1953
Thursday

My Dear Ock Soon,

I am going to send the $30.00 that you asked me for last time.  My Chaplain will receive $20 cash and a $10 bank check. He will give it to Father Houng.

When changing money over there, you must be very careful.  If caught, I will go to jail and you will not be able to come here.  You can change the $20 to won by yourself but you must be very careful.  You will have to go to the Seoul exchange bank and put your name in English on the reverse side of the check so you can get Korean won. I will send a letter to Father Houng. Either way, you must be careful and let me know right away if you receive the money.

Now I am writing your written English name. You will need this when you go to the bank. You must practice writing your name.

*Lee Ock Soon*

The reason I am not sending you cash is that I am worried it will be lost. If you are not able to exchange the bank check for won, please return it back to me.

Frank held onto the letters until the following week. He wanted Kim to write another letter to Father Houng. Once Frank had the letter for Father Houng, he would send them all to Chaplain Hart. He did not want to keep bothering the man so he decided to send everything at the same time.

On Sunday, February 22, 1953, Frank sent the letters to Father Houng in care of Captain Hart, Chaplain 76th Engineer Construction Battalion. Frank wrote the following message on the outside of the envelope to Chaplain Hart:

"Please give to Father Houng, the Korean Catholic Priest that has Mass on Sundays in the HS Company Mess Hall"

The letter to Father Houng dated February 22, 1953 follows:

Dear Father Houng,

It has been quite a while since I wrote to you. I have been very busy working. I have been working two jobs ever since I got discharged from the Army. I will have enough money to come over in May if I can get a passport.

I am seeing about it now. It would mean everything to me if I can get it and come to Korea and marry Lee so she can come to the United States with me. Miss Lee, Ock Soon, my girlfriend who you are kindly keeping at the Collumba Babies Home asked me to send her some money. I was afraid to send it to you by Korean mail. Thought you might not get it. I mailed it to Captain Hart, Chaplain 76th Engineer Construction Battalion and asked him to give it to you.

I have a Korean friend that is going to school here in the U.S. and he writes to Lee in Korean and translate her letters for me. He told me that any money sent to Korea by international mail never got there, so that is the reason I sent it as I did. Please see that she gets the money Father and say hello to her for me and that I love her very much.

Father when her time comes with the child please take her to your hospital. I am trying to get there to be married to her by then but I don't know if I will be able to get a passport. Please write to tell me how much it will cost for the doctor and things at the hospital so I can put the money in your bank account.

I have been putting $25.00 every month in your account at the Hibernea Bank in California. I also put $50.00 every month for Lee. I sent some of the receipts to you and some to Lee to give to you. I do not know if you received any of my letters, I never got an answer from you.

I wrote to Lee and told her how to change the checks and money. I guess that is all for now. Please write me just a few lines would make me very happy.

Very truly yours,

Frank Crimbchin

By sending his mail to Chaplain Hart, Frank could be certain that Father Houng would receive the letter. Although Victor had told him that the Chaplain did not approve of GIs marrying Korean girls, maybe he would help him. Frank was anxious and needed someone to be certain Ock Soon had the things she needed. Chaplain Hart was a man of God and just maybe he would be the help that Frank needed.

# 33
# O Men of God
## Frank

### March 1953

It was March. Frank had originally thought he would be back to Korea by March but he was still trying to obtain the visa and save more money. Thank God his mother said the rosary every day. Somebody needed to help him. Well, he had sent the letters off to the Chaplain Hart. Thank goodness the Chaplain was still there and could help. Frank continued to check his mailbox everyday looking for a letter from Ock Soon or Father Houng. Instead he found a letter from Roger, (Rip).

February 27, 1953

From: Roger Van Winkle

Hi Frank,

Don't faint now when you see my writing. I went to the 121 Evac the third of February and flew all the way home. I got into California the 18th so made it home the easy way. I went and saw Pega the day before I left and I had gotten the food and the big package too.

So I stayed awhile and talked about old times. You know Frank I've been trying to forget all those times you and Will and I had there. It was fun anyway. I know I don't regret it any. I've been trying to forget Rose, but you know how it is when I've been with her for so long. I really thought a lot of her and I guess I still do some. I am not writing her though. I figure on getting married in May or June so I am trying to forget. She was really swell to me the last six or seven months I was there. When you go over, look her up if possible and let me know. I'd sure appreciate it.

Pega was alright Frank. Her hands were a little chap from washing clothes for the mission though. She told me to mention it to you. Don't remember whether I did before or not so I do now.

How is work and everything coming along? Okay I hope. Don't know exactly when I will go back to work or where. I guess I probably won't be out of the Army for a month or maybe even three months. Sure hope I get out in about a month though.

Well Frank, it's almost chow time so here's hoping I hear from you soon and hope everything is going always fine.

Bye for now and good luck,
Your buddy
Rip


Frank was glad to know that Roger had visited Ock Soon before he left Korea. Frank was relieved to know she was still at the orphanage. Roger wrote that she was doing alright and her only problem was chapped hands. That was great news! It was funny how the smallest piece of information meant so much when that was all you have available. It was going on six months now and Frank could not get back to Ock Soon. He could not give up. He had to keep trying. He sent another letter to the Central Headquarters of Pacific to see what was taking so long for his visa.

It was a week later when Frank received a letter dated February 28, 1953, from Chaplain Hart. He was so excited to hear from him. Maybe he had news about Ock Soon and Father Houng. Frank anxiously opened the envelope from the Department of Army.

Office of Chaplain
76th Engineer Construction Battalion
San Francisco, CA

Dear Frank,

Your letter of February 23rd arrived today also with the contents to be given to the party you named as the addressee.

I am sorry that it is necessary to return to you the contents intended for Reverend Houng. I know how difficult it must be to get correspondence through to your Korean friends here. Moreover it is wonderful that you have such a kind and generous feeling toward them. But under the circumstances and according to Army regulations, I am not permitted to carry out your request. Should you care to help Reverend Houng with his work in the future you may do so by purchasing bank drafts made payable to him at the Seoul Catholic Mission.

I trust you are enjoying civilian in the raw now and it must be grand to do so.

More power to you and with highest personal regards,

James E Hart,
Chaplain U.S.A.
Battalion Chaplain

Frank couldn't believe it. He called the Chaplain every foul name under the sun. His heart was becoming harder and harder. He was so disillusioned by all of these men of God; Father Houng, Father Joe and now this Hart guy. They all think they are so close to God but none of them can do what is right. They should know how much suffering is going on in Korea. Yet they would not lift a finger to help him get Ock Soon out of there. They all thought they knew God, but they are all hypocrites – every one of them. In his heart, Frank wanted to hate these men. Yet he knew he could not turn against them. He still needed Father Houng. Unfortunately, he still needed him.

Sunday came and Frank picked up Kim In-sun for supper. Frank was still having a hard time with everything that had transpired this month. He was very worried since he was not certain Ock Soon had received the letters and the money he had been sending. Frank asked Kim to write yet another letter to Ock Soon. Kim wrote the following letter on Sunday, March 22, 1953.

My Dear Ock Soon,

I sent you a letter with a bank check on March 12<sup>th</sup> but so far I have not heard from you. I am deeply concerned about what is going on over there. Are you sick or has something happened to you? Please send me an answer as soon as possible.

I received the beautiful picture and embroidery from Ock Soon on March 20<sup>th</sup>. I thank you so much. Is the lady who embroidered the Rose of Sharon living with you or did you purchase the picture?

I am going to buy some clothes and send them to you. I am not sure when but I will let you know soon. The money I sent you is not a lot but it should help you with your living expenses. The money is for you, Ock Soon, but I want you to spend it carefully. At this time it is very difficult to send cash as I explained before. Therefore please spend it wisely. I do not understand the situation over there now. I need to understand what has changed with the money reformation.

I applied for my visa but I have not had a reply yet. It might take a little longer than I thought. I am not certain I am getting all of your letters, so I am suggesting that you use numbers like 1, 2, 3, 4, on each letter. I am concerned that my letters are not getting to you and your letters are not getting to me.

So what I want you to do is put 'letter No.1' on your next letter and 'letter No. 2', next 'letter No. 3', like that.

If you ever have a problem with a bank check that I send to you, ask Father Houng to loan you the money. Ask him for whatever it is you need and let me know. I will deposit the money in his bank account here.

The seasons are changing here and my parents have a cold. I want you to take good care of yourself Ock Soon.

Bye for now my Love,

Frank


**The month of March passed and Frank did not hear from Ock Soon. He did not know what was happening or what to think.**

He had originally told her he would be back in March but had to delay his trip since he was not yet granted a visa. Maybe she did not believe he was coming. Maybe she was sick and needed a doctor. Maybe she left the orphanage and that was why he had not heard from her.

Every week his mother cooked, Kim In-sun came for dinner and a new letter went out. Every day Frank checked the mail box. Every day he found nothing. The month of March would pass with not one letter from Ock Soon.

# 34
# Letters From Korea
## Frank

### April 1952

On Wednesday, April 1, Frank opened the mailbox and there was a letter from Ock Soon. Frank immediately returned to his car and drove to Pittsburgh to give the letter to Kim. He had waited so long for some news and he wanted to know what the letter said as soon as possible. The following Sunday, Kim brought the translated letter to Sunday supper.

Translated by:
In-sun Kim
South Grant St
Pittsburgh, PA.

March 19, 1953

From: Ock Soon To Frank

My Dearest,

It is spring. How tenderly and mercifully the rain falls to this thirsty earth. When the night comes and every creature sleeps, but I am awakened alone, the sound of the eaves drops and the murmuring brooks running through rocks are echoing aloud in my heart as if my love wakes me by night. I hear the baby crying. This makes me fall into the deep nostalgia of my past.

I went out for seeding the seeds in the field over the west hill with the girl students. We sang songs and danced. Everybody seemed very happy. The rain was so good to the farmers and to the dried fields. I see the new buds and leaves coming out as if the new hope promising to bring a blessing comes to us. I wonder how my love is getting along this lovely day. How are your parents? Nature certainly is beautiful.

I must apologize for not writing you the two answering letters. There was a change of money denomination in Korea and I am late for the answer because of it. I received your letters dated on the 19th of February and the 1st of March. They were very pleasing letters.

Yes, I told Father Houng about the bank note. He says that the Reverend J. E. Hart has gone and the bank note is not here, but that if money is put into the bank under my name, he can give me money here. I do hope that your bank note which you sent to the minister will be delivered to you safely.

As I said before I do not need money at the present time. I hope you will not worry about me too much. I asked about the ring to my friend. Korean gold ring seems better than the American ring. In additional some American soldiers buy Korean gold ring as their souvenir. So I just wonder how you think to buy a ring when you come over here.

I feel my baby moving in my body. It is already eight months. Very soon I will be a mother I am already excited to think of it. I am both happy and sorry. How wonderful it would be to have a child, as a girl certainly, it is a great work to have a baby.

Whenever I see my wristwatch I see your face, your body embracing me. It is my treasure for my life with my baby forever. I hope you will make a name for our baby. I am glad you will find a name for the baby.

Your sign in Korean was a pleasing one to me. I bit my lips to stop crying for such a beautiful expression of love for me. I love you. I have a good time to learn things through books and experiences recently. I learn Catholic catechism. I do wish to know enough of it so I may not be ashamed to be your wife.

I pray that God may keep you from dangers and you will be greatly successful in your work.

So long,
Ock Soon
(The night of March 19, 1953)

P.S. I apologize, my Korean friend, for not writing my letter in a random style.

Frank was so happy to finally hear from Ock Soon. He read the letter over and over, recognizing the lingo was not that of Ock Soon. Frank knew that Ock Soon did not speak like that. The poetic language and flowering tone was certainly not Ock Soon. It did not matter. He had been so worried about her but now he realized everything was okay. He immediately asked Kim to write the following:

April 5, 1952

My Dear Ock Soon,

I was so happy to receive your letter written on March 19. I asked In-sun to translate your letter as soon as possible. What am I going to do for your wedding ring? Now please do not ask me what I want like you did the last time. That is silly. I was thinking that maybe we should buy the ring when you come over here and then you can pick out your favorite one.

I deposited the $75.00 into Father Houng's bank account. I do not have the receipt as yet because his bank is in California. I will send him the receipt as soon as I get it. The $25.00 is for your room and board and the $50.00 is for you, Ock Soon. Show this letter to Father and he should give you money when you need it. Please use it wisely.

I am very glad and I appreciate that you are working hard and studying in this difficult situation. I believe that we will have a happy life together.

I wonder if you have seen the doctor yet or have you spoken to Father Houng about the baby. I really want you to listen very carefully and follow whatever the doctor tells you to do. You must go to the hospital when it is time to deliver the baby. I know that most Korean women deliver their babies at home, but not you. It is not a wise thing to do. You need to go to whatever hospital Father Houng suggests.

As much as possible, please study the Christian doctrine. It is what I want and it is especially my Mother's wish. It will be good for you too Ock Soon.

(and then Frank wrote the following words in the Hangul)

*I love Ock Soon Very Much.*

*Frank*

Several weeks later, on April 8, 1953, Frank received two letters from Korea. One was for his mother and one was for him:

To:
My Dear Frank's Mother,

Thank for the letter to you. I am glad like to see you. It is not changed over here. I am very fine now. It is getting warm day by day.

I went to the great church when the last Easter Sunday. I am helping for those poor babies and I am studying always for become a Christian. It had been very nice the crucifix and the other things.

I was received ten dollars of the bank check. I will never forget the kindness. I hope your health and happiness.

From
Ock Soon.

(I don't know how to write and explain in English. I have never written the letter in English before this. I have to learn your language more with Ock Soon.)

From: Collumba Babies Home's Housekeeper and Ock Soon's Friend,
Mi Chi

April 8, 1953
Translated by: Insum Kim

From: Ock Soon

My Dearest,

How mildly and tenderly spring grows. Oh how mysterious it is to see the fresh green new buds shooting out of the dormant willow twigs. The azaleas and the lilacs are the welcome guests with the wreath on their head in my room.

Easter Mass was one of the most glorious ones; the happy chorus of people, the hallelujah song of the little girls. Then I was one of them. I must apologize for not being prompt in answering your letters. We had quite a busy Easter week. The babies were sick, the busy choir rehearsals for Easter. Many unexpected things caused me to lag behind then, and I, as a friend of Ock Soon hope that you will excuse her and me.

I received your ten dollar bank note and I gave it to Father Houng and I got Korean money from him. I received your letter dated on the March 22 was that of your mother. It was very pleasing letter to me.

Father Houng told me that he wrote a letter to you this time. Now I just wonder whether you received my previous letter or not. I wish to know of this. I have no trouble at all with my living expenses. Did you have a nice Easter day? I believe you did.

We had a little girl baptized here on that day. I work a little and I study and I feel I am born again into a new world. I wish to learn everything before you come. Did you make a name for our baby?

I wish to get some flannel and lace with veil which will be used on my Sunday dress. I pray that God may keep you and bless you and the day of our happy union will come soon.

Your Ock Soon,

Collumba Babies Home
Seoul, Korea

Sunday April 25, 1953

No 3

My Dear Ock Soon,

How are you? Are you living comfortably? I received a very nice letter from Father Houng. Father Houng said that you are studying very hard and working diligently. I was very glad to hear that.

I bought some clothes for the baby. I bought two baby outfits, wool jacket, wool headgear, wool socks, two diapers, three white socks, six underwear and some other things. I will send them to Father Houng.

There is a Korean woman studying at the University of Pittsburgh. She is friend of Kim's (our translator) and she arrived in America a short time ago. Her name is Han In-suk. She graduated from Ehwa University where she studied English while in Seoul. Her fiancée is a history teacher in the middle school here. His name is Nan Byong-hun. Mr. Nan, In-sun and I all joined my family at the cottage today. Everyone enjoyed it so much and they all said how wonderful it will be when Ock Soon is here.

Did you get to church on Easter Sunday? I heard you are studying hard and I was so glad to hear that. By the way, I have not received an answer about my trip to Korea from Headquarters yet.

I am so lonely here without you Ock Soon. Oh. I miss you so much.

Love,
Frank

PS: I sent Father Houng the money. $25 is for your room and board. $50.00 is for you, Ock Soon. I suggest you do not withdrawal it all at once. Just take out what you need whenever you need it.

On April 27, 1953, Frank's mother wrote the following letter to Ock Soon.

My Dear Miss Lee,

I was very happy to receive your lovely letter. Hope you are feeling good. I am so glad to hear you went to Church on Easter Sunday, and that you are studying to become a Christian. Try to go to Church whenever you can. It will make me very happy. Thank your friend and housekeeper for the wonderful letter she wrote. She certainly wrote fine for writing an English letter for the first time. I hope you get along good when the baby is born. I will be thinking about you and praying for you. Frank is fine. He is waiting every day for the time when he can go back to Korea.

Take good care of yourself and God bless you. Frank received a very nice letter from Father Houng.

All My Love,
Frank's Mother

PS. Dear Housekeeper, Thank you so much for taking care of Miss Soon and please take care of her until Frank gets there. Thank you for everything.
Frank's Mother

Of course in reality, Ock Soon did not have a housekeeper nor was she going to school and studying English or the Catholic religion. Eunah was writing most of the letters to Frank and his mother at the request of Father Houng. The letters were meant to ease the minds of the Americans who were financially supporting the orphanage. The letters held very little truth and Ock Soon was unaware of the falsehoods sent to Frank and his Mother. Throughout the entire period of separation, Frank would continue to receive letters from Eunah and others at the orphanage which painted a very different picture from reality.

But as far as Frank was concerned, April was a very good month, he was finally receiving some correspondence from Korea. He was so grateful that Father Houng and others at the orphanage were willing to write to him. Frank knew that as long as Ock Soon was safe then everything else would be okay. He would find a way to get back to her. No matter how much it cost him or how long it would take; Frank was determined to return to Korea for Ock Soon. He found great comfort in the occasional letter from the orphanage. Frank had no reason to believe the information he was receiving was not true. He trusted Father Houng and he was truly grateful that the priest had allowed Ock Soon to stay there and study. Frank was very thankful for the arrangement and Ock Soon's safety.

# 35
# Chung-Pyung Orphanage
## Ock Soon

### May 1953

Ock Soon was entering her ninth month of pregnancy. She had found that carrying the jugs of water from the fresh water spring and bending over scrubbing the dirty diapers was becoming more and more difficult. Ock Soon's feet and legs were very swollen and her back ached constantly. Every day the work became harder to do and Ho Sook was very worried that Ock Soon could no longer continue to work so hard. It was Ho Sook that went to Eunah and told her that Ock Soon could no longer wash the diapers. Maybe she should get her a job in the kitchen or somewhere else that was less strenuous.

Eunah was less than sympathetic especially since Ock Soon had concealed her pregnancy for so long. Of course after several months living in the orphanage, it had become obvious that Ock Soon was with child. As long as the financial support continued, Ock Soon would be permitted to stay. It had been almost eight months ago that the soldier left Korea. Eunah knew the baby was due to be born soon.

Eunah thought about the situation and decided that Ock Soon should move to the orphanage in Chung Pyung. The older children lived there and they needed someone to help with the sewing. Many clothes needed mending and they had fabric there so Ock Soon could sit and sew all day rather than be on her feet.

Eunah spoke to Ock Soon and advised her that she would be moving to the Orphanage in Chung Pyung. Ock Soon packed her few belongings and took a bus to the new orphanage.

Ock Soon settled into the new orphanage. It is here that she would learn to sew and use a sewing machine. It was easier to sit and sew all day rather than carry the water jugs. Things were different here. Ock Soon missed the infants and toddlers she used to feed. The children here were older and could take care of themselves at meal time. She missed her little friends at

Collumba Babies Home but she was glad that she did not have to carry the heavy jugs of water or bend over to scrub the dirty diapers any longer.

Ock Soon continued to go to the chapel every day and continued to pray for Frank to come for her. She missed him more than words could say and how she wanted him to be there when the baby was born. She had believed that he would have been here by now and could not understand why the government would not allow Frank to come for her. She had not met anyone at the new orphanage that could write a letter to Frank. Ock Soon asked several people but none had ever sent a letter to America. She continued to search for someone who could help her. She wanted Frank to know that she had moved. She was concerned that he might not know where to find her.

It was on May 11, 1953 that Eunah came to Ock Soon and told her that she was doing a very good job with sewing. Eunah wanted Ock Soon to stay in Chung Pyung Orphanage after the baby was born. Ock Soon would stay there in Chung Pyung and continue mending the clothes. Eunah would take the baby back to Collumba Babies Home and place the baby in the orphanage. That was where the child could be cared for best. Eunah thought that Ock Soon would be too busy sewing to care for her baby. The woman at Collumba would be able to care for the baby just as they did for all of the other children.

Ock Soon was stunned by what Eunah saying. It had never occurred to her to give up her baby. She would never think of placing the child in the orphanage. Ock Soon wanted this baby. What would Frank think if he came back and the baby was gone? The women at Collumba did their best for the babies but so many were sick and some even died. Ock Soon would never let Eunah take her baby from her, never!

Ock Soon listened to the women but said nothing. After they left the room, Ock Soon prayed and prayed. She did not know how she would survive but she knew she could never stay there and let them take her baby from her. Ock Soon was frantic.

Oh how she wished Frank was there with her. If Frank was there she would not have to depend on any of these people.

That night Ock Soon came up with a plan. She would go to see Father Houng in the morning. She would tell him that she needed the money Frank had sent to him. She knew Father Houng had Frank's money. She had never gone to him for anything – not even one dollar in all the months she was living there. But now she needed the money. She would let him know that she wanted the money for the baby. After she got the money, she would leave this place. If she wanted to keep her baby, she had to get away from here. If she stayed, her baby would be taken away from her and be placed with the other orphans. She could never let that happen. She had to go and find a safe place for both her and her baby.

Early in the morning on May 12, 1953, Ock Soon took the bus back to Collumba Babies Home. She waited for Father Houng on the steps outside of his office. When he arrived, Ock Soon asked Father Houng for some money. She told Father that she knew Frank had been sending him money every month. She knew that money was supposed to be for her. Frank had told her that if she ever needed money, she should go to Father Houng. She told Father that she needed some money now to buy some things for the baby.

Father Houng was very surprised that the girl had come to him at this time for money. She had never asked for any of the money before but today she seemed adamant. Father attempted to give her $20.00 but the girl said, "No.", she needed more than that. Father reluctantly gave her $60.00 and Ock Soon abruptly left his office.

Ock Soon took the $60.00 and walked to the market. She purchased a bathtub for the baby. In addition, she purchased some diapers and baby clothes. Ock Soon then went to the fish market. There she bought a big fish, shrimp, rice and all kinds of vegetables and spices. Ock Soon put everything in the baby bathtub and carried it on her head. She walked several miles to the only person she knew she could count on. Ock Soon went to see her dear Halmeoni, (Hana's mother) near Seoul.

Halmeoni could not believe her eyes when she saw Ock Soon standing in front of her with the bathtub full of food on her head. She let out a loud scream and just wept to see the girl was still alive. She brought Ock Soon into the home where so much had taken place. She remembered the young girl from the train station that so many years ago had come to live with her. She recalled the many years Ock Soon had cared for her grandsons, Shin and Min Ho. She remembered the terrible killings and the long journey they made to Taejon. Now here stood Ock Soon who was obviously going to have a baby of her own. Halmeoni grabbed her and brought her into the house.

Ock Soon explained to Halmeoni everything that had happened. She told Halmeoni that Frank had not yet come for her and now Eunah was trying to separate her from her baby. Halmeoni listened to the story and told Ock Soon to stay with her. Together they would care for the child.

Ock Soon was so happy to have a safe place to stay. She was very hungry now and wanted to cook a meal and invite Halmeoni to eat with her. Ock Soon built the fire in the pit like she had done so many times before. She cleaned the fish and shrimp and then prepared the vegetables with special spices and hot red pepper. Ock Soon cooked the rice and the fish over the open fire. The fresh food smelled so delicious. Together they sat down and ate and ate. Ock Soon cleaned up after their meal and found she was simply exhausted.

She went to the old room and lay down on the mat with Halmeoni just like she had done many years ago. Ock Soon remembered the many nights Halmeoni and she had slept together in this old room. She remembered when she first came to this house starving and Halmeoni gave her some hot tea and rice. Halmeoni was always there to help her. She had grown to love this old woman.

She lay there remembering Chin and Min Ho growing up in this house before the terrible war came. She remembered playing with Min Ho when he was just a little boy; the long walks and the fun little games they played together. Those were such kind days. She was safe in this home back then. Min Ho was such a fine young man. He was like a little brother to her. Ock Soon lay in the dark room remembering.

Ock Soon then recalled the day the communists came and destroyed their town. She remembered the killing, the horror and the death. So much had happened to each of them since that awful day. Everything was different now. Even without gunfire, peace was gone. Life had become very difficult for everyone.

Ock Soon lay there remembering her love for Frank and how much she needed him to come for her now. How she longed for him to come for her and help her. Tears ran down her face as she thought about him and as she fell into a deep, deep, sleep.

It was in the middle of the night, that Ock Soon was awakened by terrible abdominal pains. Immediately Ock Soon thought that she had eaten something that made her very sick. Maybe the fish was bad or the vegetables were sour. She was moaning and crying. She had never been this sick before in her life. She remembered her father and his death after he returned from the party. She remembered how sick he was and how he never recovered. Everyone said he had died from something he had eaten. Ock Soon was certain she had eaten something bad and now she was dying too.

Halmeoni was awakened by her crying and moaning. Ock Soon told Halmeoni she was going to die. She must have eaten something bad. Her stomach was so sick and the pains were very bad. Her back hurt and the pains would come and go. Ock Soon was in so much agony, she did not know what to do.

Halmeoni just laughed at the girl. "My daughter" she said. "You are going to have your baby!"

Ock Soon was in labor throughout the night. She never did see a doctor during her entire pregnancy and she had never gone to the hospital as Frank had instructed. Even though Frank had sent money and had been explicit in his desire for her to deliver the baby in the hospital, under the care of a physician neither

Father Houng nor Eunah ever considered this. Korean women delivered their babies at home and Ock Soon would do the same.

Ock Soon had never felt so much pain in her life. She had never seen anyone deliver a baby so she had no idea what to expect. The labor went on for hours and it was not until ten hours later that the baby would be born.

It was dear Halmeoni who would deliver Ock Soon's baby, a sweet baby boy. Ock Soon looked at the infant and wept. He looked just like Frank. She had never been so happy as when she held that little baby boy in her arms. Yes, together Halmeoni and Ock Soon would care for this little boy. There was no need to go back to the orphanage where Eunah intended to separate her from her son. She would stay with Halmeoni and together, they would care for the child.

Ock Soon would never return to Collumba Babies Home again.

# 36
## The Deception Continues
### Chung Pyung Orphanage

#### May 16, 1952

Since Ock Soon left the orphanage, things had become very complicated for Eunah. After she had advised Ock Soon that the baby would be placed in the Collumba Babies Home, Ock Soon simply left. When Eunah learned that Ock Soon had left the orphanage, she became very angry with Ock Soon. Eunah had warned her once before that if she ever left the orphanage again, she would not be permitted to return. So that was it. She would never let that woman return to the orphanage.

But Eunah's problems were bigger than that. If Frank found out that Ock Soon had left the orphanage he would stop sending support. If the support stopped, Father Houng would become angry. Father Houng urgently needed that financial support for the 300 children for which he was responsible. In an attempt to cover up the problem, Eunah composed a letter on May 16, to Frank indicating it was from Ock Soon. Eunah was unaware that the baby had already been born on May 13, 1953.

May 16, 1952

My Dear Frank,

It is the time of year when bright sunlight is blazing in the early summer. Also, it is getting deep green on the mountains and the streams flow boundlessly. The frogs are in the rice fields singing like the world is theirs.

I am replying quite late this time, after having received your Letter #3 with your mother's letter. How have you been? There is no other word except "Thanks" for your mother's love for me.

These days I am having some physical problems so I will be in the hospital. This was discussed with Father Houng.

I left Seoul with my sister (ghostwriter) to go into the far away country for recuperation. I am having an interesting and unforgettable time in the country side. I will be staying with my sister until recovered from the baby delivery.

Oh! I am feeling so alone, how happy I will be and glad if we see each other after the baby is born. I will wait until that time.

Tomorrow, I am going to leave here and go to Seoul. I will send you a letter after I arrive in Seoul. The time has come to finish this letter. I am looking into the sky away, imaging your appearance.

Love,

Ock Soon

Eunah sent the letter to America. She knew she would have to inform Father Houng about Ock Soon leaving, the next time she saw him. Eunah would have that opportunity the following Sunday. When Eunah informed Father that Ock Soon had left and she did not know where she went, Father became very upset with her. Eunah should never have told Ock Soon that they were taking her baby. Father told Eunah that the girl had come to him requesting money for the baby but she had not mentioned that she was leaving the orphanage.

Now Father had a bigger problem since he was still receiving letters from the soldier with money. The soldier wanted to know what Ock Soon was doing and how she was feeling. Father did not want to tell the soldier that the girl had left the orphanage. Father knew if he found out she wasn't there, the money would stop coming and the soldier would be very angry. Although Father never once believed the soldier would return to Korea, he did not want to anger the man and he certainly did not want the "donations" to stop. Someone had to answer the soldier's letters. Father had accumulated several letters from the soldier that remained unanswered. Father Houng told Eunah to handle the situation and to immediately write back to the soldier.

Eunah was disgusted.  Now it was her job to write to the soldier. There was no way she was going to tell him that the girl had run away. Eunah knew the soldier was never coming back anyway.  He said he was coming in March and that never happened. Here it is almost June and still no soldier.  On May 22, 1953, Eunah did what the priest asked and she wrote the following letter to Frank.

May 22, 1953

To Mr. Frank,

I, as a friend of Ock Soon for whom I have a responsibility of answering your letter, must apologize for being late for the answer. I hope you will excuse me. I have been very busy, and I just can't rise up my head.

Ock Soon wanted to stay at my home which is outside of Seoul, and I gave her room at my house. She and I had a very pleasant time at my home. She stayed at my home for a few days, and she left my home for Seoul expecting a child. After Ock Soon left my home, I received your letter No 4. It was a very nice letter and I forwarded it to Father Houng. I believe he will do everything for Ock Soon and you; the report of the birth of child, education in the Korean language and in the English language and Catechism.

Again I wish you to come here soon for Ock Soon, and have a happiest time. I couldn't write a letter for your mother. Ock Soon asked me to write a letter to her. I hope your mother and father will be fine.

I think Father Houng will take care of all about Ock Soon. Again I thank your friend who writes letters for you. Father Houng will answer your letters for Ock Soon. May God bless you.

Sincerely,
Eunah Kwang

Eunah was still unaware that Ock Soon had already delivered a baby boy.  She did not know where Ock Soon went after leaving Chung Pyung Orphanage, nor did she care. She wanted no part of this anymore. She did not intend to write any more letters to Mr. Frank. Ock Soon and Mr. Frank would now be Father Houng's problem.

# PART FOUR

## Pega and Frank

# 37
# TOKYO, JAPAN
## Frank

### July 1953

Marunouchi Hotel
Maruhote, Tokyo

July 9, 2:30 AM

Dear Family,

I have been in Japan about one hour now. This is the hotel that I am staying at. You can talk about traveling but it is too much for me. We left Alaska and flew half way across the ocean and the island that we were to land at had too much fog. So we turned around and flew all the way back to Cold Bay Air Force Base[15]. The Air Force guarded the plane and everything; but they would not let us go. The Commander wanted it in writing from some General that it was okay for us to take off. That took five hours there besides flying back and forth. But we finally got here.

You do not get a booth to sleep in unless you ask for it when you buy your tickets. It costs $35.00 more. There were only about 12 berths on the plane, there was 40 people on the plane. So it is pretty rough sleeping all the time in a seat. Northwest had reservations made at this hotel for me.

I am supposed to be at 8th Army at 8 o'clock tomorrow to get clearance for Korea. My plane takes off at 1:30 tomorrow afternoon. It takes 3 ½ hours from here to Korea so I ought to get there about five in the evening. I am all right. Hope you both are the same. Outside of what I wrote in the letter, everything is going fine.

Love,
Frank

---

[15] *Cold Bay Airport (originally Fort Randall Army Airfield) was constructed during World War II during the military buildup of Alaska in 1941. Several Fighter Squadrons were assigned to the Airfield during the war. The base was set to close after WWII but remained open during the Korean War to support transport demands by Military Air Transport Service with flights along the Great Circle Route from Japan.*

# 38
# Seoul, South Korea
## Ock Soon

### July 1953

Ock Soon loved that little baby boy. She did not want to put him down. She always wanted to hold him and rock him and sing songs to him. She could not believe the baby actually belonged to her. Oh how she longed for Frank to come to Korea and see his son. He would be so happy. This was what he wanted also – a baby boy!

Halmeoni loved the child as though he was her own grandson. He was such a sweet little boy, and oh so beautiful. Halmeoni was so happy to have a baby in the house again. It had been a long time ago that her grandchildren were infants and she just loved babies. Both women spent their days playing with and caring for the child.

The baby was born at a wonderful time of year in late spring while the weather was warming up. It was so much easier to have a new baby in the spring rather than the dead of winter. The baby was a pleasant little infant who rarely cried except to be fed or changed. Both women would rush to his side anytime the child made even a little whimper. They enjoyed caring for him so much!

The war had been so dark and so much death and destruction had surrounded both of the women; having a newborn baby brought them both hope and joy. Ock Soon continued to pray and ask the Lord to keep her Frank safe, believing in her heart, he would come for her someday. It continued to be her daily prayer although Ock Soon had not received any contact from America for several months. Of course she had no way to write to Frank and tell him that she had left the orphanage or to let him know where she now living. When she was strong enough, she would find someone who could send a letter to America and tell Frank that she had moved out of the orphanage and was living with Halmeoni in Seoul.

Ock Soon could only hope that he would understand. She certainly understood how the people at the orphanage thought. Frank did not understand what was happening at the orphanage. She knew they never believed Frank was coming back for her. Ock Soon knew they intended for her to give up her baby to the Collumba Babies Home. She understood they intended to separate her from the child so that she would not become attached to him and spend all of her time with her own baby. She knew they wanted her to work at the Chung Pyung Orphanage to break their bond. She had to leave that place. She could not give up Frank's baby. That was all she had in life. Although she had promised Frank that she would never leave the orphanage, she could only hope that he would understand and forgive her for not staying there any longer.

It was early in the morning on Sunday, July 12, 1953. Ock Soon rose up, fed and dressed her baby boy, tied him on her back with her podeagi (baby carrier) and walked the twelve blocks to Myeongdong Cathedral. Ock Soon had not been to Mass since she delivered the baby boy about eight weeks ago. This would be her first visit since she felt well enough to carry the baby tied on her back to the church. Ock Soon was so thankful that she had her son and somewhere to live safely. He was growing so big so fast and was such a healthy baby. She knelt before God and humbly thanked Him for all of the blessings He had so graciously bestowed on her. She asked Him once again to keep her Frank safe until his return. This was her daily prayer and one she always lifted up to the Lord. She knew she had to wait patiently on the Lord. God had given her peace many months ago that Frank would come back for her. She just knew he would. She did not know how he would or when he would, but she knew that someday Frank would come for her. She loved him so much and she knew that he loved her too. Frank was a strong man and he would do anything he needed to do to bring her to America with him. She would have to be strong too.

The baby was so peaceful during the Mass. He slept during the entire ceremony and Ock Soon was able to worship her God in her quiet spirit.

By the time Mass was over, the sun had risen and the town was awake. It was a beautiful summer morning as Ock Soon returned home. She had planned to go to the well to get fresh water. Ock Soon missed the well that was in the yard. It had never worked again since that day long ago when the bullet missed her head but shot through the pump. Ock Soon thought about that day when war was at their doorstep. She now knew that it was God who protected her all those harrowing days. She now understood that God was watching over her all the days of her life and He cared for her when no one else would. She had grown to love Mother Mary and her son Jesus. She was so happy that they loved her back.

Although Ock Soon had to walk several blocks to get the water, it did not matter. Walking a little further to get the water was such a small thing. Ock Soon had witnessed so many people, both young and old, who had been killed during the war. She had walked the streets of Seoul and looked upon the bloody soldiers – both Americans soldiers and Korean soldiers, lying dead or dying all over the sidewalks and streets. In her escape from Seoul, she had watched the people desperately clinging to the train and then watched them as they were crushed to death. She had walked over one hundred miles on icy winter trails and saw many dead or dying along the way. She had awakened to find dead bodies surrounding her in the little house on the way to Taejon. Walking several blocks to get the water every day was such a small thing. Ock Soon never even considered it a burden. She was so grateful to be living with Halmeoni again. Since the war, everything was more difficult now for everyone, but at least she and Halmeoni had survived.

Ock Soon stopped at home to get the water jug. She and her baby continued on their journey to the well. After pumping the water, she carried the jug on her head, her baby sleeping in the podeagi on her back and returned to their home. Ock Soon started the fire and began to cook a fresh pot of rice. The family could eat rice and vegetables this morning. She always liked to cook for Halmeoni since Halmeoni appreciated it so much. Halmeoni was getting older now and moving around much slower. She had loved Ock Soon like her own child and now she loved the baby boy just like a grandson. How grateful Ock Soon was to have Halmeoni in her life.

It was on this very same Sunday morning that Frank had returned to Seoul. Ock Soon was totally unaware that Frank had been traveling for days. She had not heard from him for many, many weeks. Frank had arrived early that morning and had taken a cab to the Collumba Babies Home. He wanted to be sure Ock Soon was not at Collumba before he traveled to Chung Pyung Orphanage. Frank told the driver to wait for him outside the orphanage gates.

Father Houng was in the chapel when he heard the soldier had returned. He was completely shocked that the soldier had come back for the girl. He was actually dumbfounded. He *never* believed for *one* moment that the soldier would actually come back. This had never happened in all the years he was taking care of these women. Never before had the soldier actually returned to take the woman back to America. Father was startled since he knew the girl was not there and yet he had continued to accept the room and board payments without notifying the man. He had instructed Eunah and his assistant, Father Park, to write letters to Frank without telling him that Ock Soon had left the orphanage. Father Houng needed that money to feed the starving children. He had become accustomed to the $75.00 a month and was not about to give it up. Father knew he was being deceptive but it was deception for the sake of the hundreds of babies he was responsible for. God would forgive him.

Father Houng immediately decided he was not ready to see the man. He told Eunah to tell the soldier that he was not there. It was not a complete lie since Father was about to leave the premises to go to Camp Sykes for Mass anyway. He would just leave a little sooner than planned.

Eunah was disturbed and just as upset.  She had no idea where the peasant had gone and she did not want to see the soldier.  She became suddenly afraid the soldier would learn of her deception and her repeated requests for money that she had kept for herself.  What would he do when he found out it was her, not Ock Soon, asking for money every month?  If she could have avoided the confrontation she would have, but Father had once again put the responsibility on her.  Eunah went out to greet the soldier and told him that Ock Soon had left and she did not know where the girl had gone.

Frank was confused since the last correspondence he had received indicated that Pega was studying hard and doing well.  The letter indicated that they would take Pega to the hospital when the baby was born.  Frank knew by now, Pega had to have delivered the baby.   Where in God's name was she?   Eunah continued to deny any knowledge of where the peasant was now living.

Frank was absolutely furious.  He told Eunah to take him to Chung Pyung Orphanage immediately to see if Pega was there.  Eunah tried to explain to the soldier that she was certain the girl was not at Chung Pyung Orphanage.  Eunah would know if she was there since she visited there frequently.  Ock Soon had left the orphanage several months ago and she had no idea where she was.  Several months ago!  How could that be?  Why did he receive letters indicating Ock Soon was still going to school and learning catechism?

Frank was exhausted.  He had been traveling for days and now after he arrived, he learns Pega is gone.  He was so furious it was all he could do to restrain himself from picking up the furniture and throwing it across the room.   Why didn't this woman know where Pega had gone?   His blood pressure was rising and his face was as red as a beet.  He was raising his voice and literally screaming at her.  He simply could not believe that they had allowed Pega to leave the orphanage and could not tell him where she went.  Before he completely lost control of his temper, Mi Chi came running into the courtyard.  She had heard the soldier was back and was very excited. She knew where Ock Soon was staying and offered to take the soldier to the house.

Frank was immediately relieved and told Mi Chi to come with him. Frank and Mi Chi hurried to the cab and drove off to find Halmeoni's house. Mi Chi had never actually been to the house but some of the other students had told her that they had seen Ock Soon sitting outside the house on the porch with her baby. Mi Chi had the driver go up and down several roads looking for the house. Every time she thought she found it, it turned out to be someone else's home. Finally Mi Chi became very excited - she recognized the old home.

"There it is. That is where Ock Soon is staying!" Mi Chi shouted. Mi Chi was so excited she could not contain her joy. She jumped out of the cab and ran down to the house and called out, "Ock Soon, Ock Soon, he is here, your soldier is here. Come quickly. Hurry, come quickly!"

Frank wanted to run with her but had to pay the cab driver while Mi Chi ran ahead. Ock Soon could hardly understand what Mi Chi was saying but she hurried to join her outside the house.

Ock Soon could not believe her eyes. Walking down the road was the man who she had been waiting for; the man she so loved, her Frank. She stood there in absolute shock and remained utterly speechless. She was so astonished, she could not move and she could not speak. Frank ran up to her, put his arms around her and tried to kiss her. Ock Soon started to respond but suddenly became aware that they were standing outside in public. She immediately grabbed Frank's hand and the two went inside the doorway of Halmeoni's house where she finally was able to kiss the man she had been longing for. It had been almost ten months since she had seen him. Although she believed he would return for her, she was physically shocked to actually see him standing before her. Her prayers had been answered. He had come for her just as he said he would. He was finally here, in Korea, once again. Tears of joy ran down her cheeks as she wept. She did not have to worry anymore or wonder how she would survive. Frank had returned and everything was going to be just as he said it would be.  He would take her to America with him, just as he had promised.

Everyone in the house was very excited.  Pega ran and got the baby and showed Frank their son.  Frank was so happy to learn he had a baby boy and so relieved that he had found them.  Everything was surreal.  The couple was together once again and Frank was meeting his son for the very first time.

Halmeoni had never met the soldier and she too was amazed that he had actually returned to Korea.  Although Halmeoni had never said anything to Ock Soon, she herself never believed the soldier was coming back to Korea.  It had been almost one year and Halmeoni thought Ock Soon was just a foolish girl to believe the American would come back for her.  Word traveled quickly throughout the community that the soldier had returned for Ock Soon and Ock Soon was going to America.  For some women in the community, hope was renewed. They would believe that their American would come for them also.  For others, who had long ago realized, their American would not be coming back for them, jealousy grew in their heart.

Ock Soon was nothing but grateful.  God had been so incredibly good to her.  When no one else believed in Frank, Ock Soon trusted and believed that God would bring Frank back to her.  She knew someday Frank would come back and he really did.  He really had returned to take her to America.  Even Ock Soon was amazed.

After all of the greetings and introductions, Frank wanted to go see Father Houng immediately to make arrangements for the wedding.  He did not want to delay his goal to get married and get back to America as soon as possible.  Ock Soon and Frank walked back to Myeongdong Cathedral but the priest was not there.  Ock Soon was not disappointed.  Nothing could spoil this day or this moment.  Only joy and happiness filled her heart and soul.  The couple walked back to Halmeoni's house full of love for each other and love for their infant son.

They ate supper together with Halmeoni, her three children and their families.  It was a very happy day and not unlike a celebration. During supper the conversation turned to the baby. Halmeoni was trying to explain to Frank about the day the baby was born and how she delivered his son. Frank thought he misunderstood what Halmeoni was trying to say. Frank asked Ock Soon, "What hospital did you deliver the baby in?" Ock Soon and Halmeoni tried to explain that the baby was born right here in this house. Halmeoni had delivered the baby boy.

Frank was utterly shaken. The blood drained from his face and he turned as white as a sheet. He could not believe that Pega had delivered the baby without seeing a doctor. Frank had sent extra money to Father Houng every month and asked him to take Pega to the doctor for checkups and make certain she delivered the baby in the hospital. Frank was disgusted to think that Father Houng made no effort to see to it that Pega was cared for by a doctor. Oh, he took the money alright, and even had the gull to write to him to tell him that Pega would go to the hospital. None of that happened. Frank felt like such a fool. He had been so deceived by these men of God. Here all along, he found comfort in believing Father Houng was taking care of Ock Soon. Father Houng did not take care of Ock Soon. He never took her to the doctor, not even once. He never intended to get her to a hospital. Frank's heart was filling with anger and rage. If he didn't need these people to help him get out of this country, he would never deal with any of them again. But Frank knew he was still at their mercy and he would have to keep quiet about all of the anger he felt. He swallowed his rage and decided he would not confront these people about the deception. Unfortunately, he still needed their help.

In addition to never having seen a doctor as Frank had requested, it was obvious that Ock Soon had not learned any more English. She actually understood less now than when he left her last year. That was the arrangement he had made with Father Houng; Ock Soon was to go to school and learn English. She would need to be able to speak English in order to survive in America. Frank was totally disgusted and dismayed at all of the broken promises.

Although angry, Frank did not let his anger interfere with his joy on this day. He was so happy to be with Pega again. It had been so very long ago that he had seen her. He had missed her tremendously and finally after so many months, he was actually here in Seoul and was going to bring Pega back to the U.S. with him. No, he would not let the lies and deceit of the people he had trusted so foolishly interfere with his joy on this day. He was simply too happy.

Later that evening, before the electricity went out, Frank wrote the following letter to his parents.

Sunday, July 12, 1953

Dear Mother and Dad,

I finally got here all right. I am writing this from the house where Pega is staying. She and the baby are all right. The baby was born May 13th, it is a boy.

She is a very religious girl. We went down to the priest this afternoon but he was not there. As you go in the yard to the church there is a big statue of Christ there. She stopped in front of it going in and out and said a prayer.

I got in Seoul at 7:00 o'clock this morning but it took me until 10:00 to find her. She had gone to the 6:00 o'clock Mass this morning. The electric did not come on last night so I had to finish this letter this morning.

I had the taxi three hours and it cost $8. There is so much to tell I don't know where to start. It is now 9:00 o'clock in the morning. We are going over to see the priest at 10:30. He might be there then.

I got through customs of Korea and Japan okay but they did not look at my things very close. If they knew I had clothes for her and the baby I would have had to pay a tax on them. When I was in Japan I repacked everything. I put all the things at the bottom of the duffle bag and just had my things on top of it.

I do not know how much the baby weighs, I guess it is about average size for an American baby, but the lady next door has a Korean baby ten months old and it is the same size as my baby that is two months old.

I hope you and father are alright and be sure to take care of yourselves.

Pega is the same except she is a little heavier from having the baby. Everything is alright here. I am fine. Take care of yourselves. Say hello to Don for me. I will close now and if I have some time I will write more in the next letter.

Love,

Frank

P.S. Send letters to Father Houng. I will get them there. We are about twelve blocks from the church.

The couple could not be happier. Their dream of being together had actually become a reality. Frank had never been so happy to be with the only woman he had ever loved. Ock Soon's heart was filled with joy and thanksgiving to the Lord, her God who had promised to bring Frank back to her and through His mercy, Frank had returned. Nothing and no one would ever separate them again.

# 39
# Bribery and Corruption
## Seoul

### July 1953

The next week passed quickly. Frank had only one thing on his mind and that was to fulfill all the requirements to get Pega out of the country. He knew they must get married and of course Pega needed her visa and passport. He had tried several times to see the priest but Father Houng had always been unavailable. Frank was able to meet with his assistant, Father Park, who was truly happy that Frank had returned for the girl. Father Park always had a tender spot in his heart for Pega. She worked so hard, much harder than any of the other girls. She was very quiet and humble and never asked for anything. He was also impressed with her genuine love for God. No one prayed more than Ock Soon. He had grown very fond of the girl and was so happy for both her and Frank. Father Park would have been delighted to marry them, but he could not do so. It was Father Houng who would marry the couple. Frank would have to wait until he could meet with Father Houng to make those arrangements.

Before leaving the U.S., Frank did his research and learned that a foreigner could get a visa to enter the U.S. in about 90 days. Frank was very anxious to complete all the necessary paperwork as soon as possible. The sooner he applied for her visa, the sooner they could go to America. He had brought $500.00 with him to live on while in Korea for the next three months. Frank knew the American dollar was worth a lot more in Korea and he could live very inexpensively there. Frank calculated that $500.00 would be more than enough for Pega and him to live on; but he could not waste any time.

On Wednesday, July 15, Pega and Frank walked to the courthouse to find out how to get a visa and a passport. Frank learned that the consulate from the U.S. Embassy came to Seoul from Pusan once a month. On his monthly visits he would stay in town for about three days while he handled the local government business in Seoul.  After three days he would return to the Embassy now located in Pusan.  The consulate was expected to arrive at the courthouse the following Monday, July 20th.  So Frank would return on Monday to see the man and obtain the necessary forms for marriage and the visa.

Once this was done, then Frank would be able to focus on getting married.  Although he thought they would be married in the Catholic Church, the Korean government did not recognize or even care about that.  They required them to be married in a civil ceremony by the mayor.  Frank had so much to do but everything was on hold until Monday when the consulate arrived.

Pega and Frank spent their days getting to know each other again.  Pega had not yet registered a name for her baby since she believed that Frank would return and name the child.  Frank had been thinking about a name for the baby.  He knew that if the baby was a boy, he would name him after his brother, Donald.  If the baby was a girl, he was going to name her after his mother, Kathryn.  The baby boy was officially named Donald Crimbchin or Donnie.

Until the forms could be submitted, the couple spent their time caring for Donnie and helping Halmeoni around the house.  While Frank was there, he learned that the well in the courtyard was not functional.  As a first class machinist, fixing the pump would be a very simple project.  Frank just needed the right tools and replacement parts.  He was able to find a tool shop in town where he could rent some hand tools and pick up a few parts.  Frank walked to the tool shop and showed the man what he needed.  He gave the man fifty cents to rent the equipment.  Frank took the tools home and began to work on the pump.

The main pieces below the ground, the cylinder and pipes, were just fine.  Even the spout had sustained no damage.  Apparently the gun shot through the head part and pump handle.  Frank knew he would need a gasket and adapter, handle links, nuts and some link bolts.  Fortunately the old store had most of the parts that he needed.  Frank was able to form the handle links from other thin steel rods which he purchased.  Although it only took about an hour to actually fix the pump, it took about four hours to find the store and make the parts he needed. By late afternoon the pump was fixed and spurting water again in no time. Everyone was very excited to see the water splashing out of the spout once again!

Halmeoni and her family were utterly amazed that Frank was able to fix the broken pump. Ock Soon thought back to that long ago September day, when the U.S. Marines marched into Seoul and pushed the Communists out of the city. She was almost killed during that battle while standing at that very pump. She thought about how this man, Frank, came all the way from America, is now in her life and repaired the broken water pump for Halmeoni and her family. It was truly an amazing thing. God had blessed her in an incredible way. She had to marvel at all the miracles He had done for her throughout her life.

The week passed quickly and on Sunday, Pega assumed that Frank would go to confession and communion with her. Although Frank was a Catholic, he was not a really good practicing one. It was his mother who was the devoted Christian. He had not gone to confession and communion since his encounter with Father Joe at St. Mary's. Pega was surprised that Frank indicated he would not go to confession but she insisted. In order to keep peace, Frank submitted to her requests and went to confession that Sunday. He found it so odd that during the Mass, all the women sat on one side of the church while the men sat on the other side. Frank was so amazed at how devoted Pega was to God. Her faith was evident every day in all she did. Every night before she went to sleep, she took out her rosary and said her prayers. She prayed more than anyone he knew. He would be sure to write his mother and tell her that her prayers had been answered. He had found a good Catholic girl just as his mother had hoped.

On Monday, July 20, Frank was first in line to see the consulate. He spent about thirty minutes going over everything that needed to be done. The form required for Frank and Pega to be married was simple enough. But Frank was amazed at the number of forms required to begin the process of applying for a visa through the Office of Immigration and Naturalization. There were forms for Biographical Data, Affidavit of Support, Petition for Alien Relative, Report of Medical Examinations and Vaccination Records, the list went on and on. In addition to submitting the forms to the United States Consulate, endless sets of documents had to be completed and submitted to the Ministry of Foreign Affairs in Korea.

Apparently this was going to be much more complicated than Frank had anticipated. After receiving the completed Application for Visa, The Office of Immigration and Naturalization would then investigate Pega's background to make sure she was not a criminal or a Communist. This could take several months. Frank was prepared to stay in Korea for three months but according to the consulate, the process could take six to nine months. There was no way Frank could stay in Korea for nine months! He simply did not have enough money and he had to get back to work at Taylor and Wilson's Manufacturing Company. His parents still depended on him financially and he certainly needed to work. Frank gathered all the required forms including Marriage to a Foreigner and headed home. Frank was not prepared to stay in Korea for more than three months. He had believed that if he didn't waste any time and completed everything as soon as possible, he would have been able to leave Korea in ninety days. Now he was learning it really could take six to ninth months! This was very discouraging news. Frank would have to find a way to survive in Korea if he had to be there for more than three months.

Frank read through and completed the form for marriage which they would take to the mayor's office the following day. If there were no problems, Pega and Frank might actually be married in the morning! They had to be married before they could complete the visa indicating Pega was his wife. By being married before they left the country, it would be much easier to get Pega into the United States.

Frank and Pega rose early on Tuesday, dressed in their best clothes and walked to the Mayor of Seoul's office. They were both so happy that their long awaited dream was coming true. Hopefully there would be no snags and when they left the mayor's office they would be husband and wife. Pega was so happy she could hardly contain her joy. She proudly walked the fifteen blocks to the mayor's office. Frank had dreamed of this moment for months. Finally, he would be able to call Pega his wife. He had thought about the moment when the mayor would say, "You may now kiss the bride." He had worked so hard for so many months to get to this point in their lives. It was like a dream coming true. Halmeoni was more than happy to watch over the infant while the couple started on their journey to see the mayor.

When they arrived at the mayor's office, Pega explained to the clerk that they had come to be married. The clerk asked for the completed documents which Frank turned over. The clerk reviewed the documents thoroughly and then asked Frank to follow him. Pega was directed to wait in another office while Frank and the clerk moved to the inner room. Once inside the room, the clerk asked for 1,000 won which was equivalent to about $5.00. Frank paid the man and then sat down on the hard wooden bench waiting to be called into the mayor's office for the marriage ceremony.

Frank sat waiting nervously, hoping everything was in order. There had been so many difficult snags and delays that he hoped nothing would get in the way of today's ceremony. About forty minutes passed and the clerk returned with the papers. Frank was startled. He handed the papers back to Frank and said, "It is completed, you may go." Frank did not understand. What was happening? He asked the clerk; "Isn't the mayor going to see us?" "No." replied the clerk. "It is completed." "But I want to be married." Frank said. "You are married." the clerk answered.

Frank was shocked. He was married and he never even saw the mayor. All the mayor had to do was sign the papers. "Wow. What a country!" Frank thought. He started to laugh out loud but caught himself when the clerk shot him an angry look.

The couple left the mayor's office as husband and wife. Frank laughed to himself when he thought, "I didn't even get to kiss the bride!" Frank and Pega walked back to Halmeoni's home as a married couple.

Frank would find that throughout Korea everyone was desperate for money and financial support. The Korean people believed that all Americans were very rich. Everywhere he went with his forms, he was required to slip money to the man behind the desk. Frank found that if he did not pay the bribe or "tip" as it was called, he would not get the information or the signature he needed. Over and over again, Frank was forced to pay a "tip" from his meager $500.00.

One of the forms required a signature from a Korean official at the police station confirming Pega had not committed any crimes. That simple form would be the beginning of enormous stress and frustration. Frank and Pega went to the police station and were advised the official was not available. In addition, there would be a fee due for requesting his signature. Frank paid the man the "fee" and was told to return the next day. This process of demanding a "fee" and asking for the American to return the next day went on for weeks. Frank actually returned every day for two solid weeks and the process was always the same. Pay the man and come back tomorrow, pay the man and come back tomorrow. Finally at the end of two weeks, he had had it.

Frank was twice the size of any of the Korean policeman in the room. After two weeks of no progress and no signature, Frank exploded. He repeatedly picked up the desk and slammed it to the floor all the while, screaming and shouting at the policemen. Frank demanded a signature immediately. The Korean policemen were very frightened. The man behind the desk was visibly shaking and said; "OK, OK, I sign, I sign." He quickly signed the papers and asked them to never come back. As they were leaving the station, one of the policemen turned to Ock Soon and said; "I could have you arrested you know." Ock Soon meekly looked at the policeman and simply shrugged her shoulders. There was nothing she could do. Frank was a stubborn man whom they had pushed to his limit. Silently she hoped they would never have to come back to this police station again.

Next they had to take the documents to the Korean Embassy where once again, money was expected. It would take weeks to work through the corruption and bribery of the Korean officials and get the necessary documents completed for a visa to the U.S.

Frank continued to work through the enormous amount of paperwork required. Answering the questions regarding Pega's background turned out to be very difficult. Pega's personal history was both scattered and undocumented. Pega did not have the addresses of where she used to live or even her parents' full names. She did not know her own date of birth since no one had ever celebrated her birthday. Nor did she know her parents names or their dates of birth.

In Korea, it is very disrespectful to address someone by their given name. There is a social hierarchy by which people are referred. Just as one is called, mother or father, so it is with other members of the family and society. People are referred to by their position. A male would call his older brother, *hyung*, but a female would call the same older brother, *obba*. While a male would call his older sister, *nuna*, a female would call her older sister *unni*. Your mother's brother (your uncle) would be called *Sahmchon*, while your father's brother (also your uncle) would be referred to as *Eemohboo*. Never is a person referred to by their given name. At that time, a woman could marry a man and never hear the name of her mother-in-law spoken aloud. Pega had never heard either of her parents' names spoken aloud and therefore she could not provide that basic information. She knew her parents as Eomeoni and Abeoji, Mother and Father.

The only good thing was that many people did not have documentation following the bombing of the city. Records and documents had been lost in the war so it was not unusual for people to no longer have the certificates or proof of identity. Frank worked on the forms for several days creating information like names and birthdates.  As soon as the forms were complete, Frank would plan a trip to the U.S. Embassy in Pusan.

In the meantime, Frank and Pega were planning on making a move in a different direction.

Halmeoni had been very kind to the young family and Frank was impressed with how much she truly loved their baby. Halmeoni loved children and had practically raised her two grandsons.  She was so delighted to have baby Donnie in her home.  She was always quick to run to care for him anytime he needed changed or bathed.  It was good that Pega had someone else to help her especially when she had been alone.

Frank appreciated Halmeoni's hospitality very much but there were several families presently living in the home.  Frank was disturbed at how the Korean men treated their wives.  One night Frank heard one of Halmeoni's sons, Min Kyung, come home intoxicated and started yelling and beating his wife and kids. Frank wanted to intervene but Pega told him not to get involved. It would be very disrespectful if Frank said anything to the man. This was Min Kyung's home and they were his guests.  Frank asked Pega if he did this often.  Pega told him, "Yes.  Many nights the men come home after drinking and beat the wives and children."  Frank was upset and told Pega that he felt like he should stop the man from hitting her.  Pega pleaded with him not to intervene; it would be so disrespectful if either of them said anything to the men in the house.  It was then that Frank decided they needed to find somewhere else to live.  The next day Frank and Pega began their search for a place for their little family to move into.  Frank was hoping that they could find a small apartment with two bedrooms.  It would be great if they could rent it month to month.

After the destruction of Seoul, there was a shortage of apartments.  They searched locally finding that all of the nicer rooms were occupied.  Eventually, they did find an old woman with one room to rent.  The house was just several blocks from Halmeoni's home. Amazingly, the rent was $1.50 per month!

Frank, Pega and baby Donnie would move into the little room and make it their home.

There wasn't much in the room since Korean people slept on mats placed on the floor. In addition, they sat on the floor to eat their meals so there really wasn't a need for a lot of furniture. Halmeoni allowed the couple to borrow some bedding from her house. She helped the couple get set up. They did not have much to move, mostly clothing and some baby items. Even though there was next to nothing in the room, Frank and Pega loved having a place to call their own. Frank was so glad to get out of Halemoni's home. Even though she was a very kind and gracious woman, he was not used to having so many people around all the time. The little room felt like heaven.

Frank and Pega lived together in that one room for the next several months. Halmeoni sorely missed the baby and she would walk over at least twice a day to check on him. The ladies had a little ritual they played that made Frank laugh every time. Halmeoni would come into the room and the first thing she did was check the baby's diaper. Of course, even if Pega had just changed the baby, the diaper always seemed to be wet when Halmone checked it. That's when Halmeoni would teasingly scold Pega and go about changing the baby herself. She never put the baby down for the entire visit. How she loved that little child!

Frank didn't know anything about babies and had always kept his distance anytime someone brought a baby around. He certainly did not understand all the cuddling and he truly believed the old adage that the women were 'spoiling' the child. Frank found it totally annoying that the women were always kissing the baby and fussing over him. Every day Frank would tell Pega to stop kissing the baby; they were putting their germs all over him and that is why the baby always had a cold. Neither of the women ever listened to him and continued to fuss over the child which only aggravated Frank even more.

Besides the twice daily visits from Halmeoni, Frank had daily visits from the young Korean girl who lived in the same house with her mother. Her name was Chu In Soon. In Soon was a very beautiful Korean girl who had fallen in love with an American soldier, Paul Winters. The soldier was from North Dakota and had left Korea about four months ago and had promised to return for In Soon. Although she had not heard back from Paul for the past two months, she continued to write to him every day – that is – she continued to have *Frank* write to him every day. Frank was not a patient man and found her continual request to write to Paul very bothersome. On the other hand, he remembered how happy he was to get correspondence from Pega so he continued to pacify the girl and write the letters. He only hoped that this Winters guy truly intended to come back for In Soon. She would be heartbroken if he did not come for her. She was hanging onto the promises he had made to her. Since he rarely wrote back, Frank had real concerns that the guy was backing off of his original promises.

July 1953 had been a very rainy month in Seoul. Rain had fallen 22 of the 31 days leaving the ground saturated. On July 31 it rained another twelve inches in six hours. The rain water poured down the mountainside, overflowed the drainage system and took out a bridge near their house. Water was backing up throughout the streets. Pega urged Frank to hurry and gather up the clothing and move back to Halmeoni's house. She was terrified that she and the baby would be caught up in the flooding. But Frank was a stubborn man and there was no way he ever intended to go back to live at Halmeoni's house. He told Pega they were going to stay right where they were. Pega was distraught but humbly obeyed her husband's wishes. She kept watching outside the room as the waters rose higher and higher in the streets. She tried to remain calm but all she could do was pray that God would keep them safe.

By the time the storm was over, part of the flooring in the house had caved in and the porch ceiling had fallen down. Frank didn't care. It was simply a project he could work on to stay busy. He would patch the floor and the roof as best he could with the materials at hand and they would continue to live in the one room 'apartment'. The landlord was thrilled to have Frank stay there and work on the room. The old woman was hard pressed to do the work herself. Frank was glad to have something to do during the next week. He had been working every day of his life since he was a young man and lying around doing nothing was very difficult for him. He knew it was going to be very challenging for him to spend week after week, just sitting around, and waiting for all of the paperwork to get processed by the American government.

# 40

# The Visa

## Pusan, South Korea

### August 1953

Frank and Pega went to Mass on Sunday, the 2<sup>nd</sup> of August and immediately following Mass, they were able to meet with Father Houng. Although Father Houng was surprised the soldier had come back for Ock Soon, Father still had difficulty believing Ock Soon would actually go to America. Father was aware that the laws had changed in America regarding marriage and immigration of Koreans but he had yet to witness any Korean woman going to America with a soldier. Father knew that in reality there existed a lot of prejudice and Asians had been barred from immigrating to the United States for decades. Father also knew that although the laws had changed there were very few Koreans who would be permitted to immigrate to the U.S. He did not believe that Ock Soon would be one of them.

Because of this, he had deep concerns in regard to marrying the couple in the Catholic Church. The Sacrament of Marriage was considered an unbreakable bond between a husband and wife. If Father married the couple and the U.S. government denied Ock Soon a visa, Ock Soon would never be able to marry again. Father had to be absolutely certain Ock Soon was going to America before he would marry them. In addition, Father had to be certain that Frank was a Catholic in good standing. That would require certificates from Frank's church in the U.S.A.

Father Houng advised the couple that he could not marry them unless he had a copy of Frank's baptism certificate and proof that he had never been married before. This was very frustrating since Frank had no idea where his baptism certificate was and how could he prove he was never married before? Father Houng agreed to accept a letter from his priest at home stating his baptism and marital status. Frank would have to write to his mother and ask her to go to St Mary's Church and have Father Joe write the letter. That should not be a problem.

On Monday, August 3, Frank took the train from Seoul Station to Pusan to speak with the consulate at the U.S. Embassy and submit the application for visa. It was a twelve hour journey. The train departed the station at 7:00 p.m. Monday and arrived in Pusan at 7:00 a.m. Tuesday. He found his way to the embassy and met with the consulate who appeared much more annoyed with him than during his first encounter. Apparently the guy had never actually processed this type of application and didn't want to be bothered. Frank encountered one problem after another with the information the consulate was providing. First he learned that processing the paperwork would take at least another six months. Frank was getting agitated just listening to the guy. He asked if there was any way to get the paperwork rushed through. Frank tried to explain that he did not have six months. He was prepared to stay no longer than three months.

No, there was no possible way the process could be rushed along. After submitting the Application for Visa, all of the documents would be sent to the U.S. Embassy. After the U.S. Embassy reviewed the information, an investigation would take place to ensure Pega was not a Communist. If there were no criminal findings, Pega would have a face to face interview at which time a decision to approve or deny the visa would be made. In addition, although the McCarran and Walter Act of 1952 abolished the ban on Asian immigration, there was a quota of 100 immigrants from each Asian country that would be permitted to enter the U.S. each year. If the number was reached before the end of the year, they would have to wait until 1954. All of this was very disturbing news to Frank.

There was no possible way he would be getting her out of the country in three months. Frank knew he could not leave Pega alone again and trust Father Houng or Father Park to make certain she got out of the country. Although both priests, especially Father Park, were treating him very well since he returned to Korea, Frank realized he could not trust them to help Pega if he left her there alone. Frank knew from his past experience that even if they said they would care for her and get her to the airport, they would not do that. Frank would have to stay in Korea until he could bring Pega home himself. Frank was not prepared to stay there and his parents would be very distraught but he felt he had no choice. He almost lost Pega once before, he was not going to lose her again.

As the consulate was reviewing the forms, he questioned Frank about Pega's education which had been left blank on the application. When asked, "What school did Pega attend?" Frank answered, "None." At that, the consulate advised Frank that Pega would not be able to enter the country unless she could demonstrate basic reading comprehension in any language. The law reads that a person must be literate to enter the United States. If she could not read and write, she would not be able to pass the written test that all applicants must pass in order to enter the country. In addition, Korea is part of the Asiatic Barred Zone and although the U.S. has opened up the doors for immigration, extreme care must be given to those people permitted to enter the U.S.

Frank was totally disgusted, and he started arguing with the consulate. The consulate told Frank that it was a privilege to live in the United States and illiterate people are not permitted. That is why there is a process in place to determine who can enter the country and who cannot. Rules are rules and they are there for a reason.

Frank told the consulate that Pega would learn to read and write during the next six months and she would be able to pass the damn test. The consulate did advise Frank, "You could return to the U.S. and take the baby with you. Your wife could come later." Now there was no way Frank would ever consider taking the baby without the baby's mother! The more the man talked, the angrier Frank became. He asked the consulate, "What am I going to do with a baby?" And that was certainly the truth. What would Frank Crimbchin ever do with a baby? He had never been around babies before and just the thought of being alone with a baby, well it just didn't sit right with him. There was no way he would leave the country with the baby and not take the baby's mother!

After speaking to the consulate and completing the forms, Frank needed $4.00 for the processing fee. Frank had the traveler's checks with him but the consulate needed cash and he would not accept a traveler's check. Frank would have to get the cash and return. He headed down to the black market and found a money changer. He was able to sell the $10.00 traveler's check for $8.00 in greenbacks and return with the $4.00 application fee. Frank was not a patient man and the entire process was frustrating and sometimes infuriating to him.

When Frank returned, the consulate told him he had some good news to tell him. The consulate said that he had read a little further in the manual and learned that any wife, husband, children, parents or grandparents did not have to take the written test in order to obtain a visa. If her background was clear of any criminal activity or communist involvement, his wife could get a visa based solely on her marriage to Frank. Well, this *was* good news but Frank couldn't believe the man was just now getting around to reading the guidelines! He was so aggravated thinking; "This guy gets paid good money for not knowing his job. This is the only government job available over here – Visa and Immigration. He should know the laws backward and forward again. By the time Pega gets to the States, I will know his job better than he does!" Even though he was annoyed at the consulate's lack of knowledge, he certainly was glad that Pega would not have to take the written test after all. That was one less thing to worry about.

Frank submitted the application but one thing was missing, Pega's fingerprints. The consulate advised Frank to go back to Seoul, go to the local police station and get her fingerprints taken. He would then have to take the fingerprints to the clerk at the U.S. Embassy office in Seoul. The clerk could mail the fingerprints back to Pusan and that would save Frank a second trip to Pusan.

Once the Pusan office received the fingerprints, they could begin processing the application.

That seemed easy enough. At least the police department already knows that he was not going to wait for weeks to have this done. He planned on making one visit and one visit only.

After his dismal trip to Pusan, Frank realized he was not going to get out of the country in ninety days after all. He would never leave Pega alone again and his meager $500.00 would not be enough for six or nine months. Frank had to find a way to make some money while he was staying in Korea. This was going to be very difficult. He did not speak Korean and even if he did, jobs were very difficult to find. Plus he needed to earn real American dollars, not Korean won– finding work was going to be a difficult challenge.

As soon as Frank arrived back in Seoul, he and Pega went to the police station and obtained the prints. Pega was very nervous to go back to the police station where Frank had had an outburst, but she had no choice. She prayed all the way there hoping there would not be a scene. She did not want to be arrested! The couple was able to enter the station, obtain the prints and leave peacefully. Pega was so happy and relieved; God always watched over her and answered her prayers. They left the police station and immediately walked over to the U.S. Embassy office in Seoul and provided the fingerprints to the clerk. The clerk agreed to mail the prints to Pusan as directed. With that, the application for the visa would finally be started. There was nothing else Frank could do but wait. He could now begin to earnestly looking for work.

On the International front, after two years of ceasefire talks between the United Nations (UN) and Communist forces, the Korean Armistice Agreement was signed on July 27, 1953. For two years the main stumbling block in peace talks had been the issue of the prisoner exchange. The Communists were insistent that ALL prisoners be returned while the UN insisted that any prisoners who wanted to remain in South Korea may do so. Finally in July of 1953, the Communists relented and signed the agreement.    Operation Big Switch, the actual exchange of prisoners began early in August of 1953.

Frank and Pega's "apartment" was near the helicopter landing pad where the soldiers would be exchanged.  The 76th Construction Battalion had been working twelve hour days to complete the pad. Every day from August 5, 1953 until December 23, 1953, helicopters took off and landed exchanging prisoners of war.  From the landing pad, prisoners were taken to Panmunjom, Freedom Village.   By the end of December 1953, 75,823 Communist prisoners and 12,773 UN prisoners would be returned to their homelands.

Although Frank could hear the sound of the helicopters day in and day out for months, he was fighting his own war.  His own battle to bring Pega to the states had not been resolved.  The world was rejoicing that the Korean Conflict had finally come to an end but Frank could not take part in the celebration.  His battle had not yet been won and the challenge was growing more and more complicated.

Frank continued to write to his parents, keeping them informed of what was happening.  He knew they would be very disappointed to learn he was going to be in Korea much longer than originally anticipated.  He hoped they would understand but they worried about him and they needed him at home too.  Everything was piling up and Frank tried to remain positive.  He would have to find a job - any job- very soon.

## The Party

The following weekend, Frank and Pega were invited to join in the celebration for Father Houng.  It was quite a party.  They were celebrating Father Houng's Anniversary.  Priests from all over the area arrived as well as the Bishop from Seoul.  Frank could not understand much of what was being said but it was nice to get out and do something entertaining for a change.

Father Houng had been responsible for over 300 children between The Babies Home and Chung Pyung Orphanage. Throughout the entire war, Father Houng had cared for hundreds of orphans, doing his best to keep them fed and safe. Although some had died, Father had been able to save many.

All of the orphans attended the celebration and sang and danced for the priests. The children were very happy to get special treats and Frank was delighted to find they were serving beer, wine and even whiskey. It was a nice celebration and Frank was careful not to indulge too much in the spirits.

# 41
# The Salesman
## Tradewell and Company

### August 1953

Pega never really understood all of the difficulty Frank was facing. She was so happy and so full of joy that he had returned that nothing else was going to bother her. Her days were filled with delight in caring for her baby, happiness in being married to the love of her life and the joy she found in knowing God and how much he cared for her. She continued to worship and praise God for all the mercies He had bestowed on her throughout her lifetime. Pega believed that all of her suffering was for a reason. God had chosen to bless her more than any other. She had never been happier in all of her life.

Frank on the other hand was feeling more and more stress based on the extended time frame and additional monies needed. Although he needed to find a job, he did not have a car or even a bicycle so all of his job hunting was done on foot. He had been walking up and down the streets looking for anything that might hold promise but was not finding anything to pursue. He remembered that some of the officers from the base who wanted to stay in Korea after they were discharged from the Army, talked about getting into sales. Frank hated sales. He did not have the kind of personality that people would embrace right away. He tended to be an abrupt and inpatient man and did not like to 'butter up" to people or put on airs of friendship if he did not like you. All of the qualities that would make up a good salesman; good people skills, communication skills, friendly personality, outgoing, well that did not describe Frank Crimbchin. But the man was worried. After looking for a job for several weeks, he knew he had to do something. Frank started to look for a sales job since nothing else was available.

The first place he looked into was a trading company called Baleon and Company. Frank stopped in to see the owner but learned the man was in Japan. Frank visited with one of the supervisors and talked about the job. Baleon and Company sold a variety of items; household items, furniture, bedding, bar and restaurant equipment. Frank learned that one of their biggest sellers was beer. Baleon sold a case of beer for $5.35. Frank immediately wanted to buy a case from the supervisor but learned it was illegal for the company to sell beer to him. Due to regulations surrounding imports, they were only permitted to sell the beer to GIs and even then an officer had to sign for it.

Frank stayed for about an hour discussing the details of the job with the supervisor. The supervisor felt that they could really use another salesman but the final decision would have to go through the boss. If he was hired, he would be paid a base rate plus commission. There were lots of bars on the Army base and they could always use another person to contact them and get more orders. At one point they had four salesmen but now they were down to two. The supervisor felt the boss would certainly hire Frank.

The two men hit it off great and by the time the interview was over, the supervisor gave Frank a case a beer and told him to come back on Sunday when the boss got in from Tokyo. He could probably have the job. Frank was excited. Finally a prospect for work and a case of beer too! Frank returned the following Sunday but the boss was still in Tokyo. The supervisor told him to try back on Wednesday.

Frank was anxious for work and didn't want to wait until Wednesday so he decided to try another company called Tradewell and Company. This company sold all types of manufactured goods from a catalogue. There were literally thousands of items to sell. Everything used in bar rooms such as tables, chairs, linens, glassware – if the item could be found in the bar, Tradewell could supply it. The catalogue also had furniture, bedding, lamps and even cars!

The salesmen generally sold to Americans and GIs stationed in Korea. Although they were permitted to sell to Koreans, there was an import tax of 180% on everything. So if a car sold for $2,000, it would cost the Korean man $5,600. But if they sold the same car to an American for $2,000, it could be waiting for him at the dock when he got home.

Although the boss preferred to hire someone who was planning to live in Korea for a while, he really liked Frank and offered him the job. He told Frank that he could start immediately. He would be paid $250 a month plus commission. Of course, just like Baleon and Company, one of Tradewell's biggest sellers was beer. Frank would be paid ten cents on every can of beer he sold. The boss told him that after a month or so he should be making about $500 - $600 a month! Last month the boss sold 11,500 cans of beer and his commission was $1,150! Frank couldn't believe it. He found a job and it was going to pay some good money.

After meeting with the boss, Frank met the secretary in the office, whose name was Louise Maser. She was a very beautiful German girl who hated being in Korea but could not get out of the country. Apparently in 1948 she met a Korean man, Park Sung Jin, who was studying to be a doctor. During his years in Germany, the couple met and fell in love. They soon wanted to marry. Her parents begged her not to marry the man and promised her the world if only she would break it off. Louise was a stubborn girl and nothing her parents could promise would tempt her to stop seeing the man. When she informed her parents that she was getting married and would be moving to South Korea they practically disowned her and broke off all communication.

After completing medical school, Sung Jin and Louise left Germany and moved to Seoul. They opened a small medical clinic within the city. The building was big enough that the couple was able to live in several of the rooms and to care for patients in the adjoining exam areas. Louise helped her husband by assisting him with his patients, ordering supplies and keeping the books. Louise also helped by doing everyday tasks such as washing the bandages and hanging them out to dry for reuse by the patients. Over the next several years Louise would work diligently at the clinic supporting her husband in his work.

The couple eventually had beautiful twin daughters who were the delight of the doctor's life. The family was happy and the girls were a sweet addition to their busy home. Some looked down on the family due to the interracial marriage but this did not bother Sung Jin. He knew that he had broken the Korean guidelines for marriage but Louise and he loved each other so deeply, nothing else mattered. Their life was happy and joyful until the day the Communists entered Seoul. The North Korean Army went door to door and captured all of the educated men. Sung Jin was taken captive in order to provide medical care to the injured North Koreans and Louise had not seen him since that dreadful day.

Life immediately became unbearable for Louise. Since she had married a Korean man, she had lost her citizenship in Germany. She was not permitted to return to her homeland since she was considered a Korean citizen. She found herself alone in Korea to feed and raise her two daughters. The three were struggling and Louise decided she had to take the girls to the orphanage. She would have to find a job and she had no family that could help her care for her children. Louise was broken hearted. She had no idea where her husband was and now she had to give up her daughters in order to keep them from starving to death. Louise grew to hate the country that had taken so much away from her.

Eventually she was able to find work at Tradewell and Company. Louise handled the books and ordered the merchandise. She was very busy keeping records of sales and salaries as well as calculating bonuses. Louise worked six days a week. She would do anything to get out of the country not unlike so many of the Korean women. Louise wanted to get her girls back from the orphanage and take them to America.

Working at Tradewell proved to be a great setting for Louise to meet American soldiers. Most of their business and sales were conducted with the Americans and Louise being a beautiful "single" woman found love easily among the men.

By the summer of 1953, Louise had become involved with a high ranking officer from the U.S. Army. Although Officer Bradley was married to his high school sweetheart in the states, he had moved into the medical clinic to be with Louise. He had the power to order simple conveniences to be built at the clinic for his personal use. Suddenly, Louise had the comforts of water delivery on a regular basis to her cistern. There was additional plumbing added to the facility, a generator and new electrical wiring throughout. Officer Bradley had many of the western comforts to which he had been accustomed installed in the clinic. Life had become much more affluent with the arrival of Officer Bradley.

Frank was surprised to find a German girl working at Tradewell. He and Louise hit it off right from the beginning. Louise was delighted to learn that Frank's parents were from Germany. She found it interesting that his brother, Donald, was currently, serving in the Armed Forces in her homeland. Louise was happy to have someone to talk with at the office besides the boss and the Chinese boy who helped out there. She found she had a lot in common with Frank and was excited to have him in the office every day. Louise finally had something to look forward to when she went to work.

On August 28, 1953, Frank wrote the following letter to his family.

Dear Mother and Father,

I hope this letter finds both of you in the best of health. We are doing all right over here. Pega and I took the baby to an army doctor over here and he checked him all over. He said he was a very healthy baby and we should not worry about the little cold that he has. He told me to give him a tablespoon of orange juice every day and to bring him back when he is five months old and he will give him a vaccination and all the shots that they give the baby at that age back in the states.

Well I have been working at my job two days now and it is not too bad. It has been hard getting used to that kind of work. We sell just about anything, which makes it so tough. And when you do sell something there is so much red tape involved.

I will get my first check the end of September. I will send $100 of it home. My boss said he will put $100 of it in my bank account at home and then you will be able to take it out as you need it. I am concerned that Father was laid off. I know he is getting only $30 a month on his unemployment so I hope this helps. So please send me the bank account number and the bank name and address so I can give them to him (the boss).

I am guaranteed $250 a month. He said I ought to make $500-$600 after I get onto the way it goes. If and when I start making that, I will be able to send $250-$300 a month home.

The outfit I am going to work for has only one car but he has a jeep coming in- in a couple of weeks. He said when the jeep comes in I can use it to get around. In the meantime I am to do most of my selling on foot. I go around to all the army camps and I try to sell them beer and things for their club.

Like I wrote in the other letters they said it would take about six to eight months before we can come to the United States. So if it should take that long please take care of yourselves and don't worry. When a person worries it makes them age so fast. So please don't worry about us over here. As long as I am here, I can take care of the things here.

I will send money home as soon as I start to get it. So don't worry about this end of it. Don is big enough to take care of himself and is in no great danger in Germany so try not to worry. The baby is feeling alright and so is Pega.

Do not say anything to anybody about me having a job. If you told anybody that I would be hunting one, then tell them I did not find one because if I work while I am off from Taylor and Wilson, I will lose my nine years seniority.

Don't forget to send me Don's address as soon as you get it. I hope you and father are alright.

The lights go out at 11:00 o'clock. I have only seven more minutes so I will close.
Love to all,
Pega, Don and Frank

Several days earlier, Pega had asked Father Park to please write the following letter to Frank's parents.

Dear Mother,

I am so sorry that I could not write to you sooner. When I received your letter, even though I haven't seen you face to face, I feel like seeing your gracious face. We are all alright; we think is because of your prayer.

While I was listening to Frank reading your letter I was dreaming of you and our happy future family with all together. I think you cannot even imagine a country like ours.

How do you feel when you saw your first grandson who was born from a foreigner? Baby is almost one hundred days old and start laughing very nicely. After Frank got here he is always busy taking care of his son and in every moment he is thinking of you and the long days you took care of him.

In some quiet night he is telling me old stories and I am listening very happily. However I am always thinking that you may have quite a time because of me since I do not know anything. But I'll promise that I try very hard.

Mother I imagine you'll be very lonesome because your both sons left from you. When we think all these things, we feel hurry back home very soon but things are not as well as we hoped. We worried very much when we heard father was sick, but we were very happy when we were informed that father was alright.

I have millions of things which I would like to tell you but I will tell them some other time. I hope both of you will be happy until we meet all together.

May God richly bless you.
With love, Daughter-in-law

Frank had started his new job and was so glad to have somewhere to go and something to do every day. Until the jeep arrived, Frank would be traveling on foot going from camp to camp, trying to sell beer and merchandise. He and Louise became

265

very good friends since he himself enjoyed having someone to talk to who could speak English well.

Louise could not believe that Frank had actually returned to Korea for a girlfriend. She was very much aware of all the Korean women who got involved with American soldiers and were left behind. She found it very honorable that Frank would actually come back for the woman. Louise found a lot to admire about Frank and took a strong liking to him.

After several weeks, Louise finally had the opportunity to meet this Pega. She was utterly shocked. She could not believe that Frank came back for this peasant. As soon as Pega opened her mouth to speak, Louise realized the woman was uneducated. Her Korean language skills were very poor. Louise could not believe Frank had fallen for such a woman. Did he understand what kind of person she was? If she couldn't speak Korean properly, how would she ever learn to speak English? Louise despised the woman immediately. She did not hesitate to let Frank know he was making a huge mistake. Louise would continually remind Frank, that Pega wouldn't last two weeks in America. How could he even think of taking her there? She was going to be a burden to him for the rest of his life. For his own good, and his own wellbeing he should really think about what he was about to do. The peasant would never be able to help him get ahead in America. He deserved so much better!

Although Louise spoke poorly of Pega, Frank did not let her opinion affect his commitment. He knew Louise meant well and was only trying to look out for him. He also knew that Louise wanted to go to America more than anything else in life. She dreamed of being reunited with her girls and moving to America, the land of the free and the wealthy.

Frank thought that maybe someday in the future, he would be able to help Louise. Maybe he could sponsor Louise and get her out of Korea but he was not going to promise her anything. He had to focus on getting Pega there first. He had to take care of first things first.

# 42
## Life in South Korea
### More Red Tape

Fall 1953

Fall was coming and Frank realized that he would have to find someone to supply more wood to keep the family warm this winter. Boy, he hated the thought of another winter in Korea. Life in Korea for him was torturous. Cooking over an open flame, keeping the house warm with wood, bathing at the public bath house, no electricity after 11:00PM, all of this was more and more burdensome as time went on. If only he had a solid end date to look forward to, waiting might be more tolerable.

The red tape and government delays were so frustrating. Frank thought again about asking Pennsylvania Congressman Fulton to write a letter to help them but he believed the government official had little interest in helping him and it would be another waste of time. The last time he asked for help, Congressman Fulton forwarded his questions to another government employee who checked into the situation and wrote him back, telling him to read the newspaper to find out what was happening. Frank did not believe writing the Congressman would help.

Well, at least he had a job and he was with his wife and son. Someday this would end and he vowed he would never return to this country again.

Frank would never make it big in sales in South Korea. He was thankful to have a job and the boss was very good to him. Over the next several months, the boss would be sure to deposit $100 a month into Frank's bank account in the U.S. so Frank's parents had money to live on. Frank was aware that his father was receiving only $30 a month for six months through his unemployment and his parents really needed the extra money to survive. In addition, the boss faithfully paid Frank the $150 plus whatever commissions he earned.

Without transportation, Frank continued to walk on foot to the various American camps and bars. Frank always had a variety of items he could sell; plastic and glassware, dinner sets, silver ware sets, refrigerators, ice cube makers, pop and of course beer. He was peddling waitress uniforms, gas stoves, electric stoves and boilers. He never did sell a Chevy or a Buick car. That would have been a windfall!

His sales volume was mediocre and over time he really grew to dislike his job. Frank didn't mind working hard, but he found sales to be very stressful. He simply did not have the personality to talk easily to strangers or the ability to convince them to buy things they really didn't need. Selling the merchandise was just the first headache; the red tape following the sale was unbelievable. A career in sales just wasn't Frank's specialty.

Frank did work long hours, usually 10 hour days. Long before Frank arrived, the boss had hired a Chinese boy to work in the office. Since Louise did not drive, the boy acted as a chauffeur for Louise. He would pick her up for work in the morning and drive her home every night. The boss had become annoyed with the young man since in the past two months, he had wrecked the car three times. The boss had grown weary of the young man's poor driving habits.

As soon as the new jeep passed through customs, chauffeuring Louise everyday became part of Frank's job. Frank didn't mind, it broke up the day and he enjoyed riding around the countryside in the jeep. Louise loved having Frank as her new chauffeur. She was still hoping to find a way to get to America and this could be her ticket if only the man would come to his senses! Frank had never thought of himself as good looking and was not a "ladies" man so he never fully understood Louise's intentions. Frank would write his parents and tell them of the nice German girl in the office and how someday he hopes to help her get to America.

In every letter to his parents, Frank would remind them not to disclose to anyone that he had found a job. He was still very concerned about losing his seniority at the machine shop where he had worked for almost a decade. Frank knew it was against company rules for anyone who was on a leave of absence from the company to work for anyone else during that time. He would sure hate to lose the seniority he had worked for since he was fourteen years old.

Frank's parents continued to write to him regarding their concerns that he was going to have to stay there so long. They really wanted him to return to the U.S. and go back to Korea at a later date to get Pega. They really missed him at home and were still hoping that he would be able to come home while waiting for Pega's visa to be approved.

Frank finally wrote his parents the following:

"I know how you and father feel about me coming home as soon as I can and I would like to leave today for home. But I would be afraid that she might not get there if I left her here to come over on her own.

There is the baby too. When I am here to look out for him- it is not too bad. But I would never have any peace of mind if I were to come back and leave him here for some time to come later with her.

The priest treats us very good, but you know how they were when I was home. They would be the same after I left. No matter how much he would tell me that he would see that she got on the plane, I could not trust him to do it."

The next several months would seem to drag on and on. There was nothing Frank could do but continue to wait on the government to approve Pega's visa. It could not happen soon enough!

In mid-September, Frank's landlord informed him that she would need their room for a family member who was returning home to live with her. She asked the couple to begin looking for another place to live. Frank and Pega were both very disappointed.  They had grown fond of the little 'apartment' and the location was great.  Sure they were now cooking on a portable gas stove and still had to get water from several blocks away but Frank had grown used to it.  In his mind he likened it to camping.  Pega thought their 'apartment' was wonderful and never knew anything else.  She thought the gas stove was really incredible since all her life she cooked over an open fire.  Pega had never been happier in her entire life.  Neither wanted to leave their little room, but realized they had to begin looking for somewhere else to live.

Frank had been searching for a new place for several weeks but he had not been able to find anything.  Time was passing by and he had to be out of there as soon as possible.

When Louise learned of Frank's dilemma, she had a brilliant idea.  Since Frank was already chauffeuring her to and from work every day, why not just move into her place?  Louise had some extra rooms at the clinic and would be glad to rent one to him.  The rooms were once used as exam rooms for patients and were somewhat removed from each other granting each couple privacy.  The rooms at the clinic actually had beds in them.  They could live in one of the patient examination rooms and share the kitchen with Louise.  The clinic had one bathroom with a toilet and even a shower.  Anytime they needed water Officer Bradley would simply call the Unit and more water would be delivered within 24 hours.  It sounded perfect to Frank.  The place was very nice and much more updated than the old thatched roof house he had been living in.

Although Louise really enjoyed Frank's company, she continued to have a very strong dislike of Pega.  After Frank moved in, Louise told him that he was more than welcome to use her shower but not Pega. She would not allow that woman to shower in her home.

Frank learned to overlook Louise's harshness towards Pega.  He believed that once Louise got to know Pega, she would get over her dislike.  In the meantime, Frank would not use the shower either. They would both continue to go to the public bath house as they had been doing for months.

Louise had a Korean housekeeper whose name was Ye Seo Yeon. Seo Yeon had two daughters named Jin and Yuna. Seo Yeon and Pega became good friends while Pega lived in Louise's house. Pega really enjoyed living at the clinic with all the new conveniences. She missed seeing Halmeoni every day but spent a lot of time with Seo Yeon.

Frank was so happy to have somewhere comfortable to live. It was so much nicer than anything he would have been able to find. Louise was very happy too. She knew that given time, she would be able to win Frank's heart over to hers. Her competition was nothing to be concerned about. Louise wanted to go to America too.

# 43

## The United States Embassy
### The Fingerprints

### December 1953

Early in December of 1953, the U.S. Embassy moved their office from Pusan back to Seoul. That was great news to Frank who figured he would be able to monitor the status of Pega's application for the visa more closely.

On Friday, December 7, Frank stopped into the U.S. Embassy in Seoul to inquire about the status of Pega's request for a visa. He met with the consulate who informed Frank, they had not started to work on her case yet. WHAT! He had submitted all of the documents four months ago and they should be ready to finalize the visa by now. Frank was incredulous. Four months had passed and things should be finalized soon but he is hearing that they never even started to investigate the case. WHY?

The consulate informed Frank that he had never received the fingerprints which he had requested back in August. He was still waiting for Frank to submit Pega's fingerprints before they could begin to work on the case. Without the fingerprints they could not begin to research the alien applicant. Frank could not believe what he was hearing. Why didn't the consulate receive the fingerprints? Frank had taken Pega to the police station back in August and she had her fingerprints taken. He then brought the prints to this very office and gave them to the clerk. The clerk said he would send them to the U.S. Embassy in Pusan. What happened to the prints? The consulate informed Frank again that he had never received the fingerprints.

The clerk Frank had spoken to in August had recently left Korea and went back to the states. No one else at the Seoul branch knew anything about the fingerprints. They opened the drawer of the clerk's desk and there sat Pega's fingerprints. The clerk had never sent them to Pusan. Unfortunately, it would take another six to nine months before a visa could be issued.

Frank lost all control of his temper. He began screaming and shouting, cursing and threatening all of those in the room. He told them there was no way he could stay in this filthy country for another six to nine months. They screwed everything up and they would have to make it right. Frank continued to rant and rave, calling them every evil name he could think of – everyone in the room was afraid of the man.

Finally the consulate, in an effort to calm the man, told him they would do everything they could to move this along and get him out of the country as soon as possible. He was to bring Pega back to the office in the morning. They would speak to her and see what could be done.

Frank left the office, still in a rage. He could not believe the utter incompetence he was dealing with. He had to get out of this country. He just couldn't take it anymore.

When Frank told Pega about the fingerprints and the delays, she too was devastated. But unlike Frank, Pega took all of her concerns to the Lord. Pega did not sleep that night. She stayed awake all night praying to God to help them.

The next morning Frank took Pega back to the office. Upon arrival, the consulate told Frank he was going to do something to help them get out of the country but he must never tell anyone what he was about to do. It was against all regulations to provide a visa to anyone before completing an investigation. But the consulate felt confident that Pega was not a Communist, therefore, he was going to interview her and if possible, issue the visa. He would do the investigation afterwards. If anything came up after she had left the country and records revealed she was a Communist, she would be deported and have to return to Korea. By doing this, they would be able to leave the country in three or four weeks. The consulate asked the interpreter to come and assist. They interviewed Pega for about two hours. When they returned, the consulate told Frank to come back on Friday and he would have Pega's visa ready for her.

Frank couldn't believe it. They were finally going to be able to go to the United States. After five long and burdensome months, he was hearing that Pega could leave in about three or four weeks. It was amazing news. They were so happy and excited. He couldn't wait to write to his parents and ask them to purchase the airline tickets. They were finally coming home!

# 44
## Marriage for a Lifetime
### Baptized For Eternity
January, 1954

Baptized and Married on January 2, 1954.

Front Row: Left to Right: 1. Father Park's Sister-in-Law. 2. Ye Seo Yeon-the German Girl's Housekeeper. 3. Ock Soon Lee. 4. Frank Crimbchin. 5. Friend of Father Park's Brother. 6. Father Park's Brother

Back Row Left: A partial picture of Halmeoni, the woman Ock Soon was living with when the war broke out. Although Ock Soon referred to this kind woman as Halmeoni (Grandmother), she was not Ock Soon's biological grandmother. She was the kind woman who allowed Ock Soon to live with her and her family. She treated Ock Soon with genuine love and Ock Soon helped her with her two grandsons.

(Actual names of some of the people in wedding party are unknown).

December 24, 1953
From: Reverend John Park
To: Frank's Mother and Father

Merry Christmas
Happy New Year

I greet your son's happy marriage on the second of January 1953. The bride and the baby will be baptized on the same day before the marriage. They are very lucky because, it is very hard for Korean to get married with American.

So far as I know Frank and Ock Soon are very good minded. As we kept her for a long time, we are sure she is a very good girl. I believe their marriage will be happy and blessed by our Lord.

They will leave Korea for the states on the fourth of next month 1954 with their baby boy. I will baptize them and Father Houng will say Matrimony Mass on second day.

Thanking you for the Christmas card,

Rev John Park

Hothership
Kaulchino
Seoul, Korea

And so it was. On January 2, 1954, Frank and Pega put on their rented bride and groom attire and headed for the church. Just as Father Park described in his letter, Pega and the baby were baptized into the Catholic Church. Father Park was so happy to be able to perform the Baptism Ceremony and Pega who had waited so long to be baptized into Jesus was full of peace and joy.

Father Houng performed the Catholic Ceremony of Marriage which Frank's mother had so long ago requested. He had put the couple off until the very last minute because he had seen so many marriage arrangements fall apart. He had wanted to be certain that Ock Soon was truly going to America with Frank before he would marry them. And now the visa was granted, the passport obtained and the airline tickets had been purchased. Father Houng finally believed that Ock Soon Lee was really going to America.

Halmeoni attended the ceremony with both great joy and great sadness. She was certainly happy for the young girl and her new husband but she also knew she would never see Ock Soon again. She knew that once Ock Soon left the country, she would never return. Halmeoni had grown to love the girl just like her own daughter and she loved the baby just like a grandson. She would never forget the first time she saw the young woman who came to her home starving and cold. She remembered how she gulped the cup of hot tea and bowl of rice. How sad she felt for the girl that first day.

She remembered how the young woman served her family so faithfully over the years. She would never forget how Ock Soon carried her grandson on her back for over 100 miles in the freezing cold temperatures to escape the Communists. She would be forever grateful to Ock Soon for all of her sacrifices. Yes, she was a very special girl and Halmeoni would miss her for a very long time.

Father Park was so happy for the couple that he provided a celebration dinner for everyone after the ceremony. Father Park had arranged for his own brother and sister-in-law to serve as witnesses during the ceremony. They all joined together after the wedding for dinner.

For Ock Soon, she could only give thanks and praise to the God above who rescued her and blessed her more than any other. She knew it was God who brought this man to her, this very strong man, who would have the courage and determination to do everything that was necessary to marry her. Ock Soon knew that there would never be another such man. Only Frank would do what he did for her love.

And it was God that brought Frank to her that day so long ago when the old woman tried to sell her.  She would be forever grateful to the God above who saved her from death and provided her a life full of mercy and blessings.  Her prayers had been answered in God's time, just as she knew they would be.

# 45

## Departure: Seoul, South Korea
### Arrival: U.S.A.

### January 1954

On the 3$^{rd}$ of January, the couple went through customs and then flew to Japan. Pega had never been on an airplane before and still spoke minimal English. Everything was strange and new. Frank guided her through the airport and customs. Pega followed him just as she had done so long ago on that day when she first met Frank and he took her to Sunja's house where she was bathed and groomed. This time everything was different. She had grown to love the man who promised to come back for her. Like a princess whose dream was being fulfilled, Pega was becoming a new person. Lifted out of sheer poverty and starvation, Pega was truly going to America.

The couple had a stopover in Japan. They would spend two days in Japan before leaving for the U.S. While there, Frank found a tailor and ordered a suit to be made for Pega to wear on the plane. The tailor took all of her measurements and then stayed awake all night and made that suit. The next day he arrived at the hotel with the most beautiful suit, Pega had ever seen. It was a beautiful deep purple and it fit her just perfectly. The tailor had done a fabulous job. Pega looked in the mirror and thought she was actually starting to look a little like an American. Everything was utterly amazing to her.

Frank had wanted to find a special gift to take home for his mother. He searched for a jeweler and eventually bought a beautiful necklace made of the finest cultured pearls. They were so gorgeous. Pega knew that Frank's mother would be so happy to receive such a beautiful gift.

On January 4, the couple boarded a Northwest Airlines flight to Seattle, Washington. Frank could hardly believe the journey was finally over. He was finally able to bring his love, his wife, back to the United States. The road had been so very difficult, so long and so burdensome, but it had finally come to an end. They were actually on a flight heading home.

The entire flight was a learning experience for Pega. Frank did all the speaking and Pega barely spoke a word. She could not understand anything those around her were saying. Everyone was speaking English so fast, she could not keep up. She slept quietly on the plane and cared for her baby.

Once they landed in Seattle, things became even more of a puzzle. Pega had never seen anything like this before. She could not even imagine some of the things she was seeing. Everywhere, people were rushing around her. In America, people did not even have to walk up the steps. She was amazed that the steps moved them up and down. Pega found the new environment quite shocking. One thing was for sure though. Everyone in America was wealthy beyond belief. And now that she was going to be an American, she would never be poor again.

As soon as they landed in Seattle, Frank showed Pega where the ladies' room was located. She had to use the bathroom and change Donnie's diaper. They had to hurry to catch the connecting flight to Pittsburgh. The only problem was that Pega had never seen anything like this restroom in her life. There were rows and rows of toilets and sinks. She did not know how to use these appliances. They were different than the ones at the hotel. Everything was so bewildering to her. She finally used the toilet as best she could (not closing the door or flushing the commode). She sat on the toilet with the door open and her baby in her arms. When she got up, she forgot to flush. She was looking for somewhere to change the baby and eventually put him down next to the sink.

She took off Donnie's dirty diaper and was looking for some place to put it. She had never seen big silver trash cans before and had no idea these beautiful containers where for dirty diapers. Pega just stood there with the dirty diaper in her hand, looking around and around, simply puzzled as to what to do with it. Women were looking at her oddly- some disgustedly- and passing around her to use the sinks and wash their hands. She watched as they discarded the paper towels in the beautiful containers. She still didn't know what to do with the dirty diaper. Everything was so difficult, she just wanted to cry. Why didn't Frank come and help her? He knows she doesn't know what to do!

Suddenly a very kind woman noticed her bewilderment and approached Pega. Without speaking she tapped Pega on her arm and pointed to the trash can. Pega was so happy that someone stopped to help her. She felt like an angel appeared before her that day. Everything was shocking beyond anything Pega ever imagined. Although she was hurrying as best she could, none the less, everything was taking too long. Frank was getting worried and sent another woman in to get her. When Pega finally came out of the restroom, they had missed the connecting flight to Pittsburgh. The couple ended up sleeping in Seattle for one night until they could get the next flight out.

The entire trip from Seoul to Pittsburgh would end up taking three days. But finally they were on the last leg of their trip. The next evening they arrived at the Greater Pittsburgh Airport. As soon as they got off the airplane, Frank telephoned his mother. He was so happy to finally get back to his hometown. His parents would be coming to the airport from McKees Rocks and it would take less than an hour for them to pick up the young family. Frank spoke to his mother giving her the latest updates about their trip and arranging for a pick up spot. After a brief conversation, he handed the telephone to Pega. Frank told her to say, "Hello, how are you?"

Pega took the telephone and spoke into the receiver saying, "Hello, how are you?" Kathryn could not believe she was actually speaking to Pega after all of this time. She was so happy and excited, she said, "I am fine! I am so happy you are finally here! How was the flight?" Pega did not understand one word of what her mother-in-law just said to her. She simply repeated, "Hello, how are you?" There was dead silence on the other end of the telephone. Kathryn was learning for the first time that Pega did not *really* speak English. She was so startled; she simply hung up the phone in shock and disbelief.  When Pega realized Kathryn had hung up, she gave the phone back to Frank. Kathryn, just like Pega, was about to embark on a new journey unlike any before.

Frank and Pega waited at the airport for Frank's parents to pick them up.  The old 1950 Chevy arrived, introductions and hugs were exchanged and the family packed the luggage into the trunk and headed out to what would become their new home for the next six years.

The couple would be living with Frank's parents, Frank and Kathryn, in McKees Rocks, Pennsylvania.  The home was a three story brick house with a detached garage.  It was a very typical home for a middle class family at that time.  As far as Pega was concerned, she thought the home was a castle.  Every couple had their own bedroom, *even the baby*!  The house had hardwood floors and beautiful wool oriental rugs in each room.  The furniture was unbelievable.  They had a beautiful couch and two chairs in the sitting room.  The dining room had the most beautiful wood carved furniture Pega had ever seen.  Each bedroom was just gorgeous with a chest for clothes and a high bed to sleep on. Pega had never been in a home like this in all of her life.  The house even had *two* bathrooms!  Pega could not believe she had married such a wealthy man!

That night it was very difficult for her to sleep in the house.  All night long Pega heard strange noises.  She had no idea what was making the noises.  Was someone in the house?  Should she wake Frank up to find out what was happening.  Later, Pega would learn that the furnace turns on and off all by itself.  They do not build a fire in the house like they do in Korea.  Somehow the house stays warm when the machine turns on.  That was the strange noise that had frightened her so much the night before.

The next day, Pega watched as the family took food from a large cold closet.  They called it the refrigerator and it was so amazing that it kept all the food cold so it did not spoil and rot. She watched as her father-in-law cooked on a large beautiful stove with an oven to bake in. Her father-in-law would laugh and laugh at her as she was so amazed at such simple things in life.

The most incredible thing was the washing machine. People did not have to go to the river to wash the clothes in America. The machine did all the work! All she had to do was put the clothing through the wringer to get the water out. Oh how she loved it! What fun! No more dry and bleeding hands from cold river water and pounding rocks. She felt like a Queen doing the laundry.

Over and over again, Pega would find her life in America the most amazing journey. Each day brought new experiences and each experience brought new learning. Pega's mother-in-law and father-in-law grew to love her deeply. They thought she was a remarkable young girl who learned very quickly.

In Korea, the tradition is to please your mother and father-in-law. Korean women are taught to obey them and give them great honor. That is exactly what Pega did. She would work very hard to do anything and everything to please them. Any time visitors came to the house; Frank's parents would continually brag about Pega and praise her skills. They would tell their family and friends just how wonderful she was and how fast she learned. Pega took great pride and joy in their approval and tried even harder to please them.

Pega's journey in America over the next six decades would be one filled with great joys, sorrows, trials and tribulations. But just as her Lord watched over her during her youth, so He did over the next sixty years. Pega would go on to raise seven children, build a machine shop business with her husband and build a small Korean fellowship of believers in Butler, PA. The Korean women, who would attend Pega's Bible Studies and worship together at the Korean Church, would grow to love the Lord, just as Pega does.

On January 4, 1954, Ock Soon Lee's journey to America was just the beginning of a life full of service to her family and her church. It would be the beginning of an incredible journey provided to her by her Lord and Savior, Jesus Christ.

## Korean Women Immigrants married to American men

- In 1954, Ock Soon Lee was one of only 116 Korean women admitted to the U.S. as the wife of an American citizen.
- In 1953 – 96 Korean Wives of American citizens entered the U.S.
- In 1952–101 Korean Wives of American citizens entered the U.S.
- In 1951 – 11 Korean Wives of American citizens entered the U.S.
- In 1950 - 1 Korean Wife of an American citizen entered the U.S.

Source: U.S. Commissioner of Immigration and Naturalization, *Annual Reports*, 1947-1975, Table 6 (Washington, DC).

## Korean War Statistics

- More than one million American service members served in the Korean War. The United States led a coalition of twenty nations. A total of 36,574 American troops died in the war, and another 103,284 were wounded. http://www.koreanwar-educator.org

- South Korean Military Casualty Summary: 227,800 dead; 717,100 wounded; 43,500 MIA – Total 984,400
  Total Enemy Military Casualties exceeded 1,500,000 of which 900,000 were Chinese and 600,000 North Korean.
  http://www.koreanwaronline.com

- While accurate numbers for deaths are imprecise, various sources approximate the war's South Korean civilian casualties – dead, wounded and missing – at about one million people. North Korean civilian casualties were perhaps twice that, many of them as a result of the U.N. bombing campaign. The numbers vary, but it's probably safe to say that there were somewhere between three and four million Korean civilian casualties; this at a time when the total population was some 30-40 million people! Civilians died at a ghastly rate in Korea.
  http://www.calvin.edu/news/2001-02

# EPILOGUE
## THE ORANGE

### July 20, 2012

I went to visit with my mother today. I was just starting to write Part II of her memoirs which she had recorded thirty years earlier on audio tape. I wanted to read some of the chapters to her. It was very odd, my reading her own story to her.

Tears ran down her cheeks as I read the chapters, describing their first meeting and my father arranging for her to stay with a friend. She cried as I read of their falling in love and their inability to marry.

After a period of time, the chapters ended and we sat there quietly. I couldn't determine what she was feeling; anger, sadness, I just didn't know. I asked her, "What are you feeling?" She told me she was sad. It was a very sad story.

She sat there with tears on her cheeks. I cried too. It was a very touching love story but also filled with so much sorrow and so much pain.

My mother proceeded to tell me she recently remembered something she had completely forgotten about. Her memory was about an orange. She went on to tell me that when she was about eight years old and living with the difficult family with nine children, the father of the house went on a trip. When he returned, he brought a gift for everyone, one orange for each person. All the children were so very excited and delighted as he passed the oranges out, one by one. She sat there quietly, waiting for her orange but he did not give one to her. Everyone got an orange - everyone but her.

When she realized that he did not have an orange for her, she ran out to the barn and sat on the hay crying and sobbing; calling out to her dead father. She missed him so much. She had never seen an orange before and had no idea what it was. She saw them peeling the orange and eating it but had never tasted one herself.  It was at that moment in her life with this difficult family that she knew she would never be a part of any of them.  She would always be an outsider.  She would never taste of their oranges.

It broke my heart.  Here next to me was my eighty year old mother, tears streaming down her face, crying over a moment in her life over seventy years ago that still cut her to her core.  She went on to tell me that she is remembering things she never took time to think about before.  The orange was just one of them.  She believes if she had taken the time to dwell on these things before, she would not be the person she was.  She did not have time to be sad about all the terrible things that had happened to her in her life.  After she came to America, she was always busy having babies and taking care of her husband and their seven children.

But now for the first time in her life, she is alone here in this big old farm house.  It is in these quiet moments, when she sits alone, that she remembers these things.  And it is only now that she has found the time to cry.

# AFTERWORDS

Life is difficult. Every day, every one faces challenges of different kinds and different intensity. For some, the challenge might be physical such as a serious illness or disability. For others the challenge might be emotional such as mental illness or deep sorrow. Many face financial difficulties, marriage struggles or problems with teenagers. How we confront and deal with our challenges makes all the difference.

My father, Frank Crimbchin, faced challenges in this life just like everyone. He suffered from serious depression for which most of his generation did not seek medical help. Many who suffer from depression will treat their depression with alcohol, as did my father.

Alcoholism is a disease which destroys families, relationships, careers and will even steal a person's life. Sadly, my father suffered from depression and treated his depression with alcohol which did damage many of his family relationships. He was a man with a good heart; strong convictions, incredible work ethic and skills, yet alcohol robbed him of the joy and love waiting for him from his children and grandchildren.

I wrote this book, not knowing my father, before alcoholism. God in His infinite mercy allowed me to see my father as the young man he was before his addiction. How merciful is our God. I have been blessed with the privilege of sharing this person, my father, with my siblings and all of our family members who would otherwise have only know him in his illness.

I did not see my father the last year before he died. But my mother, who always prayed fervently for my father to turn to God, saw him do so prior to his death. On the day he died, my daughter, Bethany, and I gathered in prayer over my dying father and prayed for forgiveness for all the hurts I may have caused him and vice versa. Although unable to speak or respond, I believe my father heard that prayer and embraced it. I believe my father accepted the Lord as his personal Savior when he lay dying for many months and I believe I will see him again – healthy and whole.

When I see my father again, I believe I will finally meet the man I never knew. I will meet the man whose heart will be filled with a *Love Beyond Measure.*

The Letters.

The Spirit of the Sovereign Lord is on me, because the Lord has anointed me to proclaim good news to the poor. He sent me to bind up the brokenhearted, to proclaim freedom for the captives and release from darkness for the prisoners, to proclaim the year of the Lord's favor and the day of vengeance of our God, to comfort all who mourn, and provide for those who grieve in Zion- to bestow on them a crown of beauty instead of ashes, the oil of joy instead of mourning, and a garment of praise instead of a spirit of despair. They will be called oaks of righteousness, a planting of the Lord for the display of his splendor. Isaiah 61:1-3

\*\*\*\*\*\*

At the request of Ock Soon Lee, Pega Crimbchin, 10% of all proceeds from the sale of this book will benefit drilling wells for fresh water in undeveloped countries in memory of Frank F. Crimbchin.

# BIBLIOGRAPHY

Crimbchin, D. (2012). Oral History. Interview by K. Schell in Butler, PA.

Crimbchin, O. (2012-2013). Oral History. Interview by K. Schell in Cabot, PA.

Goulden, J. (1983). *Korea-The Untold Story of the War.* New York: McGraw-Hill Paperbacks.

Granfield, L. (2003). *I Remember Korea.* New York: Clarion Books.

Kenny, E. (2011). Oral History. Interview by K. Schell in Fairview Park, Ohio.

MacQuarrie, Genevieve Sonnett, (n.d.). *Frederick Sonnet Family History.* (Unpublished research).

O'Donnell, P. (2010). *Give Me Tomorrow*, Philadelphia: Da Capo Press.

Savada, A. & Shaw, W. (1990). *S Korea: A Country Study*, Washington: GPO for the Library of Congress.

Sloan, B. (2009). *The Darkest Summer*, New York: Simon & Schuster Paperbacks.

Stewart, R. (2000). *The Korean War: The Chinese Intervention,* Washington, D.C. Government Printing Office.

Walker, J. (n.d.). *A Brief Account of the Korean War*, Antioch: Korean War Association .

Willem, R. (2011). Oral History. Interview by D. Hunter in Conroe, TX.

Yuh, J. (2004). *Beyond The Shadow of Camptown*, New York and London: New York University Press.

21C Military Tactical Research Agency. (2000). *The 50$^{th}$ Anniversary of the Korean War.*

*A Song Every Korean Knows.* (03-18-10). Retrieved from
    http://thekoreanway.wordpress.com/2010/03/18

Campi, A.J. (June 2004). *The McCarran-Walter Act: A Contradictory
    Legacy on Race, Quotas, and Ideology.* Retrieved from
    http://www.immigrationpolicy.org

*Communist forces to re-take Seoul.* (01-04-1951). Retrieved from
    http://www.news.bbc.co.uk/onthisday/hi/dates/stories

Crumley, B. (07-12-11*). Marine Corps Armor in the Battle for Seoul* .
    Retrieved from http://www.mca-marines.org/blog/beth-
    crumley/2011/07/12

Evanhoe, E. (November 2002). *Withdrawal to the Pusan Perimeter;
    Defense of the Pusan Perimeter, The Inch'on Landing & Pusan
    Perimeter Breakout.* Retrieved on 04-28-12 from
    http://www.korean-war.com/TimeLine/1950

*Fulton, J.G.* (n.d.). Retrieved from http://bioguide.congress.gov
    /scripts/ biodisplay

Grey, J. (n.d.). *Fact Sheet Operations Big and Little Switch.* Retrieved
    from http://www.nj.gov/military/korea/factsheets/opswitch
    Operations Big and Little Switch

*Immigration and Nationality Act.* (n.d.). Retrieved from
    http://www.uscis.gov/portal/site/uscis

*Kimchi.* (n.d.). Retrieved from http://www.lifeinkorea.com/ culture/
    kimchi/kimchi.cfm

*Korean War After Action Reports, Lessons Learned Documents, Battle
    Assessments. (n.d.).* Retrieved from
    http://www.paperlessarchives.com

*Korean War – Casualty Summary as of May 16, 2008.* (n.d.). Retrieved
    from http://www.koreanwar-educator.org/topics/casualties /
    pdfs/korea.pdf

*North Korea Invades – The Outbreak of Insanity*. (n.d.). Retrieved from http://www.koreanwaronline.com/arms/NKAssault.htm

Savada, A. & Shaw, W.  Editors. (1990). *South Korea: A Country Study – Korea under Japanese Rule.* Washington. GPO for the Library of Congress. Retrieved from http://countrystudies.us/ southkorea

Popovic, M. (n.d.). *Death Anniversary*. Retrieved from http://traditionscustoms.com/ death-rites/death-anniversary

Rhem, K.T. Staff Sgt. (06-08-2000). *Korean War Death Stats Highlight Modern DoD Safety Record.* Retrieved from http://www.Defense.gov/news/newsarticle

Roberts, J. (n.d.). *Hq & Hq Co 2nd Engineer Group (Construction).* Retrieved from http://home.hiwaay.net/~stargate/korea.html

*The Immigration and Nationality Act of 1952 (The McCarran-Walter Act). (n.d.).* Retrieved from http://history.state.gov/ milestones/1945-1952 /ImmigrationAct

*The Important Role the U.S. Army Corps of Engineers Played during the Korean War. (n.d.).* Retrieved from http://www.usace.army.mil /About/History

Truman, H.S. (1950). *Truman's Veto McCarran Act (1950).* Retrieved from http://wadsworth.com/history

*USNS  Marine Phoenix (T-AP-195). (n.d.).* Retrieved from http://navsource.org/archives

*USNS Sgt. George D. Keathley. (n.d.).* Retrieved from http://navsource.org/archives

*USS General Henry W. Butner (T-AP-113).* (n.d.). Retrieved from http://navsource.org/archives

# ABOUT THE AUTHOR

Kathryn (Katie) Schell is the firstborn daughter of Ock Soon Lee and Frank Crimbchin. Katie recalls, as a very young child, the tragic stories of survival her mother would share with her. These stories would not only shape the person Katie would become, but also left an indelible mark on her heart for the suppressed and needy around her.

Katie studied Nursing at Sewickley Valley School of Nursing in Sewickley, Pennsylvania and went on to earn a Bachelor's Degree in Human Resource Management at Geneva College in Pennsylvania.

Katie served people with developmental disabilities for over twenty years and went on to serve the community through Nursing.

Her love for her mother and the desire to share her mother's incredible journey remained alive in her heart which culminated in the writing of these memoirs.

Katie lives in Harrison City, Pennsylvania, is married to William Schell, the love of her life. Katie has two living children, Thomas Jay Dunn and Bethany Joy Friel. Katie has one son who went to be with the Lord at the young age of 19. His name was Jason Lee Dunn.

Made in the USA
Middletown, DE
21 September 2015